TRAVELING THROUGH TIME

TRAVELING THROUGH TIME

How Trauma Plays Itself Out in Families, Organizations and Society

M. Gerard Fromm

PHOENIX
PUBLISHING HOUSE
firing the mind

First published in 2022 by
Phoenix Publishing House Ltd
62 Bucknell Road
Bicester
Oxfordshire OX26 2DS

British Library Cataloguing in Publication Data

A C.I.P. for this book is available from the British Library

ISBN-13: 978-180013-025-8

Typeset by Medlar Publishing Solutions Pvt Ltd, India

www.firingthemind.com

For

Maryjane

Contents

Acknowledgments

The travels—intellectual, emotional, and literal—that this book represents have involved far too many people to acknowledge here. I trust they know how fortunate I feel to have worked with all of them. Basically, this is a book about the Erikson Institute of the Austen Riggs Center. That "of" is important because the interdisciplinary learning of the former is, as the reader shall see, intrinsically linked to the clinical work of the latter. So, let me acknowledge the two parts of this one incredible institution, first by thanking the patients and their families for joining us in the intimate, difficult work of treatment, and then by thanking Ed Shapiro for his vision and leadership in creating the Erikson Institute, Jim Sacksteder for his steady, loving support of it, and Jane Tillman, its current director, for nurturing it so imaginatively before and during the pandemic.

Many others have contributed to the Institute over the years, and thereby to this volume: Kai Erikson, Tom Kohut, and Kim Leary, board leaders who energetically encouraged this work; Mary Carswell and Dan Schwartz, who invented the Erikson Scholar Program; Donna Elmendorf, John Miner, and John Santopietro, whose contributions are reflected in Part II; and a host of Erikson Scholars, including Diane

O'Donoghue, Yuko Okamoto, and Jessica Stern, who collaborated with me on some of the following chapters. A number of others offered advice and comments on parts of the text, including Lee Watroba, program manager of the Erikson Institute, Angela Sowa and Chuck Brandes of the Psychoanalytic Institute of Northern California, and International Dialogue Initiative friends, Lord John Alderdice, Robi Friedman, Frank Ochberg, Ford Rowan, Regine Scholz, and Lydia Wilson.

I am especially grateful to my friend and colleague, Vamık Volkan, who founded the International Dialogue Initiative during his tenure as Senior Erikson Scholar. Vamık's intrepid desire to understand groups in conflict has brought him to troubled places all over the world, and his willingness to commit himself to that work, to empathize with both sides, and to tell their stories in writing has made him a model for all of his students, including me.

Of course, behind everything is Erik Erikson, as foundation and inspiration. The Introduction and subsequent chapters take up his importance to the field of human development and to the Erikson Institute. Here let me simply say that it has been an honor of a lifetime to have worked with—and through the Institute, for—him.

Finally, to my fellow traveler, counselor, muse, and life partner, my wife, Maryjane, thank you for being there every step of the way. I'm so grateful to have shared these adventures with you. I love you with all my heart and dedicate this book to you.

Permissions

I would like to thank the following for their permission to reproduce material from my previously published work:

Prologue: Adapted from a chapter originally published under the title "Of whom shall we speak: psychoanalytic reflections on dignity," in: S. Levine (Ed.), *Dignity Matters: Psychoanalytic and Psychosocial Perspectives,* London: Karnac, 2016. Reproduced with the kind permission of Taylor & Francis Ltd.

Chapter 1: Adapted from an article originally published under the title "Fear of breakthrough" in *Modern Psychoanalysis, the Journal of the Center for Modern Psychoanalytic Studies, 41*(1), 2018. Reproduced with the kind permission of Sam Dash, managing editor, *Modern Psychoanalysis.*

Chapter 3: Adapted from a chapter originally published in: Y. Okomoto, Y. Kamite, & Y. Takano (Eds.), *Perspectives on Generativity Research: From Identity to Generativity*, 2018. Reproduced with the kind permission of Nakanishiya Publishing Co. Parts of this chapter were also published in the Introduction to M. G. Fromm (Ed.), *Lost in*

Transmission: Studies of Trauma across Generations, London: Karnac, 2012. Reproduced with the kind permission of Taylor & Francis Ltd.

Chapter 5: Parts of this chapter were originally published under the title "Potential space and maternal authority in organizations," in: *Organisational and Social Dynamics, 9*(2), 2009. Reproduced here with the kind permission of Phoenix Publishing House.

Chapter 7: Originally published in: *Organisational and Social Dynamics, 17*(1), 2017. Reproduced here with the kind permission of Phoenix Publishing House. Also published in: R. Frie (Ed.), *History Flows through Us: Germany, the Holocaust and the Importance of Empathy,* New York: Routledge, 2018; and in: A. Zajenkowska & U. Levin (Eds.), *A Psychoanalytic and Socio-Cultural Exploration of a Continent: Europe on the Couch,* London: Routledge, 2020. Reproduced here with the kind permission of Taylor & Francis Ltd. Excerpts published in: E. Schreiber (Ed.), *Healing Trauma: The Power of Listening,* New York: IPBooks, 2018. Reproduced here with the kind permission of IPBooks.

Chapter 9: Adapted from an article originally published under the title "Psychoanalysis and trauma: September 11 revisited," in: *Diogenes (23),* 2004. Reproduced here with the kind permission of Sage Publishing.

Chapter 11: Adapted from an article originally published (with V. D. Volkan) under the title "We don't speak of fear," in: *Georgetown Journal of International Affairs,* January 28, 2016, https://georgetownjournalofinternationalaffairs.org/online-edition/we-dont-speak-of-fear. Copyright © 2016 Edmund A. Walsh School of Foreign Service of Georgetown University. Reproduced here with the kind permission of Johns Hopkins University Press.

Chapter 12: Excerpts originally published under the title "Psychoanalytic approaches to social trauma," in: A. Hamburger, C. Hancheva & V. D. Volkan, *Social Trauma: An Interdisciplinary Textbook,* Cham, Switzerland: Springer, 2021. Reproduced here with the kind permission of Springer Nature Switzerland.

I would also like to thank the following for the use of the words of W. H. Auden:

Prologue—Lines from "In Memory of Sigmund Freud," Copyright © 1939, 1940 by W. H. Auden, renewed. Reprinted by permission of

Curtis Brown, Ltd. All rights reserved. Also, Copyright 1940 and © renewed 1968 by W. H. Auden; from COLLECTED POEMS by W. H. Auden, edited by Edward Mendelson. Used by permission of Random House, an imprint and division of Penguin Random House LLC. All rights reserved.

Chapter 6—Lines from “Musee des Beaux Arts,” Copyright © 1939, 1940 by W. H. Auden, renewed. Reprinted by permission of Curtis Brown, Ltd. All rights reserved. Also, Copyright 1940 and © renewed 1968 by W. H. Auden; from COLLECTED POEMS by W. H. Auden, edited by Edward Mendelson. Used by permission of Random House, an imprint and division of Penguin Random House LLC. All rights reserved.

Afterword—Lines from W. H. Auden’s poem, “In Memory of Sigmund Freud,” Copyright © 1939, 1940 by W. H. Auden, renewed. Reprinted by permission of Curtis Brown, Ltd. All rights reserved. Also, Copyright 1940 and © renewed 1968 by W. H. Auden; from COLLECTED POEMS by W. H. Auden, edited by Edward Mendelson. Used by permission of Random House, an imprint and division of Penguin Random House LLC. All rights reserved.

About the author

M. Gerard Fromm, PhD, is a distinguished faculty member of the Erikson Institute of the Austen Riggs Center and a fellow of the American Board and Academy of Psychoanalysis. He was the first Evelyn Stefansson Nef Director of the Erikson Institute, and directed the Therapeutic Community Program at Riggs for many years before that. Dr. Fromm has taught at, and consulted to, a number of psychoanalytic institutes across the country and has served on the faculties of the Yale Child Study Center and Harvard Medical School. He is president of the International Dialogue Initiative, an interdisciplinary group that studies the psychodynamics of societal conflict. He is also a past president of the International Society for the Psychoanalytic Study of Organizations and of the Center for the Study of Groups and Social Systems in Boston. Dr. Fromm has directed or served on the staff of Group Relations Conferences in the United States, Canada, Europe, and Israel. In addition to an independent practice of clinical and organizational consulting, he is also a partner in College Health and Counseling Services Consulting. Dr. Fromm has presented and published widely, including the edited volumes, *Lost in Transmission: Studies of Trauma across Generations*; *A Spirit That Impels:*

Play, Creativity and Psychoanalysis; and (with Bruce L. Smith) *The Facilitating Environment: Clinical Applications of Winnicott's Theory.* He is also the author of a book of clinical papers called *Taking the Transference, Reaching toward Dreams: Clinical Studies in the Intermediate Area.*

INTRODUCTION

Traveling through time

> *"Bullets don't just travel through skin and bone. They travel through time."*

These words were tattooed onto the shoulder of a young woman whose father was shot during "The Troubles" in Northern Ireland. This wrenching, volatile, but also binding truth is the subject of this book. It's a truth about traumatic experiences that happen to a family, but also to a society and to the organizations that link these intimate units with the larger context of history and culture. It's also a truth about the way trauma plays out over time, including between generations. This book, organized in the midst of the Covid-19 crisis, is a collection of stories and reflections on this phenomenon.

Trauma is a vast subject, and there has been considerable research on its various aspects over the last several decades (Brenner, 2001; Caruth, 2014; Coates et al., 2003; Fromm, 2012a; Hamburger et al., 2020; Herman, 1992; Van der Kolk et al., 1996; to name just a few). My focus will be on stories of trauma: the conditions that lead to it, the forms it takes, the ways it affects a person's life and the lives of others, and how that fallout might be addressed. Etymologically, trauma is a *wound* to an organism, a puncturing of the physical, but also the psychological "skin" or boundary that protects inside from outside. When Freud took up the study of trauma, he described the "protective shield" (1920g, p. 27) parents provide for children. What makes a psychological wound traumatic is that the events leading to it are extremely powerful, existentially threatening to the core self, and happen suddenly, in a way that breaches the person's now internalized protective shield against massive overstimulation. The capacity for thought and even for feeling are overwhelmed. Instead, trauma leads to a reflexive effort to cut oneself off from the unbearable. A broader definition of trauma would also recognize the debilitating effects of cumulative traumatic stress over time, leading to sustained, self-protective warping of a person's development, to chronic self-destructive efforts at dulling the pain, and to actions that might very well traumatize others.

The stories in this book were, to some degree, gathered and certainly shaped through my experience at the Austen Riggs Center, a small psychiatric hospital in Stockbridge, Massachusetts. The treatment program is unusual in today's world; quite troubled patients are seen in intensive psychotherapy in an open therapeutic setting. The reader will learn more about this program in the chapters that follow. Suffice it to say for now that the very personal data from such intensive work, and from the breadth of activities patients and staff engage in together, are quite rare these days. Mental health professionals do not usually get to know the patient as a person in such depth, don't usually learn about the sufferings of their parents and grandparents, don't see their artistic work in the local gallery or on the local stage, and don't tend to discuss problems of living and working together in patient-led community meetings.

It is this rare and precious data that led Riggs to create the Erikson Institute, which I had the good fortune to direct for many years. Named for Erik Erikson, the Institute's job was to bring this data into dialogue with others to see what all of us could learn in the overlap of our interests. We did this in many different ways: fall conferences on subjects like war trauma and the psychological effects of social media, an annual creativity seminar, a pro bono consultation service for local human service organizations, an annual conference for college counseling centers, interdisciplinary forums, clinical workshops and, perhaps most importantly, a program of Erikson Scholars-in-Residence. We learned from these events, and so did our partners-in-dialogue. In particular, academicians interested in psychoanalysis, who tended to be already extremely knowledgeable about its concepts, found Riggs case conferences to be transformational learning experiences; as one Erikson Scholar said, Riggs was "where the theoretical rubber meets the clinical road."

Throughout all of this, we held, as our North Star, Erikson himself, this restless, creative man who, with his own wounds from a complicated growing up and only a high school degree, became the pre-eminent developmental psychoanalyst of the mid-twentieth century. Erikson spent ten years on the staff of the Austen Riggs Center. He was a full-time clinician, but also an intellectual traveler. In a sense, while keeping one foot in the psychoanalytic consulting room, he put the other into a different discipline—history, anthropology, sociology—to see what could be learned at those intersections. His first major psycho-historical work, *Young Man Luther* (1958), was to some degree inspired and informed by his treatment of a patient at Riggs, whose breakdown, like Luther's four centuries before, occurred in the seminary.

Erikson's insight was that a child's development is not only profoundly influenced by the family context, but that that family context is profoundly influenced by its historical and sociocultural context (Erikson, 1950). And that a young person's struggle toward identity may also include influencing the next phase of that larger context, for better or worse. Witness his work on Gandhi (1969) but also on Hitler (1950), both of whose lives were shaped by the traumatic conditions—the brutality, humiliations, and pervasive losses—of their societies. The French psychoanalysts, Davoine and Gaudilliere (2004), write about how trauma associated with the "big history" plays itself out in the "little history" of ordinary families, some of whose members become the patients we see in our consulting rooms. A startling finding from their work is how often the patient's troubles have to do with how a family's traumatic history has been "cut out" (p. 61), so to speak, from the official narrative, in response to which madness becomes a research instrument for finding the truth.

This book, like an earlier one (Fromm, 2012a), grew from this clinical finding, as did three Erikson Institute conferences on the intergenerational transmission of trauma. The experience of that young woman in Northern Ireland has much to teach us, even if we don't necessarily recognize trauma in our own family histories. Indeed, it tends to be the fate of trauma that its effects slip below the surface when bad times have passed. "Men learn from history only that men learn nothing from history," said World War II general Francis Braceland (1946, p. 587), paraphrasing Hegel, a sentiment also documented in the work of the trauma theorist, Judith Herman (1992). There are, of course, good reasons for this: the relief people feel when the horror is over, the wish to protect other family members from their suffering, the desperate need to forget, and so on.

But sometimes, what can't be emotionally contained, thought about, or spoken in one generation is passed on, in one way or another, to the next. Sadly, in some cases, an unspoken, perhaps unspeakable truth about trauma is taken out on, and thereby *communicated*, to the next generation in action, the consequences of which can be devastating. Viewed from this angle, we see trauma and its effects all around us. In American society, "deaths of despair" from opioids and horrific explosions of violence generate enormous trauma but also spring from it. We see again and again how abuse begets abuse. And, of course, natural disasters, which often include a man-made element—like the coronavirus disease and the mismanagement of its treatment—have traumatic consequences, which may be passed along in one way or another.

The ubiquity of trauma risks diminishing its importance; if everything is traumatic, nothing really is. And indeed it's important to make distinctions. Generally speaking, the effects of trauma from natural disasters differ from trauma at the hands of other human beings. Some events that might be traumatic for one person—given that person's history and resources—might not be for another. Resilience is real and needs to be studied along with trauma. But to minimize the latter is a step in the direction of learning nothing from history, a dangerous if all too human step, as we are witnessing now in the coronavirus crisis.

Another important distinction to hold onto, as we consider the lives of families, is that between blame and responsibility. "Blaming the parents" is often an accusation leveled at the mental health profession, and sometimes therapists act in ways that seem to do just that. In my experience, this is not helpful. But the protest against blaming parents may well have become a societally supported and politically correct resistance against really looking at what happens between parents and children. Nobody seriously doubts that parents affect children; in fact, parents want to and they should! That's what parenting means. Most want to take, and often want help in taking, that responsibility. But because they do, their vulnerability to guilt is enormous and their potential defensiveness understandable. Parents know they are in a position of great responsibility but they often feel bewildered about how to exercise it. Ideally, it's the role of mental health professionals to provide something—some alliance, some understanding—that helps parents do what they couldn't do before. The pediatrician-psychoanalyst, Donald Winnicott, did this for years on the BBC and in his consultation service. Perhaps, this book will also offer something in that direction for practitioners helping today's parents.

Simplistically ascribing a child's troubles to a parent's way of being is a mistake. It fails to consider that the developing child is also developing a mind, through which his or her feelings and fantasies about a parent's behavior are being processed and potentially misinterpreted. This sometimes leads to vicious circles of parent–child interaction that are hard to escape by oneself. There can certainly be exceptions, but parents are generally doing the best they can within the limitations of their resources. One of those limitations—the one this book studies—has to do with those parents who may be, unwittingly but powerfully, caught up in their own larger traumatic history, which can have serious effects on their children. From this angle, a child's behavior, sometimes their breakdown, may be an effort to break through to a larger set of truths and to something restorative for everyone. This is one of those clinical findings that the Riggs treatment program affirms again and again.

Erikson was a traveler, both intellectually and physically. This adopted son eventually found a professional home at the Austen Riggs Center, which became a home base for further travels. Erikson Institute activities brought us into contact with many travelers from other disciplines over the years, and have brought me into my own travels since then. To some degree, this book is a diary of those travels: a journal of the people I've met, what I've learned from them, and what I've found myself thinking about in response. When, in his later years, Erikson was asked how he envisioned the Erikson Institute, he made it clear that he did not want the Institute to dedicate itself to his theories, but rather to his stance: the "way of looking at things" (1950, p. 403) described above, to which we might add the kinds of things—in history and culture and human development—to be looked at.

This "way of looking at things" could be called "applied psychoanalysis." Even though the psychoanalytic part is no longer central to the field of mental health, ironically, its core truths have been incorporated into various disciplines and into society's thinking more broadly: that childhood is profoundly formative; that child development includes the child's relation to his body; that traumatic stress is destructive to that development—the more so the earlier it occurs; that human attachment is critical; that early relationship troubles tend to play out in later life; that people feel inner conflict; that they do things without knowing why and then resist that knowledge; and so on. Arguably one of Freud's greatest discoveries, coinciding with research occurring in the young science of psychology, was free association: that we all possess a second form of thinking—more imagistic and associative—which coexists alongside our more linear, logical, verbal thinking, and can be an enormous resource in understanding ourselves and our world.

Dreams are one example of this, and the number of articles in the popular press about dreams during the coronavirus crisis attests to another way psychoanalytic thinking is now part of the culture. Of course, the psychoanalytic task of discovering psychological meaning in human behavior no longer centers so fully on Freud's work; many other theorists, some of whom the reader will meet in this volume, have broadened and deepened his initial insights. And those who apply psychoanalysis to other fields of study are no longer happy with the word "applied"; it's too one-directional and hints at too much expertise. In my time at the Erikson Institute, we tried to maintain a stance that was curious and consultative, rather than knowing and authoritative. And whatever learning we were able to offer was repaid by the learning we received.

One extremely powerful application of psychoanalysis readers will meet in this volume is a methodology for studying organizational dynamics called Group Relations Conferences. Another is a way of studying collective anxiety called Social Dreaming (Fromm, 2000; Lawrence, 1991). Here is an example of the latter, told in a closing session of the former.

> There was a hospital that looked like a lighthouse. Ariel Sharon, gravely ill, was being wheeled in on a gurney. But the treatment in this hospital was unusual. People were hung upside-down for a while, and that seemed to help them get better.

The group's work on this dream—taken up for its collective meaning—quickly led to a startling understanding. The conference had turned members' understanding of their home organizations upside down. They had become aware of its problematic dynamics and, to some degree, of their own unwitting participation in them. Now they were going back to the so-called right-side-up world and they were frightened! I include this story here to underline that a psychoanalytic "way of looking at things" invites us to consider the upside-down world: one in which the truth people discover through their own experience might be markedly different from what is accepted as truth in the right-side-up world; one in which the apparently rational may turn out to be deeply irrational; one in which trauma is no less traumatic because attending to it would be painful.

Following Erikson, this book is not a theoretical work on trauma, even less a comprehensive survey of that field. Rather it is a way of looking at the stories I've come across, through a lens having to do with trauma and how it plays out—travels in one form or another—over time. In that last conversation, a very old Erik Erikson was characteristically modest—even, I thought, nostalgic about the wandering young man he once was—when he said that his main hope for the Erikson Institute was that it would "give a promising person a real chance, the chance I had when I came to Riggs." This book is also a record of my gratitude for the chances I've been given to hear and tell these stories.

Actually, I had one more conversation with Erikson, in a dream more than twenty years after his death. I was about to give a lecture on his work at the University of Hiroshima, having been invited by Professor Yuko Okamoto, herself an Erikson Scholar. The night before, I was chatting with two other tourists. When they asked what had brought me to Japan, I told them about the lecture, and that I had known Erikson years before. I added jokingly but also with a touch of melancholy: "You know, I'm a bit of a relic. I shook Erikson's hand. Now psychologists shake my hand,

and they feel something about that connection." A few hours later, I had a dream:

> There was a large dinner party in Erikson's honor. When I arrived, the many guests were milling about chatting and having drinks before dinner. The atmosphere was quite festive, but Erikson was sitting by himself at the head of an empty dinner table. I felt sorry for his being alone, so I went over, said hello and asked how he was. He said that he was fine. I asked what he had been doing these days, and, to my surprise, he said that he had been "teaching in the streets."

That's where the dream ended. I immediately realized that I had been "learning in the streets" during this trip and many others, indeed during my entire time at the Erikson Institute. For which I am profoundly grateful to Erik. Only later did I realize that my melancholy matched what I imagined him to be feeling in the dream, and that his aloneness reflected a risk intrinsic to his "way of looking at things." If one truly takes up the task of learning in the area between disciplines, the risk is of leaving one's own home, so to speak—which also means leaving one's area of expertise—and being a guest—or worse—in another. Even in the realm of interdisciplinary work, V. S. Pritchett's comment in *The Offensive Traveler* (1964) is worth remembering:

> By "being offensive," I mean that I travel, therefore I offend. I represent that ancient enemy of all communities: the stranger. Neapolitan girls have crossed themselves to avert the evil eye at the sight of me … And rightly: we are looking on the private life of another people, a life which is entirely their business, with an eye, that, however friendly it may be, is alien. We are seeing people as they do not see themselves. (p. 4)

"Where do I belong?" was a constant question for Erikson, a personal question from early life. So was "Where will I be accepted?" It's to his credit that he directed these anxieties toward learning about the places he didn't necessarily belong, and also—as any traveler should—toward giving something back to his hosts. Ultimately, he belonged to psychoanalysis—a discipline that helps people see themselves more fully—but to those he met in his travels, he brought both a perspective and an attitude: a profound "way of looking at things," to be sure, but also a humility—"*I have nothing to offer except* a way of looking at things" (1950, p. 403). In offering this record of my learning in the streets, I feel the risk and, to some degree, the aloneness intrinsic to Erikson's stance. But I also feel that the risk is worth taking, first of all because he did—in retrospect, the Erikson in my dream was taking care of me more than I was taking care of him—and because this book is just that: an *offering* to those whose lives have been touched by trauma.

PROLOGUE

Of whom shall we speak? Psychoanalysis and dignity

When there are so many we shall have to mourn,
When grief has been made so public, and exposed
To the critique of a whole epoch
The frailty of our conscience and anguish;

of whom shall we speak?

These are the opening lines of W. H. Auden's magnificent elegy "In Memory of Sigmund Freud" (1940a), begun just after Freud's death on September 23, 1939, three weeks after the Nazi invasion of Poland. Within these lines is the great juxtaposition of what I referred to earlier as the "big history" and the "little history," the catastrophic social upheaval of the day and the loss of one person, someone who was "doing us some good," says Auden. His poem places us at the historical end of the "long weekend" between the World Wars, when the horrors set in motion twenty-five years before were about to resume with unimaginable fury. In that context of immeasurable loss, "Of whom shall we speak?"

Auden's poem does more than remember Freud; it asserts an answer to this question: that we shall speak of someone who stands for the dignity—and, to be sure, the complexity—of the individual. Psychoanalysis as a field of study—as an institution—stands for the dignity of the individual, no matter how diminished by trauma. A corollary of the question, "Of whom shall we speak?" is "To whom shall we listen?" Psychoanalysis answers that resoundingly in favor of the individual. Further, psychoanalytic treatment embeds dignity as a clinical provision into that individual listening. In this chapter, I shall explore the nature of this provision and how it relates to the way that trauma plays itself out in families and in groups.

Who shall speak?

Just before his closing stanza, Auden writes that Freud ...

Would have us remember most of all
To be enthusiastic over the night,
Not only for the sense of wonder
It alone has to offer, but also

Because it needs our love. With large sad eyes
Its delectable creatures look up and beg
Us dumbly to ask them to follow:
They are exiles who long for the future

That lies in our power, they too would rejoice
If allowed to serve enlightenment like him,
Even to bear our cry of 'Judas',
As he did and all must bear who serve it.

In these three stanzas, Auden brings us to another question: "Who shall speak?" The answer is: dreams, the "delectable creatures" of the night, who see—indeed see with sadness—but by themselves are dumb, without speech. They are exiles—like Freud in London—whom we can bring into what Auden calls "the bright circle ... of recognition." These lines speak to a core psychoanalytic listening stance. The psychoanalyst Charles

Rycroft, in his book, *The Innocence of Dreams*, describes the exile this way: "[T]he dreaming self utters meanings from a timeless, total position … while the part of the self that receives dream-messages occupies a pre-empted, prescribed position localized in a particular time and place, and possesses a preconceived notion of itself which is at risk if it listens seriously to dream-meanings" (1979, p. 148). It was Freud's genius to recognize that these were the voices that might "serve enlightenment"—the repressed voices, the exiled voices, the dream voices.

How shall we listen?

For Auden, Freud's method was simple, and to some degree shared between the author and his subject. It addresses the question, "How shall we listen?"

He merely told
The unhappy Present to recite the Past
Like a poetry lesson till sooner
Or later it faltered at the line where

Long ago the accusations had begun,
And suddenly knew by whom it had been judged,
How rich life had been and how silly,
And was life-forgiven and more humble,

In the method of free association (Bollas, 2002), psychoanalysis dignifies both the recital and the faltering. It listens carefully to the story and to where the story breaks down, or perhaps breaks through to feelings that the storyteller had not yet told himself about. Clinical psychoanalysis rests on the good faith assumption that the patient is doing his best, and that, at the place of faltering, curiosity rather than judgment is the provision. Auden calls this provision "love"; so does the psychoanalyst Donald Winnicott, for whom love means the "positive interest taken" (1954, p. 285). Dignity is implicit in this description. Free association as a methodological foundation for clinical psychoanalysis asserts that part of ourselves is naturally working toward health, and it gives worth to—it dignifies—our seemingly less important and defensively discarded thoughts.

Further, dignity is implicit in the technical principles Freud (1915a) articulated—especially neutrality—which are sometimes controversial concepts these days. These principles and the listening stance they lead to have to do with what André Green (1999) called "the work of the negative." Beyond the analyst's basic ethic of not using the patient, these technical principles—lived out in the context of a therapeutic alliance—dignify the rejected, the negated, the hated and self-hated parts of a person, parts that are also dumb, perhaps in both meanings of that word: that is, without speech and without understanding. These are the parts of a person that lead the conscious self to accuse us of betrayal if we listen to them seriously. Our bearing the "cry of 'Judas'"—which, in Winnicott's terms (1969), means surviving and making sense of this resistance—transforms the clinical provision of dignity into something not at all thin but rather quite muscular, because of the powerful emotions experienced in the process. Feelings related to negativity become more real because they are really suffered by both parties, in the service of growth. And this provision is bi-directional: the analyst's dignifying the negative in the patient leads the patient to dignify the analyst's durability and capacity for containment.

Only hate was happy

In Winnicott's paper on regression, his full statement of the twelve features that make up the analytic setting goes on to include hate, hate "honestly expressed … in the strict start and finish and in the matter of fees" (1954, p. 285). In Auden's poem, at Freud's death,

> *Only Hate was happy, hoping to augment*
> *His practice now, and his dingy clientele*
> *Who think they can be cured by killing*
> *And covering the garden with ashes.*

Winnicott's "hate" is of a different order. It's in the service of discovery rather than covering over. The ending of the session, which sometimes triggers hate in the patient, and also fantasies about the analyst's hatred, establishes a boundary across which Winnicott hopes to meet the parts of a person they have covered over. It is both a task boundary—we are here to do this (analysis) and not that (friendship)—and a recognition of the separateness of the two participants, even as the "positive interest taken" mobilizes the patient's longing for a familial oneness. This, one might call it structural provision of the possibility of hate, authorizes the embattled negative feelings the patient is struggling with to come into the room, and it allows for the critical experience of the analyst's not being killed off by the patient's hateful feelings.

As it turns out, the patient's hate is often in the service of preserving the tenuous relationships of his inner world, a version of Auden's cure by killing off parts of oneself. For Winnicott, the analyst's survival brings a kind of joy to the patient, through the realization that the therapeutic relationship can now be trusted—almost in the engineering sense—to hold the full weight of the patient's affectivity (Fromm, 2012b1). If dignity is about worth, the "worthy opponent" dimension Winnicott has introduced into psychoanalytic theory is worth our attention.

The fosse

But as Auden says elsewhere in his poem, "To be free is often to be lonely." When we broaden our field of vision, we often discover that the patient has unconsciously participated in being killed off in the service of curing a troubled family. Progress becomes intertwined with, and sometimes seriously compromised by, loyalty, fear, and grief. The Austen Riggs Center, the small psychiatric hospital where I spent my clinical career, is, as I said earlier, unusual in today's world: a program of intensive psychotherapy in a completely open, voluntary setting. It's actually a beautiful setting, given its location in the Berkshire Hills of Western Massachusetts. But to enter a psychiatric hospital, even one on Main Street, Stockbridge, and to enter a treatment relationship with its patients, is to follow Freud, who, in Auden's words:

Went his way
Down among the lost people like Dante, down
To the stinking fosse where the injured
Lead the ugly life of the rejected,

"Where the injured lead the ugly life of the rejected." The insult of rejection is added to the basic injury, and then lived out as ugliness. We see this in our society and we see it in psychiatric hospitals. Clinical work shows us that, as we will see throughout this book, sometimes a family's inter-generational traumatic experiences simply cannot be borne by its members and are refused as "not us." But bits of this acutely painful, un-verbalized experience fall out upon and get lodged in—indeed in a sense may be unconsciously assigned to—one of the family's more vulnerable members, who lives out life as a form of refuse, across the "borderline" of what's acceptable in the ordinary social world.

These are the patients who find their way to Austen Riggs: patients with enormous ego-structure and self-esteem problems; with flagrant, scattered symptomatology, desperate for identity; or with profound withdrawal to a dark place on the other side of the fosse. One of the ironies of severe psychopathology, and of the role of outsider, which these patients occupy, is that what began as refuse—as what has had to be refused by the family—holds in a sort of trust, if you will, essential information about the family's traumatic history (Fromm, 2012a). The people who break down under this traumatic history are the ones most inclined toward—or perhaps who can't go on living without—speaking about it.

Talking it over

At the beginning of Riggs' psychoanalytic history, one of its fellows-in-training wrote a paper describing burgeoning crises among the younger, more acting-out patient population. The times were "out of joint," so to speak. The nursing staff longed for the good old days of Dr. Riggs' ten mental health commandments; the quaint New England town remained sleepy and a bit puritanical; and the newly arrived senior analysts were beginning to realize that neutrality was no way to administer a hospital. This young trainee went on to a remarkable—and quite funny—statement: "Then the historic decision was taken to talk the situation over with the patients" (Christie, 1964, p. 458). This daily "talking it over with the patients" became the core of Riggs' therapeutic community program, and dignity was explicitly embedded in its mission statement.

Here is a bit of that "talking it over." A number of years ago, patients and staff were discussing the upcoming holiday season: who would be going home, who staying, the community's plans for holiday events, which staff would be here, how people were feeling at this time of the year, and so on. One young man said that he would be visiting his family, and then added a bit contemptuously: "There, it's nothing like here. That's the real world. Here we just talk endlessly. We shelter ourselves from real life here." When he returned—having experienced enormous tension at home, lived out silently with the help of alcohol—he repeated his earlier statement, but with a twist and with gratitude rather than contempt: "There, it was nothing like here. We talk about everything here, and it's hard. There you could cut the tension with a knife, but nobody talked. Just mean remarks and another drink." Then, seeming to have realized something important, he amended his statement again: "Here, it's nothing like there. I think we are trying to deal with what really happens here. And with real feelings about that. Maybe this world is actually more real than that one. Sometimes I wish I could bring it to my family."

The outsider

In troubled families, those who find themselves in or take up the outsider role have a chance to see and even understand the suffering of the insiders, suffering that over time has unwittingly become its own system of protections, outlets, and dysfunctional roles. This kind of system is enormously costly to its members, both in terms of their well-being and their capacity to successfully carry out their roles, but it seems to get people through, at least for a while. As Auden said, those who follow Freud into the outsider fosse—and at its simplest, following Freud means being willing to take up "the talking cure"—have to "bear our cry of Judas." Talking about what's really going on or what people are really experiencing *does* involve betrayal; it involves not abiding by the unconscious rule that something important but really painful must stay outside the conversation.

And it's worth noticing Auden's word "our." We all get invested in seeing things a certain way and in avoiding personal pain in seeing them otherwise. But, as we also all know deep down, the truth not only sets free; it makes whole again. Maybe that patient in the community meeting did eventually bring healing talk to his family. Maybe in taking up an outsider status, he helped them open up, accept, bear, learn from, even appreciate those frightening, often very sad moments of family history that had forced them to, in a sense, become outsiders to parts of their own lives. Dignifying this seemingly outsider role is an embedded provision in a good psychiatric treatment program, a corrective emotional structure and point of view about people, available as a counterweight to the patient's original system.

Sense-making

As I have suggested earlier with regard to clinical psychoanalysis, engaging the negative is also a dignifying action in the daily life of a therapeutic community. Projective dynamics inevitably occur among patients and between patients and staff, as they do within a family, between the family and the outer world, and within organizations. In a psychiatric system, patients' troubles are played out and staff anxiety is as well. Dignity, within a therapeutic community's work, has to do with the staff's commitment to considering symptomatic eruption in group and systems terms. Acting out within such a system not only affects the total community; it also very likely represents something important about what is going on in the community. As in families, whose task is to facilitate the development of all of its members (Shapiro, 2020; Shapiro & Carr, 1991), whatever becomes dissociated from conscious dialogue may well be critical to learning how and why the group has gotten off its task in some way.

Understanding this in terms of the system restores what Winnicott called the "holding environment" (1960a) for development. The community's commitment must be to a stance that asks "How are they right?" (Shapiro, 2020), not an abdicating "You're right, because you are a patient [or a staff member]," but in what way is the other right? This sense-making perspective—that of an "interpretive democracy" (Fromm, 2012b2) since any member can offer the sense she sees in what's happening—lives out a "psychological equality" between patients and staff (Kennard, 1998, p. 127). It recognizes that all of us have a psychology and we are affected by what is happening around us. Again, as with families, this kind of dialogue can lead to powerful learning in the here and now for both the group and the patient (or sometimes the staff member) who might be carrying an emotional issue for everyone, with whatever degree of personal distress and compromised functioning.

Democracy

A colleague in the social conflict field commented (Waslekar, 2012) that troubled societies suffer from three deficits: a development deficit, a democracy deficit, and a dignity deficit. Facilitating the living out of democratic principles—that each person's voice matters, that finding one's authentic voice is a good thing, and that participation in decisions by which one is affected is both just and healthy—is inherently dignifying. Importantly for the mental health field, it's also inherently therapeutic. And importantly for organizations, it is inherently productive. Out of many expensive studies (Duhigg, 2016) conducted by Google, only one demonstrated strong findings about what led to the most creative teams: that each person had a voice in the discussion and that when a team member appeared to be in distress, another team member inquired about that. The silenced voice—whether from inner preoccupation or external oppression—is costly.

A number of years ago at the daily community meeting, a member said emotionally, "I feel so guilty. I'm here and others whom I care about can't be." Another said, "Yes, but when we bring our feelings to each other and share them, as you're doing in this meeting, it makes it more bearable." The former speaker was actually an experienced nurse, devastated by the loss of two colleagues who had left during a financial crisis. The second speaker was the patient chairperson, elected to lead the meeting for an eight-week term. Visitors to the community meeting often ask, "Was that a staff member or a patient who said that?" This is a powerfully de-centering, and actually therapeutic, moment—a moment of dignity, if you will. It underscores the fact that patienthood is a role, not an intrinsic aspect of the person, no matter how disturbed he might seem. Crucially, for a person in the patient role, he may begin to realize that a role taken up can also, with good treatment, be put down, and life can be lived without the ongoing undertow of an identity simply as a patient. Helping a person understand the pathological role he is in—a role that is part of a family's or an organization's or a community's troubled process—is a step in the direction of liberation and dignity for all.

Would you hold this for me?

As I wrote earlier, the irony within severe psychopathology is that what began as refuse sometimes holds in trust essential information about a family's traumatic history. The "ashes" Auden refers to, covering over the garden, are so often the ashes of death, the detritus of unbearable and unthinkable family trauma unconsciously transmitted to the next generation, some of whom live it out in symptomatology (Davoine & Gaudilliere, 2004; Fromm, 2012a). From a different context, the psychoanalyst Lawrence Gould (2002), reporting his experience as consultant to the United States Holocaust Museum, relates a frequent occurrence (reported in Fromm, 2012a2):

> An aged man, in a rumpled jacket, goes to the information desk, hands the receptionist a box, and says, "Will you hold this for me?" The box turns out to contain, in the example Dr. Gould cited, the tattooed skin that this man had cut from his arm when he was freed from the concentration camp and which he had kept hidden for 50 years. "I'm going to die soon; I haven't told my family about this and I don't want them to find it," he says; "Will you hold it for me?" (p. 212)

This is a most unusual definition of a "holding environment." Very likely, as many studies of second- and third-generation Holocaust survivors have shown, this man's family did know, in one way or another, about his suffering. But, to the degree that a traumatized person cannot think about or bear his experience, it tends to be lived out in powerful but cryptic ways within the family. And to the degree that it cannot be contained there, someone—potentially a vulnerable member of the family—or something must hold its objects, affects, and bits of the story. The Holocaust Museum serves the purpose of holding this evolving societal narrative of horror, cruelty and loss, so that an aging generation of traumatized survivors and their families, along with the rest of us, can begin to bear, in manageable doses of feeling and thinking, what has been unbearable within a family.

A psychiatric hospital can also serve that purpose for patients and families struggling with their own private holocaust (Fromm, 2012a2).

More than clinicians sometimes realize, the horrors of the "big history" may well be part of the seemingly "little history" of the patient, for whom the transmission of the family's trauma has become all too real. Discovering this in treatment opens a space for grief, in the patient and in the family, and for genuine understanding of the people on whom one's own sense of self has depended. The most profound and dignifying endpoint of this process is "the inscription of emotional truth into the narrative of the generations, honoring one and liberating the other" (Fromm, 2012a2, p. 219). When things go well, the patient, and sometimes their loved ones, become, in Auden's words, like those:

> *Long-forgotten objects*
> *Revealed by his undiscouraged shining*
> *… returned to us and made precious again*

When there are so many

If psychoanalysis stands for the dignity and complexity of the individual—and their re-dignification from the fosse of trauma—how do we take into account the problem of scale, the "so many" who suffer seemingly outside a psychoanalytic purview? A young psychologist, attending a training conference sponsored by Riggs, said at its closing: "This conference has been like oxygen to me. I'm taking a very deep breath and going to try to make it last as long as I can in my work back home." What a powerful statement, and what a daunting task! More usually, we encounter professionals who have trouble listening to a psychodynamic perspective at all, but not because it isn't persuasive to them; on the contrary, to the extent that they are captivated and moved by the deep study of cases, they must reactively dismiss it. A version of cognitive dissonance comes into play. They cannot let themselves value what they do not have the resources, within their treatment systems, to carry out because the guilt would be too great. They feel what the singer Sinead O'Connor expressed in a song many years ago: "I do not want what I haven't got" (1990).

This is the major challenge for psychoanalysis today, both clinical and applied. Indignities, humiliations, and trauma are everywhere in our world, but a person's being deeply heard goes a long way too.

A psychoanalytic framework on trauma and a process that engages the live—and often negative—feelings within individuals, families, and groups in conflict dignifies all involved, by virtue of the collective experiencing, surviving, and attempting to give words to the deep pain behind these feelings. Perhaps only psychoanalysis truly values this play of opposites—the engagement of the negative in the service of healing. Listen to Auden in his final stanza, one in which Freud has joined the delectable creatures no longer able to speak but who "long for a future that lies in our power:"

> *One rational voice is dumb. Over his grave*
> *The household of Impulse mourns one dearly loved:*
> *Sad is Eros, builder of cities,*
> *And weeping anarchic Aphrodite.*

Auden does not juxtapose Eros with Thanatos, Life and Death, as Freud did after the ashes of World War I. Rather he juxtaposes two symbols of love: Eros the builder and Aphrodite the anarchist. Eros indeed represents the love that brings together—a force of enormous creative power in human life. But what about Aphrodite? Her mythic story includes a refusal; she refused confinement in a marital relationship ordered by the powers that be *for their purposes*. If Eros says Yes, Aphrodite says an anarchic No to being trapped or killed off in a vain attempt at curing others. This is love too, says Auden, a love that weeps for what it has to do. Both shall speak, and both deserve the dignity of our listening.

Part I

Trauma in families

CHAPTER 1

Fear of breakthrough: the transmission of trauma

It was one of those soft, gorgeous September days in New York, the cloudless sky an "unbelievable blue" (Springsteen, 2002). Vic Wertz, the Cleveland slugger, at the plate: 8th inning, tie game, two men on, Game One of the 1954 World Series. In came the pitch, and Wertz crushed the ball to deep centerfield. Instantly, Willie Mays, the sensational young outfielder for the Giants, turned and raced to the deepest part of the cavernous Polo Grounds, catching the ball on a dead run, facing completely away from home plate. Instead of an almost certain loss, the Giants won the game, and went on to win the World Series. The Catch, as it came to be known, still ranks among the greatest in baseball history.

Many years later, a young man, a writer for a sports magazine, suffered a breakdown. (This and all other references to patients have been disguised to protect their confidentiality.) Diagnosed with a serious psychiatric condition by a local psychiatrist, he would obsessively and fervently talk with his therapist about The Catch. Why? What did this event mean to him? A paper by the psychoanalyst, Donald Winnicott, may have offered an interpretation. If we translate The Catch from a spatial dimension to a temporal one, here is its story: something terrible happens; instantly the affected person turns his back on this now past event, indeed runs away from it, only to run to the place *in the future* where it will fall upon him. This is the main theme of Winnicott's late career "Fear of Breakdown" paper (1974), and it is also one way to hear the story of this patient's life. The Catch may well have captured unconsciously an intuition the patient had about both his trouble and its treatment.

The clinical phenomenon Winnicott points to—that the breakdown a person is running from he may also be unconsciously running toward, so that he can finally master it—is certainly real. In this chapter, I consider this from a different angle: that a person's fear of breakdown may also include a fear of breaking *through* to trauma in the parents' life. In other words, one legacy of family trauma is often a profound fear in the next generation of re-traumatizing one's parents by opening up deeply painful experiences the parents have been trying to protect themselves from, but that have become implicated in their child's troubles.

Sky of fear

It was one of those soft, gorgeous September days in New York, the cloudless sky an "unbelievable blue." When I began with that line at a conference in New York, the listeners' first thoughts were probably not of the 1954 World Series, but of a more recent and deeply tragic September day. Despite my shift to the Polo Grounds and Willie Mays' great catch, the traces of traumatic anxiety may well have stayed with the audience for a bit, perhaps were elaborated in their thoughts just outside of consciousness, and may have taken their place as potential day residue for their dream life. The phrase, "unbelievable blue," is Bruce Springsteen's, from his 2002 CD, "The Rising." Its enormous success speaks, I believe, to its having been used, on a massive scale, to work through the trauma of 9/11. More about that later in this volume.

Winnicott too brings us into trauma in his "Fear of Breakdown" paper (1974). His description of the person's suffering goes beyond simple anxiety; rather he describes the "agony" of disintegrating as a person, of being unable to contact reality, of "falling forever" (p. 104). What has happened to the traumatized person? The Other, on whom we absolutely depend at crucial moments in our lives, has gone missing. Trauma is about the failure of what Winnicott calls the holding environment when it is most needed. The only way for the mind to survive is to leave, to shut down, to dissociate.

Winnicott's central fear-of-breakdown idea is that something extremely serious happened to a person, but that the person, as a developed entity, capable of processing intense experience, wasn't there for it to happen to. Nor was the holding environment there to contain and metabolize it. So, in a sense, this "thing of the past" has not yet actually happened because it has not yet been experienced. It is thus ever on the horizon and its traces are ever present. If we take Winnicott's paradoxical thesis literally, we could also read it as an inter-generational truth for all of us: things indeed happened to our parents; we may not have been there but we were on the horizon. The critical question is about the nature and urgency of its traces on us. How traumatic was the parent's experience and how might it have been transmitted to the next generation (Fromm, 2012a)? Winnicott speaks to a crucial gap in the parent's mental coverage of the developing child. The clinical stories that make up the rest of this chapter explore what that gap is about and what fills that gap for both the parent and the child. My thesis is that *the fear of breakdown also includes a fear of breakthrough to the traumatic history on the other side of that gap.*

Fire rain

A young woman brought up in London reported a dream after her therapist's vacation (Fromm, 2012a1).

> There were some ruined buildings. They were destroyed by fire. One was a pet shop. There were some little animals in a cage.

The next day, she remembered that the buildings had not been destroyed by fire, but by rain. Spontaneously, her therapist said: "There is a kind of rain that brings fire." The patient said, "Bombing," and remembered, for the first time, an event from her childhood. Night after night, her father would watch newsreels of the bombing of London, seemingly looking for something. His eight-year-old daughter sat anxiously beside him and repeatedly asked why he was looking at these films again and again. To her recollection, he said nothing. This occurred just after his mother's death, for whom the patient was named. She was later to learn that her father had lost his childhood home in the bombing of London when he was eight years old. After this phase of watching newsreels, the patient's father became depressed, a depression his daughter's love and liveliness were unable to cure. Over time, she came to feel that she had lost him completely, which made her extremely vulnerable to rejection in her later relationships with boys. She also came to feel that no one could stand the anger, born of hurt and humiliation, she felt inside herself.

This is a story about a gap in a parent's emotional coverage of what might be going on in the mind of his child. It highlights a father's speechlessness about something terribly confusing yet absolutely urgent to his daughter. But, from a different angle, the father's childhood trauma did indeed speak to his daughter through images, which, like their content, bombarded the little girl with emotional stimulation, including her father's unspoken grief. She may also have felt spoken to through her grandmother's name, as though some sort of link was being lived out between past trauma with one person and its being processed with a new version of that person. A crucial bit of the father's "cut out" history—the reliving of which took place in her company night after night—became intertwined with the daughter's development, and, as children do, she took it personally. To her great peril, she misinterpreted the growing estrangement from her father as her fault somehow. Indeed, she identified with his traumatic experience. It was not the loss of his home or the more recent loss of his mother he could not bear to deal with; it was *her*!

The patient played out this transmission of trauma in her relationship with her therapist by allowing herself to react to his vacation with dream images of abandonment. The buildings ruined by a fire-rain opened up a crucial bit of "cut-out" (Davoine & Gaudilliere, 2004, p. 61) history and gave a completely new context of meaning to her emotional difficulties. Getting to this history—and to what the patient had been living out in relation to her family—is one task of psychoanalytic treatment, a potentially perilous task for the patient, who may feel disloyal, even destructive, for speaking what a parent could not. After all, speaking the heretofore unspeakable separates the person from someone she needed and who needed her. In a sense, it discharges a responsibility she has been carrying for someone she loves. Something identity-defining and deeply intimate is over. In addition to both parties' fear of the feelings associated with this "cut-out" history, this real and painful separation—this differentiation out of the role of silent witness and failed caregiver—is another source of the unconscious fear of breakthrough.

Are you killing me?

At around the same time as the bombing of London, somewhere in France, a twelve-year-old French-Jewish boy took refuge in a monastery to escape Nazi persecution and remained in hiding there for the duration of the war. Years later, his son broke down into intense anxiety and depression, following three contemporaneous events: his graduation from college, his therapist's vacation, and his father's asking him to translate the journal he had kept from those years in hiding. Later, when his new therapist took an August vacation, the patient suffered a period of severe disorganization. He feared losing his place with his therapist because of how bad he felt himself to be. He imagined that his therapist might kill him, or that he might kill someone; he thought he could kill people simply by having an opinion. He remembered feeling this kind of anger at his father when his father silently refused to answer questions about why he did certain things. Suddenly he turned to his therapist and said, "Are you killing me?" His therapist said, "You may feel that there is kind of killing in speaking about your feelings toward your father."

At that moment, the patient decided that he wanted to read his father's journal to his therapist. He brought it to the next session and began reading: "August 15, 1940. Today my parents left the city." His therapist found himself saying: "Your father was left in August just as you were by me." The patient said: "Is something being destroyed?" The therapist said, "Reading your father's journal to me may make you feel that your life is different from his, and that may feel destructive." In response, the patient abruptly stopped reading. The next day, he remembered something: his father had kept a ring from his years of hiding, a family keepsake that had sustained the memory of his lost parents. But the ring had been stolen in a burglary on the day the father attended his son's graduation. The patient had always felt terrible about this. The therapist said, "Getting on with your life feels like it may destroy his." The patient then resolutely read the journal through to its completion.

To the therapist's surprise, the journal recorded the events of four years of an adolescent boy's hiding without a single statement of feeling or personal experience. Each sentence, like that initial one about his parents' departure, was dry and simply factual. Afterwards, the therapist said, "Your emotional life imagines your father's absent emotional life—what it must have been like for him during that time. It answers questions he couldn't." They then reviewed the patient's anxious fantasies: that his therapist might have him arrested; that he would stay safe by doing what the therapist wanted; that he should convert to the therapist's religion; and that the therapist was in danger from the authorities because of him. These must have been the father's precise experiences during his years of hiding. After this, the patient said, "Yes. I can't go on keeping other people safe." In subsequent months, he became remarkably less symptomatic and more real as a person. Quite strikingly, his father did as well.

Again we see how social trauma—in this case the terror of death and the loss of parents during war—falls upon the next generation. We again see silence about something urgent and enormously confusing to the child. Though this parent never spoke about his wartime experience, despite his child's repeated questions, something was sensed about the past in the present. Volkan describes this as a "time collapse" (2015, p. 13); Davoine and Gaudilliere call it "time falling into immediacy" (2004, p. 181). And again unspeakable experiences were given symbolic form and communicated to the next generation. This child was given his father's journal and asked to translate it, an action which, at some level, might have been meant to liberate the child, so that he could finally discover the experiences his father had all along been enacting. Indeed, giving his son the journal may well have reflected the father's permission for his son's discovery, differentiation, and mourning.

But taking up this authorization, as this patient demonstrates, is felt to be enormously risky. Fears of breakdown and breakthrough intermix and are highly charged. Traumatic experience is interwoven into the fabric of family life and into the child's development and sense of identity. Certain children—perhaps because of gender, birth order, physical resemblance, or some other intimate characteristic that links parent and child—find themselves in a role that more fully involves them in a parent's trauma. They may come to identify with the traumatized parent, living out a special compact in which the parent's needs and the child's desires intertwine in confusing ways.

A person's bringing this kind of experience to psychotherapy represents their seeking a relational venue for understanding what they have unconsciously been carrying for a traumatized parent. To some degree, the experience of the next generation has been "authored" by the unspoken, indeed unspeakable, traumas in their parents' histories, and sometimes they are unconsciously "authorized" to bring that trauma into the future. As I wrote elsewhere, such transgenerational experience "must come into being as emotional understanding if the [person] is ultimately to take authority for his or her own life as distinct from that of the traumatized parent" (Fromm, 2012a1, p. 113).

This patient felt this dilemma keenly as he decided to read his father's journal to his therapist. Indeed, this decision—and the anxious fantasies surrounding it—reminds us that the word "decide" has the same root as the words "suicide" and "homicide." Decisions separate; they, in a sense, kill the alternatives. For this patient, one of those alternatives had been to attempt to cure his father through identification—by carrying his emotional life for him. A major source of resistance was his profound fear, even conviction, that separating from that role would destroy his father, both by causing him to relive unbearable pain and by leaving him alone with it as his son moved on with his own life. And that latter move—to one's own life—is also risky, because the patient too is alone; if one's identity has been unconsciously organized around a family role, the question "Who am I now?" borders on identity crisis (Volkan, 2020).

This patient also played out the transmission of trauma in the transference to his therapist, through a set of reactions to his therapist's vacation and a critical decision to read his father's journal. As this process unfolded, his own highly charged fantasy life found a context for meaning: his father's suppressed emotional life. The psychoanalyst Dori Laub (2018), himself a Holocaust survivor, writes that the treatment of trauma, whether in the first or subsequent generations, involves the communication of "testimony" to a witness "[willing] to be totally present to the survivor, and [to] receive as well as experience what he/she wants to transmit" (p. 102). The transmission of trauma can be seen as an ambivalent effort at such testimony, potentially dangerous but essential to the development of the child-witness. Psychotherapy offers that person a new witness, to whom testimony can be brought in its various unconscious forms so that it can be contained, interpreted, and brought into its historical context. The potential space (Winnicott, 1971a) for understanding, that had collapsed between child and parent because containment of the unbearable was impossible, may become a generative space between patient and therapist, generative of the imagination and strength to make sense of what he has been carrying, with whatever degree of pain and confusion, for his family.

Nothing happened

A patient came to his session very upset. Without quite realizing it, he had essentially trashed his apartment over the previous two days. When he began to explore what had happened during this time, his first reaction was that nothing of significance had occurred. But then he remembered that he had gone to a medical appointment, during which he felt physically exposed to a male doctor's impersonal touch. The patient himself was a doctor. He had managed to do well in medical school, to have been part of a thriving group practice, to have married, and had a child. But when his son reached a certain age, the patient suffered a major breakdown. What happened? In essence, the patient had run to the future—a future that now included his son—and found falling upon him the little boy he was when, ages ago, he had suffered horrific sexual abuse by a parish priest. Now, the day before the session, a man had touched his body uncaringly, and in furious response, as he came to understand it, he had willfully abandoned taking care of himself. Hence, the shambles of his apartment.

But, throughout this important work, his therapist found himself thinking about what might have happened between the two of them that could also have contributed to the trouble. When he asked the patient if anything in the previous session had upset him, the patient reported no memory of it at all; as we have seen, traumatic experience leads to dissociative defenses. He asked if his therapist had anything in mind, and indeed he did. Just before that session's end, the patient had mentioned that he had just received an opportunity to return to part-time medical work, but added that his therapist probably couldn't change his appointment times, so it probably wouldn't work out. He dropped the issue there. An odd feeling of emptiness—of something important not happening—registered in the therapist, but, not understanding it, he decided to let it go for the moment. Now, in response to the patient's question, his therapist said that he recalled not answering a question in the previous session, but one that the patient hadn't asked. Instantly, the patient remembered the end of the session, and came to realize that his rage toward that outside doctor was also toward his therapist: essentially, "OK, if you don't want to take care of me (by answering a question without my having to ask it), then you'll see what happens when I don't take care of myself."

In his "Fear of Breakdown" paper, Winnicott, at his most eloquent, takes up a variation on his main theme: not of "something happening," but of "nothing happening when something might have happened" (1974, p. 106). He was referring to critical developmental moments, moments when something essential might have been provided to the child at just the right time, but wasn't. Winnicott, the pediatrician as well as psychoanalyst, thought the child registered this as an experience of intolerable emptiness, which naturally led both to the fear of experiencing such profound emptiness again, but also to the search for another person with whom to experience it in such a way that it could be tolerated, survived, and learned from.

This patient experienced a feeling of emptiness with his therapist, and his therapist did with him as well. Something didn't happen: The therapist didn't answer a question the patient didn't ask. Rather, in the next session, the therapist brought the patient back to that empty moment, acknowledged it, and both allowed and survived the patient's anger at what he felt to be the therapist's failure. From the therapist's perspective, however, had he filled that space, for example by reassuring the patient about the possibility of rescheduling his therapy appointments, he felt that he would have deprived the patient, and the two of them, of learning from this moment. He would also have deprived the patient of the opportunity to risk the profoundly strengthening question: "Would you, for me?"

This turns out to have been the precise place the historical tragedy occurred: his parents' response to that question would have been a distant No, for reasons having to do with the suffering they had come through in their lives; his priest's answer would have been a Yes, but for himself, not for this little boy. The patient avoided this question with his therapist for fear of breaking through to the traumatic history—as we now know, an enormous history of trauma for so many people—within this transference moment. Working through this moment of acute emptiness opened up the patient's shame, rage and loss, all related to his having been abused. From that tragic time forward, he felt his life was over and that he was condemned to a desolately empty future. In this vignette, the defense of "nothing happened" was less the patient's way of protecting traumatized parents—though parental guilt for their child's molestation can indeed be unbearable—as it was protection for himself and his new family. In a sense, it was his effort not to transmit trauma—so that he might provide for his son the future taken from him—but, as we have seen, such efforts can be both costly and unsuccessful.

Being the other person

In her exquisite "Fear of Breakdown: A Clinical Example" paper (1980), Clare Winnicott, a psychoanalyst and Donald Winnicott's wife, describes her first encounter with a middle-aged professional musician who suffered major recurrent depressions. The patient showed a "determination to hold her own" (1980, p. 351) in this first consultation, and, after "a rehearsed performance," spoke of the "one thing I can't do: I know everything about myself, and I can manage very well except for this one thing I can't do." Clare Winnicott found herself saying: "Well, one thing that you can't do is to *be the other person*" (1980, p. 352). Where did this rather stunning response come from? How did Ms. Winnicott have the courage to make such a bold statement in the first session? What did she mean?

The patient too was stunned. "It was touch and go," said Ms. Winnicott. "Her response was to look at me in an intent searching way for what seemed like a long time, during which neither of us moved or relaxed attention. She was in fact sizing me up and I felt the question hanging in the air was, *would I do as 'the other person' …?*" (1980, p. 352). The patient decided that indeed she would, and they began an analysis. The patient's shock at losing the "other person"—her lover's leaving her after three years—had thrown her into despair and a dissociated state for which she had no memory. After learning a bit of her history, Ms. Winnicott suggested that this loss of memory may cover up something from long ago that had also been a shock to the patient.

Soon thereafter, the patient brought in a photograph of herself when she was two and a half, a picture of a child "cringing and withdrawn, clutching her dress and sucking her thumb." Ms. Winnicott's instant thought was "autistic child." The patient said: "They tell me that's a photograph of me. I simply can't believe it; I can't recognize anything of myself in it. But my mother says, 'Don't be silly, of course it's you' " (1980, p. 352). Ms. Winnicott suggested that connecting to this part of herself may have been the one thing the patient could not do, also that keeping the photograph may have reflected her hope that someone could help her with that, and that bringing it to the session brought that request for help to her analyst. She added that the child looked terrified as though something "intolerable" had happened to her. The patient "listened intently with the whole of herself" (1980, p. 353).

Donald Winnicott's "Fear of Breakdown" paper includes a section called "Futility in Analysis." In it, he says that "There is no end [to the patient's trouble] unless the bottom of the trough has been reached, unless *the thing feared has been experienced*" (1974, p. 105). "There are moments … when a patient needs to be told" (p. 104) about "this past and future thing" (p. 105). In other words, Winnicott is telling us in this last paper that a therapist must speak from what she knows and must actively offer herself as "the other person" with whom "the bottom of the trough" might be experienced. This involves taking the whole burden of the traumatic history into the transference relationship, where there is the possibility of giving a mind to the devastating gap that had occurred between parent and child.

Clare Winnicott does this in the moment described above. And the "bottom of the trough" does indeed come repeatedly into the therapy, as the patient's early losses are worked through in the transference. These traumatic losses were directly related to the trauma of war. In that context, the patient's father left the family, never to return, and the patient's mother deceived her toddler into believing that they were going to visit a relative when in fact the child was being suddenly and without explanation left in care. Years went by before mother and child saw each other again. However the mother experienced the war and the losses associated with it, her profound denial of its effects on her child is implicit in her comment about the photograph: "Don't be silly. Of course it's you."

Later in her treatment, the patient sees that child in a dream; the little girl is lifting her arms toward the patient, who says to herself, "That child wants picking up, so I'd better go and do it" (1980, p. 355), which indeed she does. From this point forward, the patient's dissociation of her past is over. There was one final bout of near unbearable rage, again in the face of her mother's denial; the latter absolutely refused her daughter's request for information about her father. This time the patient does not break down in the face of what her mother, presumably, still could not bear. Rather, with her analyst now in the place of the truly dependable other, she *breaks through* to the actual history of her father. On her own, without her mother's help or permission, she learns everything she can about this man, who, like her, was a musician.

In a last dream image, there is a bridge and a warm reunion with a beloved pet from her early childhood. In other words, at the end of the process I have been describing in this chapter, there is not only a structure across the gap or a linking of formerly dissociated parts—represented by the bridge—there is also *a reunion with history*, an emotional encounter with what and who have been lost to trauma, a *breakthrough* to love and mourning. This patient's story, like that of the patient who dreamed about a fire-rain, tells us something about trauma to the children of the London Blitz. As Anna Freud and Dorothy Burlingham showed in their classic *War and Children* (1943), separation from parents, even though meant to be protective, was so often devastating to these children, as was—for those who stayed and fled to the bomb shelters—a mother's emotional inability to contain and comfort her child. The human "protective shield" (S. Freud, 1920g)—which on the surface can sound like a delusional reassurance that "We will be OK"—is essential to a child's capacity for resilience after trauma.

CHAPTER 2

Walking into the wild: traumatic disillusionment and identity crisis

> *Greetings from Fairbanks! This is the last you shall hear from me, Wayne. Arrived here two days ago. It was very difficult to catch rides in the Yukon Territory. But I finally got here. Please return all mail I receive to the sender. It might be a very long time before I return south. If this adventure proves fatal and you don't ever hear from me again, I want you to know you are a great man. I now walk into the wild. Alex.*
>
> —Krakauer, 1996, p. 3

The young author of this postcard was saying goodbye—temporarily or permanently—to an older man who had befriended him and given him temporary farm work. It's both moving and a sign of what he had lost that this last communication acknowledges Wayne as a "great man." The writer was a twenty-four year old named Christopher Johnson McCandless, and his fascinating, tragic story was told in a *New Yorker* article in February, 1993, by Chip Brown, then in a best-selling book by Jon Krakauer in 1996.

As Krakauer put it, McCandless' story invites reflection on "larger subjects … the grip wilderness has on the American imagination, the allure high-risk activities hold for young men of a certain mind, the complicated, highly charged bond that exists between fathers and sons" (1996, p. x). In this chapter, I will explore the nature of that "complicated, highly charged bond" between one father and son. As this volume makes clear, trauma comes in many forms and plays itself out in many different ways. In this case, what some psychoanalysts have called *traumatic disillusionment* (Wolf, 1995) seems central to the fate of this young man, as does the combination of nihilistic rage and extreme idealism that were his primary reactions to it.

The wild

Krakauer summarizes McCandless' story in the following way:

> In April, 1992, a young man from a well-to-do East Coast family hitch-hiked to Alaska and walked alone into the wilderness north of Mt. McKinley. Four months later his decomposed body was found by a party of moose hunters … He'd grown up … in an affluent suburb of Washington, D.C., where he had excelled academically and been an elite athlete. Immediately after graduating with honors from Emory University in the summer of 1990, McCandless dropped out of sight. He changed his name, gave the entire balance of a $25,000 saving account to charity, abandoned his car and most of his possessions, burned all the cash in his wallet. And then he invented a new life for himself, taking up residence at the ragged margin of our society, wandering across North America in search of raw transcendent experience … (1996, p. ix)

McCandless walked into the wild with the backpack his father had given him years before and the blue sleeping bag his mother had sewn for him, the bag in which he eventually died from starvation. He did not, however, in those pre-digital years, bring a map or a compass, and this proved ultimately to be his undoing. Indeed he rejected maps and watches, telling one of the drivers who picked him up, "I don't have to know where I am, and I don't want to know what time it is." This angry, proud rejection of convention had been part of his personality for a long time. On a W-2 Tax Form, he declared himself "EXEMPT." He described his Alaskan quest, fueled by the writings of Tolstoy, Thoreau, and Jack London, as "the climactic battle to kill the false being within and victoriously conclude the spiritual pilgrimage … no longer to be poisoned by civilization" (Krakauer, 1996, p. 163).

Being found and getting lost

The late adolescent, writes Winnicott, "has a fierce intolerance of false solutions" (1963a, p. 244), and of "being found before being there to be found" (1963b, p. 190). In a sense, this phase of young adult development recurrently offers a ritual cleansing, a renewal of ideals, to its society, especially when that society's accommodations to reality may have led to too many disheartening compromises. But this idealism needs the solidarity of peers and the shelter of a phase of freedom for its incubation. Being found prematurely—and being called, coerced, or seduced into a societal role the young person has not really chosen—is destructive to the adolescent's development and to the society that needs his inspired energy. McCandless felt it as being "poisoned by civilization."

But Winnicott added that, while "It is a joy to be hidden," it is also a "disaster not to be found" (1963b, p. 186), that is, found by another person who understands and respects this developmental process. Erikson understood this paradox, and this profound danger, as part of the young person's struggle to come to a workable sense of identity. McCandless was determined not to be found until he had achieved a purification and strengthening of the self. In this sense, his Alaskan journey constituted what Erikson called a personal "moratorium" (1959, p. 145), a time out between the demands of a person's formative years and the commitments of adulthood. McCandless' story illuminates the continuing importance of moratoria to people in the midst of identity crises, as well as the dangers one will subject oneself to in order to achieve a new self-status.

McCandless' story also makes clear that he needed to solve the identity problem before he could approach what Erikson saw as the next developmental task: that of intimacy. On any number of occasions during his wanderings, Chris took the risk of revealing himself and beginning to become attached to others only when he was on the verge of leaving. For example, on the night before he left for Alaska, he surprised the people he was staying with by a show-business worthy performance of popular tunes on the piano. On another occasion, he managed to get an elderly man to propose formally adopting him, at which point he again took to the road. He seemed to willfully break the bonds that his likable way of being, and perhaps his subtle longing, invited, especially from older men. This is a late adolescent version of an earlier developmental issue: that toddlerhood moment when attachment must also allow for the child's separation-individuation phase, or, to put it differently, when the child's first "No" helps to establish the sense of "I." For McCandless at this point in his life, it seemed as though bonds threatened to become bondage, or as though being swaddled in that sleeping bag meant that he would never get out, at least not without a willful escape.

In fact, much of McCandless' life had been devoted to the exercise of will, particularly over dependence on, or submission to, others. The themes of willfulness and of going in search echo back to age two when this child, who had not long before learned to walk, left his house in the early hours of the morning to look for candy in a neighbor's house. Years later, McCandless captained his high school cross-country team and led his group of "Road Warriors" on long practice runs—"suicide runs" he called them (Brown, 1993, p. 38)—designed to get them lost. Though a natural student and high achiever, he made it clear that the rules did not apply to him: apparently the direct legacy of an embattled relationship between his high-strung, controlling, and achievement-oriented father and his like-minded son.

The senior McCandless was an eminent aerospace engineer, who designed advanced radar and satellite systems that could map the entire earth from space, "that could practically show the beaver in the pond," says Chip Brown (1993, p. 40). He was born into poverty but worked his way through college by playing the piano and came into the aerospace industry during the post-Sputnik boom. Eventually, he started his own consulting business with his wife, but because he had a number of children from a previous marriage, both parents were forced to work long hours to eventually achieve material success. The parents' relationship was thereby deeply strained, often openly acrimonious, and the children—Chris and his younger sister—were expected to adapt, obey, and perform.

The exceptions to this severe family atmosphere—severe for the purpose of survival but also of material success—included occasional camping trips on weekends, a yearly father–son hike in the Shenandoah Mountains, and visits to the maternal grandfather's house on the Upper Peninsula of Michigan. Described by his daughter as a stubborn, dreamy woodsman and poet, this grandfather was very close to his only grandson, and the boy loved and identified with him as well. Indeed, when his mother visited the campsite where her son had died, she said that its quiet beauty reminded her of her old home on the Upper Peninsula.

Identification and identity

McCandless' story illustrates the deep, unconscious, generational interplay of critical identity elements: maps, which father created and son rejected; money, which father sought and son burned; piano-playing and camping trips, which father and son shared. It could be argued that McCandless died seeking the positive aspects of the early father–son relationship—the idealized outdoor life of those Shenandoah outings and Upper Peninsula summers—and rejecting those hated aspects of it that had to do with control, achievement, and material success. And perhaps something else. The "false being within" may also have included McCandless' identification with his father, leading him to even more fervid repudiation. For example, in his letter to the old man who wanted to adopt him, a letter preaching the virtues of taking to the road and highly critical of the settled life, the young McCandless comes across as patronizing and controlling, just the way he experienced his father. Similarly, alongside the asceticism of cross-country running, McCandless had been, throughout his growing up, an easy and crafty salesman, given to counting his money regularly.

McCandless' postcard describes his older friend, Wayne, as a "great man." The "great man" theme, and the powerful idealization that can expose a child to great disappointment, is an important one for Erikson, which he took up in his writings about Luther, Gandhi, and others. In McCandless' manifesto about his "spiritual revolution," we hear another of Erikson's themes: a person's giving himself over to "totalism," when a desperately needed sense of "wholeness" seems unattainable. As Erikson puts it (as we shall see again in later chapters), totalism "involves a Gestalt in which an absolute boundary is emphasized: nothing that belongs inside must be left outside; nothing that must be outside should be tolerated inside ..." (1959, p. 133). Erikson also notes the intense emotional "energy ... employed in inner defenses against a threatening total re-orientation, in which black may turn into white and vice versa. Only the affect released in sudden conversions testifies to the quantity of this energy" (p. 133). At the epicenter of this crisis, Erikson locates despair: "Where the human being despairs of an essential wholeness, he restructures himself and the world by taking refuge in totalism" (p. 133).

The false being within

The quantum change in Chris McCandless' orientation—"almost like a born-again Christian" his friend said (Brown, 1993, p. 40)—was noticed during college. It was preceded by a critical event. McCandless' high school graduation coincided with his father's birthday, and at the graduation party his parents gave for him, Chris gave his father a birthday gift—an expensive telescope. What a perfect gift; it not only honors his father's interests, but it could also be seen as conveying an unconscious message: something like, "I long for you to find me but from a safe distance." Amidst the partying, Chris got emotional; his sister recalls his:

> ... fighting back tears, telling Dad that even though they had had their differences over the years, he was grateful for all the things Dad had done for him. Chris said how much he respected Dad for starting from nothing, working his way through college, busting his ass to support [his] kids. It was a moving speech. Everybody there got all choked up. And then he left on his trip. (Krakauer, 1996, p. 118)

McCandless' trip was cross-country, solo, by car, and relatively well-planned. But there may have been a less conscious element to his itinerary, one that took him to the Southern California neighborhood where he had spent the first few years of his life. From neighbors and acquaintances still living there, he found himself piecing together the facts of his family's early life. His father's affair had led to his mother's pregnancy with him, which automatically implicates him in a family tragedy. This information was to some extent already known to Chris. What he had not known was that his father had continued his first marriage secretly, after having married McCandless' mother, and that two years after Chris' birth, the senior McCandless had fathered another son with his first wife. When the father's bigamy and double life came to light, both parents were engulfed in a cataclysm of pain, the open wounds seeping inevitably into their already acrimonious relationship and into their parenting.

That this disaster occurred during McCandless' toddlerhood—which parents know as the "terrible twos"—is suggestive for his enduring personality traits. His willfulness in the service of autonomy, his angry stubbornness, his being a bit of a know-it-all, and his vulnerability to shame are all traits that one sees—if things go well, rather fleetingly—during that developmental period. Family trauma, when it happens, necessarily takes place in the context of a child's developmental phase, which sometimes leads to that child's becoming stuck in certain ways of behaving and reacting. A child's fixation, if you will, often reflects the fact that parents no longer have the resources to understand him or her. In the face of their own traumatic experience—which they also can't think about—their driven reactions to the child's behavior tend to perpetuate it. More speculatively, what about that unusual pre-dawn walk on his own when McCandless was two? Might it have meant something beyond a toddler's determination to find the candy he was told he couldn't have before bed? McCandless' terrible discovery makes us wonder: Had his father taken to leaving his home at night to see his other family? Did his son notice that? Was Chris looking for candy or for his Daddy?

What the devastating story of the road trip makes clear is that the gap between "great man" and "false being" eventually became a precipice over which the father–son relationship crashed. It was the unconscious fuel for McCandless' identity crisis. To his sister, McCandless confided that the facts of his early life "made my entire childhood seem like a fiction" (Krakauer, 1996, p. 123). In college, he contemptuously refused his parents' offer to buy him a new car, telling his sister that he didn't want them to think they had bought his respect. Chip Brown writes that in Alaska, McCandless "seemed almost to revel in the power of doing without, the euphoria of dispossession" (1993, p. 38), freeing himself from being corrupted by needing someone who had betrayed him. As if enacting something about this, during his phase of random farm work on his way to Alaska, Chris often played at being Darth Vader, the great man/father whose turn toward the dark side eternally disillusions his son. In the *Star Wars* episode in which Vader reveals himself to his son, Luke lets go, seemingly to fall forever.

Happiness

By the time McCandless set off for Alaska, his family had neither seen nor heard from him in the two years since he smiled, accepted his diploma, and walked off the stage of his college graduation. The agony of losing a child had softened the senior McCandless. And something was happening to his son as well. Alaska was to have been, according to his journal, his last great adventure—the culmination of his spiritual journey and adventurous wanderings throughout the West. There were suggestions that he too had come to some form of resolution; underlining a passage in *Doctor Zhivago*, the young man wrote in the margin, "Happiness only real when shared" (Krakauer, 1996, p. 189). This generation's "dreamy, poetic woodsman" was now far less stubborn.

Indeed, McCandless had decided to end his Alaskan moratorium, but was thwarted in two ways. First, the frozen river he had crossed in April had become an impassable torrent by mid-July. Second, seeds he had reason to think were edible turned out to be poisonous. He grew increasingly weak. A note he left at his base camp while foraging for food was signed with his real name; as he was slowly starving, he gave up his traveling persona and once again became Chris. Like anorexic patients, who have internalized a struggle of wills and who play that struggle out between mind and body, what an ironic surrender it must have been when McCandless realized that his body—now half the weight it had been in the spring—no longer obeyed him. And that, in escaping one kind of poison, he had fallen victim to another. But his final diary entries suggest a peaceful and forgiving surrender as well. At the end, Chris left a smiling photograph and a note which declared, "I have had a happy life and thank the Lord. Goodbye and may God bless all" (Krakauer, 1996, p. 199).

Chris McCandless began his trek into the wilderness north of Denali by hitch-hiking into Fairbanks, a place where his father had done aerospace work in the past. He died in the sleeping bag his mother had sewn for him. Had he brought with him a topographic map of the surrounding terrain, he would have realized that it was possible to cross the swollen river a half-mile downstream. A final sad irony, very likely resulting from his repudiation of his map-making father. Chip Brown closes his article on the death of Chris McCandless by saying:

> What makes his death so memorable is the narrative he was enacting: it is an old story, the tale of the boy on the brink of manhood who ventures into the wilderness in a rite of passage. It is supposed to end with his transformation and return—the new-made man reunited with his community, a community that relies on his wise new eyes to renew itself … but this time the narrative was broken, its promise cut short. (1993, p. 47)

There is probably no clearer description than this of Erikson's concept of moratorium and of the proper resolution of identity crisis (Erikson, 1959, p. 145). Perhaps more to the emotional point, Jon Krakauer begins one of his later chapters with the following passage from the novel, *The Dead Father*, by Donald Barthelme:

> But have you noticed the slight curl at the end of Sam II's mouth, when he looks at you? It means that he didn't want you to name him Sam II, for one thing, and for two other things it means that he has a sawed-off in his left pant-leg, and a baling hook in his right pant-leg, and is ready to kill you with either one of them, given the opportunity. The father is taken aback. What he usually says, in such a confrontation, is "I changed your diapers for you, little snot." This is not the right thing to say. First, it is not true (mothers change diapers nine out of ten), and second, it instantly reminds Sam II of what he is mad about. He is mad about being small when you were big, but no, that's not it, he is mad about being helpless when you were powerful, but no, not that either, he is mad about being contingent when you were necessary, not quite it. He is insane because when he loved you, you didn't notice. (1996, p. 145)

Erikson would call this—putting it far too mildly—missed "mutuality" (1959, p. 125). As his Riggs colleague, David Rapaport, said, Erikson offered the first psychoanalytic theory of the evolving social reality with which the developing child is always engaged. Rapaport added: "His concept of mutuality specifies that the crucial coordination is between the developing individual and his human (social) environment" (1959, p. 15). While Winnicott beautifully described the mutuality between mother and infant, Erikson, perhaps more than any other psychoanalytic theorist, articulated the "crucial coordination" necessary between father and son.

The oedipal story, which is another way to read a father–son dynamic, has its mythic origins in a collision at a crossroads, a failure of a crucial coordination. Barthelme describes it as a lethal not noticing. In the McCandless case, there is more than missed mutuality between father and son; there is struggle, identification, longing, and traumatic disillusionment, all of which brought this young man—filled with angry idealism and unconscious love, in a state of impetuous vulnerability and determined independence—to a place associated with good fathers, from which he never left.

Chris McCandless' body was found in his base camp, an abandoned, rusted-out school bus in the wilderness near Denali. More than twenty-five years after McCandless' death, the bus was still there, until quite recently. A steady stream of young pilgrims had found in Chris' story their own longing for adventure and integrity, such that the "Magic Bus," as he had dubbed it, had become a holy site. Sadly, last summer, a young hiker was swept away by the Teklanika current in her effort to reach it—by no means the first to lose her life in that quest. Local authorities, both concerned and exasperated, decided to move the bus to safer ground, and in June, 2020, it was helicoptered to the Museum of the North at the University of Alaska, Fairbanks. Some locals resented the foolish young people who brought them to this decision. As they did with Chris, they criticized their disrespect for what it really meant to walk into the wild. But what shouldn't be lost in the controversy is the deep meaning of the quest itself; there *is* magic in it, the magic of renewal for the person and for society. Sometimes born of traumatic disillusionment, its goal is the restoration of ideals that are not illusions.

CHAPTER 3

A way of looking at trauma: Erik Erikson and the "cogwheeling" of life cycles

In the early 1970s, the eminent psychoanalyst Erik Erikson, recently retired from his position as university professor at Harvard, spent the spring and fall seasons teaching and consulting at the Austen Riggs Center. Erikson had been a full-time staff member at Riggs—a small psychiatric hospital specializing in intensive psychotherapy with very troubled patients—for ten years, beginning in 1951. When he returned, he attended the weekly case conference, and, at the end of the day, welcomed fellows-in-training to his home for a glass of sherry and a two-hour informal, but wonderfully rich discussion of that day's clinical case.

In his masterwork, *Childhood and Society* (1950), Erikson famously commented that the only thing he had to offer was "a way of looking at things" (p. 403). What an important perspective it was! Erikson had his theory deep inside him. In a way that seemed effortless, he was able to "read" the patient's life history, and to spell out clearly the current life crisis in which the patient had broken down, why the patient couldn't move to the next stage, how this echoed backwards through his development, and at what early phase the patient had become stuck. He paid attention to strengths as well as to conflicts and deficits, and spoke about who this person was as though he were looking through a clear mountain stream directly to the bottom. And gently, he would also read the therapist, and help us see how these two people—each with their own life histories, in a given cultural moment—were coming together, or not, within the therapeutic work. His clinical advice was simple: "You need a theory and you need a history, and then you must forget them both, and let each session stand for itself" (personal communication). In his own terms, Erikson was describing each session as a tiny but critical "moratorium" (Erikson, 1959, p. 111) for both patient and therapist.

Later, during an annual fall visit to the Center from his new home in California, I made an appointment with Erikson to discuss the connections I was seeing between his work and that of the great English pediatrician-psychoanalyst, Donald Winnicott. Erikson was uncharacteristically distracted during this conversation and eventually told me that he was having trouble thinking about my question because he was preoccupied with something: "I can't quite believe," he said, "that I am now the age Freud was the last time I saw him." That would probably have been in 1933, the year the Eriksons left Vienna. Freud would have been seventy-seven, and Erik had just turned seventy-seven before his visit to Riggs. This sweet story speaks to Erikson's attachment, not only to a great mentor, but also to a major father figure in his life. Why he needed that, how trauma played out across generations in Erikson's life, and how he used his work in the service of his own identity resolution are the themes of this chapter.

The direction of adaptation

The commonalities between Erikson's work and Winnicott's (Fromm, 1989) are striking. Both were studying—at about the same time on different sides of the Atlantic—the developing capacities or basic strengths of the child, not just the impersonal functions of the ego or the limitations of a person's pathology. Both focused on the human environment in which a child develops, and both recognized the interrelationship between an attuned human environment and the child's successful development. Both spelled out phase-specific developmental tasks and the environmental provision that facilitated or inhibited completion of those tasks. Erikson did this for the entire life cycle, and Winnicott primarily for infancy and early childhood.

In their emphasis on identity (for Erikson) or "unit status" (for Winnicott, 1954, p. 279), both placed the integrated core of the person at the center of their theories. And both elevated the concept of play to a new level of importance as the basic medium of the child's evolving integration. For Winnicott, the outcome of "good-enough" mothering, in what he describes as the transitional-object phase (Winnicott, 1951, p. 238), was the child's basic confidence in her capacity to create or to find in the world what she needs, a strength Erikson described as the achievement of basic trust. And when Winnicott, at his most eloquent, described the experience of emptiness as having to do with "nothing happening [at a crucial moment in development] when something might … have happened" (1974, p. 106), he was describing exactly what Erikson meant by missed "mutuality" (1959, p. 125). Indeed, their shared emphasis on "mutuality"—what Erikson's Riggs colleague David Rapaport called "the crucial coordination between the developing individual and his human, social environment" (1959, p. 15)—was unique to both Erikson's and Winnicott's contribution to psychoanalytic theory at that time.

This coordination is what Erikson and Rapaport meant by the word "cogwheeling" (Rapaport, 1959, p. 15). With this rather awkward word, they were trying to describe the inter-generational fit between developmental tasks of parent and child: for example, the way that the baby's need to be fed fits with the mother's physical and emotional need to feed, or the way that a mature adult's urge toward generativity meets a child's need to develop competence and industriousness. The word "cogwheeling" also captures the way that, not only do the child's and the parent's developmental tasks *fit* together, they also *activate* each other.

Of course, this ideal scenario of mutuality is not always the case in real life. Winnicott's conceptualization of the False Self (1960b)—and more recent work on the transmission of trauma from one generation to the next (Fromm, 2012a)—describes what we might call *a reversal in the direction of adaptation*, in which the child is unconsciously invited to adapt to a troubled parent, with enduring problematic effects on development. Winnicott puts it this way:

> The good-enough mother meets the (spontaneous impulse) of the child and … makes sense of it. A True Self begins to have

> life ... The mother who is not good enough ... repeatedly fails to meet the infant gesture; instead she substitutes her own gesture, which is to be given sense by the compliance of the infant. This [is] ... the earliest stage of the False Self, and belongs to the mother's inability to sense her infant's needs. (1960b, p. 145)

Erikson was aware of this problem of fit as well, and the question of who is adapting to whose needs. He wrote about "the subtler methods by which children are induced to accept . . . [their parents'] prototypes of good and evil," the way that "minute displays of [a parent's] emotion," including "minute socioeconomic and cultural panics," "transmit to the ... child the outlines of what really counts." "Every neurosis," he said, is "somatic tension," "isolated anxiety," and "shared panic," "all at once" (1959, p. 28).

The kids can feel it

The idea of "shared panic," leading to the child's being unconsciously invited to adapt to a troubled parent, brings us into the territory of trauma. In December 2001, three months after the 9/11 attack on the World Trade Center, *The New York Times* reported the following comment by a man who worked as a sidewalk Santa at Rockefeller Center on Fifth Avenue. This man, whose name was Maurice De Witt, noticed a change in people's attitudes that holiday season. Here is what he said: "The normality is not there. The parents will not let the hands of their children go. The kids sense that. It's like water seeping down, and the kids can feel it. Their reactions to Santa are not natural. There is an anxiety, but the kids can't make the connection" (Leduff, 2001).

This astute man was noticing a powerful double message in the parents' action during that troubled time. Consciously and verbally, the message was "Here's Santa. Love him." Unconsciously and physically, it was "Here's Santa. Fear him." The trauma of 9/11 was not spoken; indeed it is very unlikely that, in the moment, these parents were aware that they were carrying anxiety associated with 9/11. Nevertheless, something about that anxiety was communicated to the next generation by the squeeze of a hand, and it took someone outside the twosome, like this Santa, to see and name the trouble, someone in the position of what various psychoanalytic theorists have called the "Third" (Muller, 1996).

Following 9/11, Susan Coates and her colleagues in New York organized clinics to help children and their families with the traumatic consequences of the attack on the World Trade Center. In *Trauma and Human Bonds* (Coates et al., 2003), they tell the story of a little girl who seems to be holding not only her own terrifying experience, but her father's too. In the clinic, she drew in red, yellow, and black the burning buildings she had seen on TV, and in which she, and her family too, thought her father had died while at work in the World Trade Center's top-floor restaurant. But it turned out that her father had exchanged his shift with a friend that day so that he could do errands. It was his friend who had died in the catastrophe. The father was shocked to realize that his daughter believed he had nearly been killed by the fire. Suffering agonizing survivor guilt and recurrent nightmares about how his friend had died, this man had withdrawn from his family, leaving his little girl with her terrifying fantasies.

"So your daughter is drawing your dreams," his therapist said. This intervention put father and daughter back in emotional contact with each other. Dr. Coates and her colleagues, like the sidewalk Santa, illustrate powerfully the unconscious attunement between children and parents, especially in situations of trauma. This last story also shows how child and parent can become isolated from each other, with potentially serious consequences for the child's development as she lives out her unconscious resonance with the parent's trauma.

Parents *mind* children. Their minds make sense of what a child is feeling or imagining, and they give that sense back to their anxious child, a giving back that more often than not comforts and contains the child. But when parents lose their minds under circumstances of extreme distress, children find a way to mind their parents. They bring to their parents in one way or another—Erikson's somatic tension or isolated anxiety—something crucial that requires understanding, something related to the child's *and* the parent's shared panic. The critical question is whether the parent can hear the child's effort to make sense of what is happening, even if that effort is communicated, as kids do, in a drawing, a nightmare, or disruptive behavior.

This parental capacity to make sense of what is going on in the mind of the child crucially influences the child's proneness toward, or resilience in the face of, traumatization. That capacity for what Fonagy et al. (2002) call "mentalization" often fails because of a parent's own unbearable traumatic experience. As with the sidewalk Santa, what we see instead is the parent's panic-driven, nonverbal gesture, a gesture out there, so to speak, to be registered and made sense of unconsciously by the child. This reversal in the ordinary direction of adaptation is, to some extent, what it means for a child to grow up in a family; parents teach children consciously and unconsciously. But when the context is trauma, the transmission is both urgent and confusing to the child. Something important is happening but the child doesn't know what it is, because the parent doesn't either. This transmission, as Vamık Volkan (2004a) argues, may take many forms. For example, anxiety or other feeling states, like fear, rage, or sorrow, may be passed from parent to child. So may unconscious fantasies about the cause of the trauma. And sometimes an unconscious task is deposited into the child: for example, to avenge a parent's humiliation or to make up for a terrible loss.

Identity crisis and family tragedy

Aspects of Erik Erikson's own life can be seen through this lens. As told by his daughter, Sue Erikson Bloland, in her book, *In the Shadow of Fame* (2005), there is a poignant, at times heartbreaking, story that travels through time for Erikson. After describing her parents' first meeting at a glamorous masked ball in Vienna, Bloland writes:

> It was almost uncanny the way my parents' early experiences had prepared them to connect with each other as adults: Dad had never known his biological father. Mother had hardly known hers. They had both experienced crushing parental disapproval and had felt estranged from families and peers. Both had felt like misfits in the social worlds in which they had grown up. Yet each of my parents had also been admired and championed by one all-important adult: Dad by his mother, Karla; and Mother by her grandmother. (p. 57)

Bloland's comment about her father's not knowing his father is important. Erik Erikson was born, out of wedlock, to a German-Jewish mother and a Danish Gentile man, who was never part of Karla's life after the conception. This strong, loving woman, now compromised in her family's eyes, moved to northern Germany to raise her son. A few years later, during a routine medical checkup for Erik, she met and soon fell in love with a Jewish pediatrician named Theodor Homburger. Erikson thus first met his father-to-be in the role of patient! But Erik's mother insisted that they never tell the then three-year-old that he was Dr. Homburger's adopted, rather than biological, son. Of course, family secrets are notoriously hard to keep and can become serious problems. As Erikson described in his autobiographical paper (1970), his younger sisters were small and dark, while he was blond, blue-eyed, and "grew flagrantly tall." In public school, he was called "Jew," but at temple, he was called "Goy" (p. 743). Given this ongoing strain, it is no surprise that Erikson eventually articulated, for the first time in the field of psychology, the concept of identity crisis. For him, it was personal.

Bloland (2005) suggests that her parents' mothers each transmitted to their children a psychological task borne of personal trauma, including the pain of thwarted ambitions and shame. Erikson's mother's Bohemian lifestyle—reflecting her own intellectual ambitions—may have played its part in her pregnancy and ostracism. Her marriage to Dr. Homburger rescued her—and her son—but it also embedded her in a socially conformist way of living. According to Bloland, she inevitably invested Erik with the task of fulfilling her secret longings for an intellectual life, and even looked to him to redeem her reputation in the eyes of others.

Something similar was true for Joan Erikson. Her mother had also been thwarted in her efforts to find fulfillment in life. She was an anxious, inhibited person, fearful of anything that seemed nonconformist, and she worked hard to tame her daughter's "rebellious spirit" (p. 69). But behind that disapproval, Joan felt her mother's "secret envy" (p. 69) of her daughter's willingness to challenge convention and free herself to explore the world. Conscious embarrassment at Joan's behavior and fear about the chances she was willing to take seem to have masked her mother's secret pride and longing. Joan's mother was also quite depressed at times, and during these breakdowns, it was Joan's responsibility to care for her.

Bloland (2005) argues that Joan and Erik had "troubled mothers whom they longed to heal" (p. 70); it's no surprise that later in life, they both became healers. Both felt "oppressed by their mothers' anxious conformity to social convention" (p. 70), but both could also sense how oppressed their mothers felt too. In breaking free, they were not only liberating themselves but, less consciously, liberating their mothers as well. To accomplish this, they drew upon how special they were both made to feel by their mothers, even if they were also criticized by them. They needed to rely on this sense of specialness for two reasons: both to protect themselves as they made their leap into the larger world, and to drive them toward the success their mothers longed for but could not accomplish for themselves. The development of a powerful sense of identity, one that drives a life story of healing and great accomplishment for both Erik and Joan, was intertwined in early childhood with their mothers' transmission of their own traumatic experiences.

Neil

Bloland then describes how this remarkably successful and productive effort to transform both a parent's and a child's trauma was tragically challenged in adult life. When Sue was five years old, a son was born to the Eriksons. His name was Neil, and he suffered from Down syndrome. The doctors thought that he would live for only a year or two, and, consistent with the medical opinion of the time, they recommended that the infant be institutionalized immediately, so that he could receive the care he needed, and so that his mother would not bond with him. Joan was under anesthesia for surgery following the birth, and so Erik was forced to make a critical decision without her, something that was very hard for him. The advice of close colleagues was to accept the doctors' recommendation and to do so immediately. He followed this advice, and told his children that the new baby had died at birth.

Both decisions—to institutionalize the baby and to create a false story for his children—were fateful ones. They began a family tragedy in which depression, suppressed rage, guilt, and shame coexisted uneasily with great accomplishment and public adulation. Bloland writes:

> My brothers and I had been told that Neil had died. But there was no burial, no ritual, no ceremony to mark his existence or

> his passing from our lives. Our parents didn't seem to grieve. … [Instead] they threw themselves into frenetic activity in an attempt to assuage their pain … Worst of all for their relationship and for the family, they never talked about Neil—with each other or with us. (2005, p. 25)

There is an almost inevitable outcome to trauma-based family secrets that, as Davoine and Gaudilliere (2004, p. 61) describe, are "cut out" of social discourse: the next generation must deal with them somehow. Sometimes someone in the next generation unconsciously falls into the role of representing the trauma. About her own experience as a child, Bloland (2005) writes: "I embarrassed them all … In an odd way, it seems I took on the role of Neil. I was the child who was somehow unable to function normally in a family in which the appearance of normality was of the utmost importance. I did not conceal the anguish that pervaded our family life" (p. 30).

There is such painful irony as well as deep resonance in the transmission of trauma. Erik Erikson was the illegitimate son of a father who abandoned him. A generation later, he fathers a defective, in a sense illegitimate, son whom he abandons. He suffers all his life from the secret of his own paternity and creates a secret paternity for his children. His mother's oppressive need to regain her respectability is mirrored in his own oppressive need not to fail at that task now. Joan Erikson was the daughter of a mother who broke down into a depression so severe that she sent Joan and her siblings to be cared for by relatives in California. A generation later, Joan becomes deeply depressed and uncharacteristically passive after Neil's birth, and she leaves him—and perhaps part of herself—in care in California.

There is another kind of irony in this story as well. Bloland felt keenly as a child how emotionally painful topics needed to be dissociated from family conversation. She often complied with this dynamic; like some of those 9/11 children, she spared her parents the transmission of traumatic feelings back to them. She dreaded opening wounds that her parents could never publicly acknowledge, and she dreaded "seeing the anguish on their faces that any reference to a painful issue might suddenly evoke" (2005, p. 37). Whenever this happened, she experienced an "abrupt sense of disconnection" (p. 37) from them, which left her terribly alone. In a sense, she felt something both of her parents had felt when they were children: shunned for breaking a powerful but unwritten rule never to expose her parents to their traumatic past.

In situations like this, the next generation also, without fully realizing it, resists the dissociation of trauma and sometimes finds a way to represent it to the family, ideally in the hope of resolution. In identifying with the child she did not consciously know existed, Bloland kept Neil psychologically alive as an unconscious presence in her family. Years later in her analysis, she had a dream in which she had the facial features of a Mongolian. In her mind, she *was* this alien figure; it was her identity. But her analyst heard in this dream a reference to Neil, Down syndrome features sometimes being referred to colloquially as Mongoloid. Bloland realized how deeply her sense of identity was interwoven with her unconscious identification with Neil. Part of her had been "lost in the transmission" (Fromm, 2012a) of her family's tragedy, until this therapeutic moment. Reclaiming herself through her analysis, Bloland found the emotional distance to see the full story of her family, and make it available, in all its sorrow, for understanding and mourning. Including the very sad moment when she and her family actually buried the brother they never knew, upon his death at age twenty-one, nineteen years after the doctors had expected him to die.

In one of those clinical case conferences at Riggs that Erikson would have attended, a young psychotic patient told the staff that the hospital "is haunted by the forces of the dead. They are here as much as there are helping people here." People whose sensitivities eventually develop into serious pathology, leading toward breakdown and patienthood, are sometimes providing a chaotic alertness to feelings and events from the past that are nevertheless part of the here and now. To the degree that this process must remain at an unconscious level, a crucial part of the child, later the troubled adult, is "lost in transmission." But the story of Sue Bloland and the Erikson family tells us that this experience of being lost—of being haunted and of haunting—may, if things go well, be transformed into deep discovery, necessary mourning, and reclaimed identity, for oneself and others.

A chance

Throughout the late 1980s, I chaired the Erikson Scholar Search Committee, whose job it was to search for and select a scholar to work with us for a period of time at Riggs. During a breakfast meeting, I asked Erik what he hoped for from the program. As mentioned in the Introduction, his response was humble, generous, and had nothing to do with enshrining his theory: "Only that a really promising person gets a real chance, the chance I had when I came to Riggs."

What might Erikson have meant by this "chance" that he was so grateful for? After all, he had already published *Childhood and Society* to great acclaim before he came to Riggs. Why was this "chance" so important to him? I would argue that it had to do with something quite personal, something about his own identity resolution. We have seen how Erik's mother's traumatic experiences of shame, abandonment, and thwarted ambition seem to have played themselves out in Erikson's own life. He never felt that he had a real father—a second parental figure who could support his mother, or who could, like that sidewalk Santa or Sue Bloland's therapist, help him make sense of what was happening and see him through his own identity crisis. The question, "Who am I?" is profoundly connected to the question, "What is my name?" and Erikson never knew the last name of his biological father.

It comes as no surprise then that Erikson's longing for an identity based on a father's recognition might bring him to psychoanalysis. In his autobiographical paper, Erikson writes that, for him, Freud was a "mythical figure and a great doctor who had rebelled against the medical profession" (1970, p. 744). This combination of greatness and rebelliousness within a healing profession must have been very appealing to him. His feelings toward Freud "mixed with a search for my own mythical father" (p. 744), and Erikson easily took up the role of "adopted son" (p. 744) in the psychoanalytic movement. As he put it, "I can only surmise (not without embarrassment) that it was a kind of favored stepson identity that made me take for granted that I should be accepted where I did not quite belong" (1970, p. 744). Plus, his training in child analysis was as close as he could come, without going to medical school, to being a children's doctor, like his actual adoptive father.

In his analysis with Anna Freud, Erikson would sometimes say "I don't quite know … why I'm not with him," meaning in analysis with her father (Friedman, 1999, p. 78). Clearly the father of psychoanalysis evoked a powerful paternal transference in Erikson, including the feeling that a powerful woman, Anna Freud, was barring entry to the father figure, as he felt his mother had done by refusing to tell him about his biological father. It's interesting that the year Sigmund Freud died, Erikson dropped his adopted last name, Homburger, and invented a new name, Erikson—a Danish name—as though to distinguish himself from fathers not fully his, and perhaps to declare an independent course of development.

Before coming to Riggs, Erikson was on the faculty of the University of California at Berkeley, in the midst of the McCarthy hearings and widespread anti-communist hysteria. This was also not long after baby Neil's birth and institutionalization. Faculty members at Berkeley and elsewhere were asked to sign a loyalty oath or risk losing their jobs. Reluctant to go along with what they felt was a totalitarian demand, Erikson and a number of others refused. Erikson was not fired, but soon resigned. And so, this middle-aged man, who had a family and no formal degree, was without a job in his adoptive country.

It was at this precarious moment in the Erikson family's life that Robert Knight, the new medical director at Riggs, invited Erikson to join his staff. Knight had known Erikson from the latter's consulting visits to Menninger's. About the same age as Erikson, Knight himself had felt like an adopted son at Menninger's (Friedman, 1999), and was eager to come into his own by launching the open hospital, intensive treatment project at Riggs. He offered Erikson a "chance" that must have resonated deeply: to have a job with someone who understood him, to escape California and find a new home, to move past being an adopted son, to deepen his clinical skills and develop his own unique voice. It was a chance for which Erikson remained grateful for the rest of his life.

"It isn't me"

During his time at Riggs, inspired by a patient who had broken down while in the seminary, Erikson took up the study of Martin Luther. In Germany to give a major lecture on the 100th anniversary of Freud's birth, a memory came to him:

> ... a memory which had been utterly covered by the rubble of the cities and by the bleached bones of men of my kind in Europe. In my youth, as a wandering artist, I stayed one night with a friend in a small village by the upper Rhine. His father was a Protestant pastor; and in the morning, as the family sat down to breakfast,

> the old man said the Lord's Prayer in Luther's German. Never having "knowingly" heard it, I had the experience, as seldom before or after, of a wholeness captured in a few simple words … (1958, p. 10)

On his mythical father's 100th birthday, and under the bones of those who must have represented his Jewish adoptive father—a paternal connection he separated from in 1939 when he changed his last name—Erikson remembers a Christian father, and in the prayer to "Our Father," he finally experiences a profound sense of wholeness. "Those who have once suddenly 'heard' the Gettysburg Address will know what I mean" (1958, p. 10).

What brought Erikson to Luther? In this astonishing study, Erikson traces the resounding No of the 95 theses back to an earlier No, a No that bordered on psychosis. In his mid-twenties, Luther suddenly fell to the ground during a monastery service and roared "I am not" or "It isn't me." Erikson understood this "fit in the choir" (1958, p. 23) through the classic analytic method of restoring context. Luther's outburst, during a time when he was committed to silence, occurred as a particular Gospel story was being read: a father pleads with Christ to cure his son, who is possessed by a "dumb spirit." It was thus, as Erikson put it, the story of two cures: a father's weak faith and a son's power of speech (1958, p. 27).

Erikson took both a clinical and a cultural approach to this strange moment of breakdown. He saw in Luther's crisis of identity—his roaring declaration of what he was not—the intensity of Luther's struggles with his father. The senior Luther was determined that his son should study law and, in so doing, elevate the status of the family. He strongly opposed Luther's religious vocation and suspected malevolent, even satanic, forces behind it. But Luther was not possessed; he was striving for a mind of his own. Erikson illustrates how this father–son relationship was the crucible in which the younger Luther encountered mind-threatening doubts about himself, leading to a clinical crisis, and then to a profound No to his father and the discovery of an independent voice.

Simply as a clinical story about generational conflict in the service of identity development, there is much to be learned here. But then came the truly Eriksonian creative leap. Erikson argued further that Luther's profound identity crisis also expressed his society's need to find its voice against the corrupt power of the Papacy. Luther's No to his father was the beginning of a much greater No to the Holy Father, indeed a No to any earthly authority claiming to mediate between God and man's conscience, and also a No to a foreign language, Latin, in favor of a Yes to his own German. This was an evolutionary leap in the development of personal authority, less an oedipal victory than an identity resolution. Luther's Reformation moved European culture away from paternal power—the power to interpret scripture, to condemn as heretical and to grant indulgence—and toward the lonelier, more adult position of taking authority for one's own life and being responsible for how one lives it.

It is interesting indeed that, following Erikson's own personal act of conscience, his No to the administration at Berkeley, he took up the study of Martin Luther. Interesting too that, when speaking about Freud—his mythical father—on an anniversary occasion, Luther's German comes back to him in the memory of an "Our Father." *Young Man Luther* is a profoundly important piece of work in its own right, but it was also, it seems to me, an unconscious vehicle—from his play therapy experiences, Erikson might call it a toy (1977)—through which Erikson, identifying with Luther, could play out and work through deeply personal anxieties about the resolution of his own identity crisis. In the context of a troubled mother, on whom he depended and who depended on him, and no father, Erikson desperately needed father figures. Then, to become himself, he needed to risk differentiating from—saying No to—these powerful identity-giving men.

Like Luther, Erikson was taking a serious psychological risk. Like Lincoln, whose Gettysburg Address occurred to him upon reflecting on the "Our Father" memory, Erikson was struggling with emancipation and with keeping the disparate parts of his own identity in some kind of workable union. To do this, he had to first acknowledge and honor the "bleached bones" of some fathers, the paternal prayers of others, and the debt owed to a mythical father. Then, like Luther, he could launch a reformation of psychoanalysis, now in his own voice. Erikson believed that his reformation was fully in the spirit of Freud's work but carried further—beyond childhood into the whole life cycle, beyond the psychosexual to the psychosocial, beyond ego to identity. It's to Riggs' great credit that it gave this "promising person a real chance." It's to Erikson's credit that he took it, and let it take him into the deeply personal work of identity resolution.

Part II

Trauma in organizations

CHAPTER 4

Minding the gap: the problem of college suicide

"What Nature rent asunder long ago, man has joined today" (Friend, 2003, p. 4). With this paraphrase of a biblical quote about marriage, chief engineer Joseph Strauss announced the opening of the Golden Gate Bridge in 1937. As of 2003, when an article entitled "Jumpers" appeared in *The New Yorker* (Friend, 2003), someone had jumped from the bridge every two and a half weeks since its opening. Friend noted a suicide website's proclamation that: "The Golden Gate Bridge is to suicides what Niagara Falls is to honeymooners" (p. 3).

Of the hundreds of people who made that leap in those sixty-six years, only twenty-six survived. Nearly all report instant regret the moment they left the outermost beam, evocatively called the "chord": 32 inches wide, 220 feet and 4 seconds above the water. As one survivor put it, "I instantly realized that everything in my life that I thought was unfixable was totally fixable—except for having just jumped" (2003, p. 1). Indeed, a study entitled "Where Are They Now?" contacted 515 people who had been stopped from jumping off the bridge over a thirty-four-year period. After an average of twenty-six years, 94% were alive or had died from natural causes (Friend, 2003).

A few years after this article, the San Francisco City Council voted overwhelmingly to attach nets to the sides of the bridge, at a cost exceeding $40 million. This decision finally resolved years of stalemated debate about whether or not to build barriers so that people could not easily climb over the railings. This perhaps simplistic, protective idea was regularly vetoed by majority sentiment that a few determined people should not ruin the majesty of the view for everyone. As this drama was ending, the Great Recession of 2008 was beginning. In response to the stock market's terrifying freefall, a photo circulated on the internet showing buildings on Wall Street, with a caption exhorting business executives to "Jump."

The problem of suicide

Suicide, as the "Jumpers" article makes clear, is a permanent solution to a temporary problem, but it is also a permanent problem—a genuine trauma—for those left behind, including the clinicians who treat them (Tillman, 2006). And it is a growing global problem. Its multidimensionality is breathtaking: the extremely high suicide rates of traumatized soldiers returning from Iraq and Afghanistan, returning from the devastation wreaked by suicide bombers; the violent eruptions on campuses or in shopping malls, which so often end with what has come to be called "suicide by police"; the passive suicides in abandoned places, like New Orleans after Hurricane Katrina, or the "deaths of despair" in opioid-saturated rural U.S. communities; the suicide of health care professionals overwhelmed by pandemic deaths; the increasing numbers of suicides in various countries as policies meant to facilitate development seem to have grave, unanticipated psychological consequences. Each of these lost lives leaves traumatized spouses, parents, children, friends, and others in its wake.

This chapter builds on two areas of work done at the Austen Riggs Center, a small, open psychiatric hospital specializing in the intensive treatment of patients who have not been helped by other treatments and who have come to be called "treatment-resistant." A substantial percentage of these patients are admitted after a major life-threatening suicide attempt; it would not be overly dramatic to say that for some their treatment begins after they have died, in terms of their intention and their psychology. Thus, studying the dynamics of suicide—which includes trauma in those patients' life histories and averted trauma to their families—is a clinical imperative for Riggs.

Contagion

From San Francisco to New York. In the eighteen-month period beginning in September 2003, five New York University students jumped to their deaths—with devastating consequences for their families, the student body, and the university, as well as to the lost promise of their futures. This "suicide contagion," as it came to be called, began with two young men jumping, one month apart, into the gorgeous atrium space of the new Bobst Library. Traumatized university officials responded with a barrier of transparent Lexan; in contrast to the Golden Gate proposal, they opted for protection *and* a view. But students then began to jump from the upper stories of their dormitory apartments. Since then, many universities have responded by helping their college counseling services build a net, so to speak. This is the second area in which Riggs and its Erikson Institute have attempted to make a contribution, by bringing clinical data to a conversation about the organizational and societal contexts in which college suicide occurs.

In 2001, the counseling service of Bennington College noticed something they had not seen before and asked for Riggs' help in understanding it. They were seeing a dramatic increase in the number of new students entering college on major psychoactive medications, and they also saw a different attitude as well, an attitude of "I don't know why I'm taking this, but I need it, so please give it to me." This posed major challenges for the college's psychiatry service. Reducing or discontinuing medications requires knowing students thoroughly, but simply going along with what's already been prescribed without this knowledge is also problematic. At a different level, this trend also challenged the institution's core mission of facilitating the students' agency, development, and learning. Bennington was a pioneer in offering psychotherapy to students as a form of deeper education about oneself and one's relationships. The "I don't know" from these students was a mission challenge and also an opportunity. In collaboration with Bennington, the Erikson Institute pulled together a regional network of about a dozen counseling services for a working conference on "The Escalating Use of Psychoactive Medication by College Students: What Are They Telling Us; What Are We Telling Them?" (Fromm, 2007). The Institute has hosted similar conferences, on a variety of topics chosen by the college counseling services, every year since then.

A psychoanalytic perspective on suicide raises a number of questions. How alone is this person? What has happened in her relationships recently that might have contributed to her wish to end her life? Is there a trauma history in the person's life or family? How angry or despairing is this person? And why? Another question, more unusual from a lay perspective, is: Does the method a person chooses have a dimension of meaning beyond that method's availability or likelihood of success? This kind of question may strike the listener as distracting, even trivial, when so much is at stake. And indeed these crises first of all must be managed to insure, as best one can, the safety of the suicidal person. But people in the throes of intensely disturbed emotions don't think clearly, much less communicate effectively in language; instead they tend to speak through action, which sometimes conveys an intense, often chaotic feeling state. What might a specific kind of suicidal action communicate? And could there be collective meaning in collective behavior, perhaps a group's effort to symbolize in action what can't be thought or spoken? From this angle, how might we understand the epidemic of jumping at NYU and elsewhere?

Cutting the cord

"What Nature rent asunder ..." said Joseph Strauss. A student's going off to college is, for many, the first and most powerful "renting asunder" in his young life. It is an edge of excitement, sadness, and anxiety, and a gap that must be bridged. How many parents have sent "care packages" to, and received tearful phone calls from, their distraught offspring as that first fall away from home sinks in? The data from the Counseling Service Conferences at the Erikson Institute suggested that the movement of the sociocultural tectonic plates, so to speak, in American life has, in recent years, widened this gap into a chasm for many students, into which some despairingly plunge.

Counseling staff noted a pervasive trend. For the last several decades, both parents have had to work to make ends meet, keep up a standard of living, or fulfill ambitions in a competitive environment. In the process, parenting functions have gradually and without negotiation shifted to the educational system, which has found itself accepting this task without planning, adequate resources, or even the overt consent some European countries long ago negotiated. Parents have come to depend on the school's playing this confusing but necessary "in loco parentis" role, and indeed the dependency that naturally developed in students was generally met—until they reached college.

This was the issue at stake in the Elizabeth Shin case at MIT (Sontag, 2002). Ms. Shin's death by fire in 2000, first ruled a suicide, led to a massive lawsuit by her parents, who accused the university of not protecting their daughter from her suicidal impulses and also not informing them about the severity of her troubles. Ultimately settled, with an agreement that the student's death was an accident (she had ingested a nonlethal dose of medications and may have fallen asleep with candles burning), this case marked a turning point in the stance colleges had traditionally taken, which was that they were educating young, more or less self-sufficient adults rather than parenting late adolescents. Recognizing the dependency needs of new students as well as the gap-turned-chasm between the provisions of secondary and college educational systems, counseling services have become much more active, available, and user-friendly on campuses, initiating, for example, early assessment, prevention programs, depression screening, peer support groups, and a variety of outreach programs.

A net

Counseling services have also, relatively recently, initiated some variant of an At-Risk Student Committee, which requires greater collaboration between mental health professionals, deans, and other relevant student affairs professionals whenever a student seems to be in trouble. In the Erikson Institute conferences, developing the thinking in this area has been at the heart of the work. Among other things, counseling services have had to sort through a range of issues related to confidentiality.

The latter is extremely important to a student's willingness to talk personally to another person, which itself is an essential relational requirement for all of us, especially when we are in trouble. But a simple "policy" about confidentiality too often in practice becomes a barrier to effective collaboration rather than a textured boundary of engagement. Engaging the student around the confidentiality boundary is not only an effective intervention, it also represents an ideal model for integration, which is a key developmental task of late adolescence. Policies that become barriers, however, risk, in a well-intentioned way, an apparently small but potentially dangerous "renting asunder" of the safety net.

One way to describe the arc of a student's college years—their travel through this precious time—is from her more or less being subject to the authority of others to taking authority for herself in a world of others. The developmental challenges within this arc include: the challenge of separating from parents (which implies managing longing and loneliness); moving from dependence to independence (which implies becoming competent to manage on your own and with peers); and moving from who you are to others to a deeper understanding of who you are to yourself. The latter task describes Erik Erikson's young adult stage of coming to identity (1959): who I am and who I am not; what I think and feel as distinct from what I've been told by others. Erikson's developmental schema also means that the young adult is moving from the preceding task of *industry* (learning how to perform tasks competently in a peer context) to the upcoming task of *intimacy* (taking the risk of revealing yourself to and caring about another person).

These are ordinary but momentous developments, made more challenging by the dangers of modern life—the temptation of substances, the potentially quite hurtful dynamics of social media, the violence (including sexual violence) within the culture. Counseling services facilitate the student's development by offering a relationship with a trustworthy and knowledgeable adult, who says to the student "It's safe to talk personally to me": safe from embarrassing exposure to others, from judgment, and from having feelings and fantasies mistaken for actions. Given that people have blind spots, this safety is not just *from* things; it's also *for* something; it offers a space for the student to say things *to herself* she hasn't yet said or even known she might say. Confidentiality also provides safety for the therapist. It safeguards the therapist's identity and membership in a clinical profession, and anchors her in her work with the client and in her relationship to the institution. Confidentiality is a precious and complex provision.

But it's also important to recognize that the limits of confidentiality are a provision of safety too. Erikson once commented that it is extremely important to make the distinction between "play and irreversible purpose" (1961, p. 156). In counseling or therapy, playing out one's thoughts and feelings, even one's relationship dynamics, with another person can lead to crucial learning—as long as it doesn't lead to dangerous action. Suicide is a tragic example of "irreversible purpose." Because of what confidentiality does for both the student and the therapist, it can be difficult to think clearly about its limits, especially given the heat of the moment with students, and also given what might be being played out between the student, the counseling service, and the college itself.

A diagnostic distinction

One bit of learning from the clinical work at Riggs and the counseling service conferences of the Erikson Institute is a diagnostic one. The more healthy the student, the more they expect the adults around them to work together on behalf of their growth. They take for granted that confidentiality doesn't preclude staff good judgment and discretion about when they talk to each other and what, at a general level, they talk about. So, they easily and thoughtfully sign informed consent forms, which authorize appropriate sharing of information. But more troubled students have had different experiences leading to different expectations. They are much more inclined to expect the adults around them not to be able to work together—to have potentially unbridgeable gaps between them. The more they feel this, the more they test it because, deep down, they know they need a working team. Sadly, in many cases, their family system has fragmented under the weight of its own traumatic experiences and been unable to provide emotional containment, reflective functioning, and usable speech to the student. So the student plays out this unfinished business within the college community.

This is, first of all, a developmentally important effort to get what is needed from adults, but it can also lead to splits or gaps between parts of the college community, including between the counseling service and the dean's office. Either/or choices (like empathy for the student or accountability to the college) take center stage when a both/and perspective is needed. Ironically and sometimes tragically, this too often replicates the split between parents who have not been able to work together to raise their child. Added to this is the fact that "students of concern" often feel they have not received what they needed in their growing up. They are understandably angry about this, about what may have caused it, and about the failures that have resulted from it. Their acting out in the college setting discharges some of this built-up anger, at the same time that it spreads the anger around to various people so that no one person has to bear it all. And it communicates something to its targets, often the authorities in college who represent parental authority.

Confidentiality moments

All of this is actually hopeful because it invites both containment of and communication about the trouble, provided that everyone survives in a working relationship with each other. For this to happen, these students need a clinical team, each person holding to their role. The therapist and student are the first and most critical "team." Their therapeutic alliance is crucial, including their capacity to explore what the student's acting out might mean within their own relationship. Other members of the staff team, within and outside the counseling service, form a safety net of people and important functions surrounding and supporting this team.

For this team to work, it should be understood by all, including the student, that clinical information is shared as needed and with discretion within the clinical staff group. Beyond that, confidentiality should not be seen as a barrier to communication with school authorities, but rather as a boundary around which extremely important work can occur. Confidentiality moments, when they come into the foreground between student and therapist, are not simply procedural, not simply about signing forms. They are an opportunity for discovering meaning at the boundary between the authority of the student and the authority of the therapist. In that sense, they are a primary site for the work of negotiating boundaries between self and other, which is a huge part of the student's developmental task more broadly.

In other words, confidentiality moments in the therapy relationship are primary developmental moments for the student. How to handle them is an important training issue for staff. For example, a student might ask for a guarantee that the therapist won't report what he says to anyone else. Rather than the therapist's giving a simple Yes or No answer, this is an opportunity for both exploration and for speaking personally. Questions like "Who are you worried I might speak to?" or "What's been your experience with telling personal things to people?" can open up important learning conversations.

Of course, the student may eventually want an answer from the therapist, and one possibility, noting of course exceptions based on emergency, would be: "I'm very happy to keep things between us. If, for some reason, I ever feel I need to bring something from your therapy to someone else, I'll talk with you about that first. And, if you don't feel you can trust my judgment about something, don't tell me yet. But can we talk about what you're worried about between us?" This kind of receptiveness at the boundary highlights the student's feelings and decisions, holds to a "How is the student right?" stance, and pays attention to the therapy relationship, including how the confidentiality dilemma might make sense in the student's history and family context.

I never thought of myself as ...

None of this is meant to minimize the importance of confidentiality to a student's coming to speak personally to another person and, indeed, to himself. A very good argument can be made that any shakiness in the provision of confidentiality risks students not coming to counseling in the first place. But other gaps in coverage are also risky. In a counseling service conference, a clinician said: "I never thought of myself as an employee of the college. I always thought of myself as in private practice." Other counseling staff tended to feel that they were "working for the student" while administration "worked for the institution." This oversimplified view, understandable as reflecting the staff's deep commitment to the student, splits counseling from the institution, thereby creating potentially serious gaps: for example, the gap sometimes felt by the international student who may bring anxieties to the health service but is too ashamed to go to counseling, so never gets there; or the gap for the student sent home on disciplinary suspension by the administration without their having consulted with counseling about the student's mental health problems.

Also, as mentioned earlier, splitting therapy from administration unwittingly splits the disciplinary function from the caretaking function. The risk here is failing to take seriously the student's aggression, which generally has been played out in some part of the college arena and found its way to the dean's office. Lost in this scenario is the meaning of the student's destructive and potentially self-destructive action, including its possible meaning within the therapeutic relationship: for example, as an anxious response to what has gotten opened up in the therapy or to an inadvertent injury by the therapist. Other potential risks include missing how students use the array of available authority figures in college to play out multiple, and often troubled, relationships to parental figures. The confidentiality barrier can unwittingly replicate the unfortunate and not uncommon situation of two parents who can't talk to each other, especially when it comes to developing a shared way of raising their child.

Finally, the split between counseling and the institution—which operates in-the-mind and often without anyone realizing it—risks missing the student's deep connection to her educational aspirations and task. If one holds onto that connection, a student's suicidal feelings, for example, could be heard, among other possibilities, as a way of saying, "I desperately want to get out of a school I once really wanted to get into." The treatment task then includes taking the student seriously and examining how her impulse might be deeply right. This opens up a whole series of important questions: What happened? Where is her family in this? Is there something the student cannot bear to bring to her family? What does the student really need and from whom?

The mission of college is, very broadly, the education and maturation of its students. Because this phase of human development has its unique emotional challenges, colleges have created counseling services. Thus, the mission of the counseling service is an extension of the broadly developmental, and even educational, mission of the college. From this perspective, confidentiality is a provision to the student *made by the college* through its counseling service in order to support the student's development. It's the college's *authorization* to counseling based on the college's understanding of an expertise their students need.

Sometimes colleges drift toward a hands-off stance with counseling for fear of intruding on an expertise they don't understand well. Sometimes they do intrude, and counseling turns to its professional guild to buttress itself against the college's perhaps misguided power. Sometimes liability concerns of both clinicians and administration become intense and confusing. In these situations, a well-developed relationship with the college's legal counsel is a very important part of the safety net. But as a legal colleague with much college experience put it, he has never seen a case won because college personnel spoke to each other about a student's difficult situation, and he's seen many cases lost because they did not. In all of these situations, the director of counseling has the crucial role of negotiating the boundaries between the college and the service, including a textured understanding of what information goes back and forth and what happens with that information.

To speak or not to speak

There is another form of "renting asunder," more vertical than horizontal, that relates to creating a safe space to talk. During NYU's dark days, there was much debate on campus about whether or not staff could, and students should, speak at all about what was happening. University officials, understandably concerned about stemming the contagion and about the reputation of the school, opted for muted dialogue. Especially with regard to the latter concern, the issue of "brand" was at stake—in the double meaning of that term. In the competitive marketplace of American higher education, each school wants to present itself in the most appealing and distinctive way: to create a positive brand. And each school fears that what happens on campus may get the school's name branded in a negative way. This gap between a college's desired and actual, or external and internal, representations of itself can also become a dangerous chasm because it can lead to silence about serious difficulties.

Ironically, the gap between how one wants to be seen versus how one might actually be seen is also one of the major stresses an adolescent-becoming-young-adult faces. Students so often have strong desires to impress parents, teachers, and friends, and to live up to something in their own eyes as well. When this fails, as it must to some degree, the student must come to terms with this personal gap between the desired and the actual, or between the external image he is striving for and the much more deflated internal image he feels to be the truth. For vulnerable students, this sense of failure can lead to an identity crisis and to suicidal feeling, a feeling that "I have to get out of here, but I can't bear how others will think of me for that. And I certainly can't bear how I will think of myself." In other words, there is a mirroring interplay between this emotional dilemma—the dilemma of image and reality—for students and for the college itself. To the degree colleges can reconcile the tension between these internal and external realities—can face internal problems honestly and empathically, develop realistic solutions, and engage in open examination of emerging issues—they provide a context of maturity for their students to do so as well.

Not long after the "Jumpers" article was written, a group called The Icarus Project emerged, which promoted this kind of open communication about stresses and emotional dilemmas. Its motto at the time was "Navigating the Space between Brilliance and Madness." The Icarus image captures this second kind of gap students and institutions must negotiate—the gap between achievement and limits, between aspiring and falling.

Minding the gap

Some of the gaps that develop in any system can be thought of at a "tectonic" level, so to speak, that is, as having to do with unseen forces affecting everyone but at a level no one grasps or can intervene with. At a conference for counseling services on the subject of sexual violence on campus, a discussion took place that suggested a major struggle at a much deeper level than any one person or group could encompass. The Title IX culture, meant to protect sexual trauma victims, was coming up against what that group saw as a "fraternity culture," supported by alumni. The deeply felt mission of Title IX staff—and perhaps the rage some carried on behalf of victims or from their own traumatic experiences—led to their intense wish to "dismantle the system."

This struggle at what seemed like the "parental" level was passionate and clearly gender-toned. Two different kinds of authoritarianism could be heard as seeping into the conversation. A stereotypically "paternal" authoritarianism—"Do it because I say so"—was attributed to the male powers that be, and a stereotypically "maternal" authoritarianism—"Do it because I say it's good for you and I need you to"—seemed to find its way into the attitudes of mostly female Title IX staff. Indeed, the "kids" in this system were seen as "defiant" if they didn't file complaints or if they kept their distance from Title IX procedures. What the students said about this was telling: "If I get on that train [the "train" of Title IX procedures], it will pull away and take me someplace I don't want to go." Unfortunately, the result for this dedicated Title IX group of staff was frustration, and for the students it was being left on their own. The gap between two groups at the "parental" level left a sad and even dangerous gap for students. Fortunately, the progression of discussion in this particular conference led to the emergence of younger staff voices who seemed not so caught up in this generational issue, related to trauma, and very able to engage with and really hear from students.

As in this example, the Erikson Institute's Counseling Service Conferences illuminated how systemic dynamics within institutions meet the dynamics of students, sometimes in ways that make things worse for both. At the same time, given that representatives from different schools were talking to each other at these conferences, these dedicated staff members were able to relax concerns about liability, guilds and institutional image in favor of honest, deeply felt communication about their students' struggles. The fortunate result was the major contribution these staff members could then make to minding the gaps within their back-home systems, thereby building both bridges and nets.

CHAPTER 5

Potential space and organizational trauma

In January, 2002, the annual Group Relations Conference of a regional organization was held as it had been for many years. GRCs are intensive group experiences, designed to study leadership and authority in the unfolding dynamic of the conference itself. Members engage with the tasks of various conference events and study how they relate to each other and to the staff in that process. One of those events is called the Institutional Event, and this one began ordinarily enough. The conference director described the task to members, which had to do with their using their authority to decide which aspects of the conference they wanted to study further (e.g., how gender differences were playing out) and with what other groups they wanted to engage in that study (for example, a group reflecting on gender might want to engage with a group reflecting on leadership).

After the task of the IE was spelled out and questions were responded to, the director left, and two staff members stayed behind to consult to how the group was taking up its task. Generally, because this large group is often unnerved about being left on its own, a relatively tumultuous period tends to follow, which might include confusion, excitement, frustration, laughter, power struggles, the emergence of leadership, and somewhat disjointed efforts to form smaller work groups. Instead, in 2002, four months after 9/11, members exploded out of the room as soon as the director left. Even though that recent disaster was not mentioned at all, the group acted as though the public space had become "Ground Zero." The seven or so people left in what felt like the debris spontaneously decided to study the effects of 9/11 on the conference. It seemed clear that trauma, and the fear that it would happen again, had been enacted by the whole group. This small group was thus taking up a piece of work on behalf of everyone.

The pediatrician-psychoanalyst Donald Winnicott developed a concept he called "potential space" (1971a, p. 47). Winnicott was a theorist of the unnoticed obvious; for example, in his articulation of what a teddy bear has always meant to a child at a certain developmental moment. The concept of potential space was, in his theory, an extension of a child's use of transitional objects (1951), and describes an area of maximal in-touch-ness with one's own creative potential. More about that later. For now, whatever eventually happened in the smaller groups of this IE, the potential "potential space" of the large group was not sustained. People could not contain themselves long enough to sort things out together nor could they reflect on why they couldn't. The public space in that particular moment could not become a space for play, for a vitalizing sense that "something could happen" or that "we could do something together." Rather, members acted as though they *knew* disaster *would* happen. What Winnicott would think of as the space for creative illusion was filled, instantly and paralyzingly, with the certainty of delusion (1951).

The external context of disaster—a disaster, not only of enormous loss, but of boundary rupture on many levels—seemed to have collapsed the boundaries necessary for the IE to become a potential space, used fully by members through the exercise of their own authority. But perhaps a second, internal context also contributed to the hole in the boundary. The conference director had announced that she would be leaving temporarily for the funeral of a close colleague. In this emotional context of insecure leadership—and echoes of death—neither members nor consulting staff could bring their weight to bear on building new boundaries in an environment no longer felt to be holding either group. Trauma had collapsed potential space.

Potential space

What Winnicott eventually called potential space began with his discussion of transitional objects (1951). Potential space was the heir to the earliest scenario of human relatedness, the phase of an infant's life when, if things go well, the infant's basic needs meet good-enough adaptation by the caretaking other. The outcome of this adaptation is that the child, Winnicott thought, comes to feel a sense of ordinary omnipotence or basic confidence; as the caption on a Jerry Seinfeld mug said: "Want a cookie; got a cookie!" The child's confidence reflects a developing trust in the beginning-to-be-sensed reliable partner to this magical experience. In the beginning, the infant's relatedness to this other is part and parcel of his subjective experience, not only of meeting the world, but of creating it. From the infant's point of view, it's the wanting that creates the getting.

The overlap between this need-driven gesture of the infant and the need-gratifying response of the caretaking other is what Winnicott called a space of illusion, which he meant in a positive sense. It is an "intermediate area … allowed to the infant" (1951, p. 239). Over time, this space takes concrete shape as the child's transitional object, for example, a teddy bear, which the child invests with the power to soothe himself, and over which he "assumes rights" (p. 229). "*Of the transitional object it can be said that it is a matter of agreement between us and the baby that we will never ask the question: 'Did you conceive of this or was it presented to you from without?' The important point is that no decision on this point is expected. The question is not to be formulated*" (pp. 239–240; italics Winnicott's).

This space of illusion—and of transition to relating to the other as a separate person in her own right—Winnicott eventually called potential space (1971a), the word "potential" highlighting the experience of creativity as a central experience of the well-cared-for infant. What he found in the external world, at the beginning the mother's nourishing breast, was there waiting to be found by the infant, whose need created it in the first place. Optimally intense experiences, enriching the developing sense of self and of the world (the world as one's oyster, so to speak) were the regular outcome of an optimal human relationship in potential space.

Winnicott's ideas about potential space were original but not fanciful; they developed in the course of consulting to tens of thousands of children and parents over forty years. One implication of the potential space concept for organizational life is that Winnicott's assertion of the infant's "rights" implies an authority relationship. The caretaking other lends herself—her physical, mental, and emotional responsiveness—to the infant's budding agency. Through what Milner calls her "answering activity" (Milner, 1937, p. 184; Parsons, 1990), that is, her sense-making response to the infant's "spontaneous gesture"—the recognition, for example, that this cry means hunger and that cry means fatigue—she facilitates the infant's *creation* of the need-satisfying world. Her authority in the role of "mother" is exercised by lending it to the nascent authority of the infant, and the "agreement" between baby and mother not to disrupt this positive illusion implies a contract, including elements of the mother's responsiveness but also her restraint.

This question of authority is taken up again by Winnicott in his discussion of the True and False Self (1960b). There he talks explicitly of leadership and followership roles. In healthy development, it is the mother who follows the infant's lead by making sense of his "spontaneous gesture" (p. 148), thereby shaping the infant's bodily aliveness into a sense of true self. As we have seen in Chapter 3, should the need-driven gesture of the parent substitute for the infant's, a sense of falseness and alienation develops in the child, along with dissociative defenses against this rudimentary breach of trust.

At the end of his discussion of transitional space, Winnicott says that it "widens out" (1951, p. 233) into, on the negative side, pathologies of omnipotence (like lying and addiction), but more usually, into play, artistic creativity, culture, and religious feeling. Indeed, it is in his theoretical paper on playing that Winnicott makes his first reference to potential space. "In order to give a place to playing, I postulated a *potential space* between the baby and the mother" (1971a, p. 47). He calls this space a "playground" (p. 47), the same word Freud (1914g) used to describe the arena of transference. Winnicott speaks of play as "immensely exciting," but always "precarious" because of "the interplay of personal psychic reality and the experience of control of actual objects" (p. 47). He calls this "the precariousness of magic itself, magic that arises in intimacy, in a relationship that is being found to be reliable" (p. 47).

Winnicott cites Erikson's work in this paper, and Erikson did indeed make the important point that, in the play phase, it is essential that the family, "in one of its exemplary forms," help the child with a critical boundary—the distinction between play and "irreversible purpose" (1961, p. 156). Playgrounds need the safety of good boundaries. A five-year-old little cowboy with a toy gun is free to give full rein to his fantasies of being in charge of his homestead. But, if he somehow acquired a real gun, the potential for irreversible purpose—for actual loss—would create a real-life danger. It would also destroy the child's ability to enjoy and imaginatively use the play space. The boundaries of a good playground distinguish fantasy from reality and wish from consequence. Play is how children develop; without a safe space for play, that development is stunted.

Applied to organizations, the authority relation described here is between human beings naturally motivated toward creative engagement with their work and their partners in facilitating that engagement. This authority is exercised in specific ways, having to do with leadership's creating conditions for a work culture and process that develops its own inherent shape and serves the organizations' task to its full, though not yet discovered, potential. This is the opposite of stereotypically "paternal," command-control authority; rather, it has more to do with "maternal" authority, that is, the authority to set the conditions for safely playing out creative alternatives and for trusting the evolving task-related partnership between leaders and workers.

A lifeline

Winnicott called one of his play techniques the "squiggle game." His colleague, Masud Khan, described how the "child uses paper as potential space in order to be privately alone with Winnicott. And this potential space of the paper is a *shared* space where both Winnicott and the child *mutually act* towards that 'significant moment' when the experience of the child can be interpreted to the child" (1983, p. 99; italics Khan's). Indeed, Winnicott once defined his work in terms of play: "*Psychotherapy takes place in the overlap between two areas of play, that of the patient and that of the therapist*" (1971a, p. 38; italics Winnicott's).

Something like the "squiggle game" can be a valuable tool in organizational consultation as well. A number of years ago, the Erikson Institute at Riggs, as part of its consultation service to local human service agencies, began work with the leadership team of a residential treatment center which was suffering organizational confusion and difficulty containing its adolescent clients. As part of the consultation, each member of the leadership team was invited to draw the current situation of their organization, and to put themselves in the drawing in some way. When they finished, EI consultants taped the drawings to the wall, so that everyone could see them, then walked the group to each drawing. The consultants asked the person who had made the drawing to stay silent, while the rest of the group was asked to associate to what they saw. Then, the person who made the drawing was invited to speak about what she intended to depict and what she thought about the group's associations.

This invariably is a powerful and illuminating exercise. In this particular example, a very dramatic moment occurred. One staff member had drawn a lake with a number of small boats on it. The boats were adrift, without oars, and going off in different directions. Some people seemed to be thrashing about in the water. Toward the top of the drawing, someone on the dock seemed to be throwing a rope with an inner tube attached to it, in an effort to save those in the water. When the group looked at this drawing, with the person who drew it remaining silent, the reaction was instantaneous: one person did not see a rope and an inner tube, she saw a noose. And indeed, once this was said, everyone saw it; the image was right there in front of us. This unnerving association opened up the organization's recent history, including the fact that its director had hung himself a few years back. This devastating event—certainly known but not discussed—was then examined as potentially a major contributor to the organization's current turmoil.

It's not necessary to conclude that the person who drew this picture was unconsciously struggling with the fallout of this trauma. That may or may not have been what was in her mind, without her quite knowing it. What is clear, however, is that her drawing brought it to mind for many others, and it did so with an "Oh my God" outburst of shock, seriousness, but also relief. This example illustrates the way that undiscussed and undigested organizational trauma leaves traces in its members and gets played out in organizational dysfunction. It also illustrates that one way out of this trouble—a genuine lifeline, if you will—is finding a potential space to bring the traumatic experience into consciousness and conversation. Key conditions for that are the consultants' ability to create this space, to manage its boundaries, to contain the group's feelings, and to facilitate their effort toward a genuine conversation. The consultants are certainly not leading the organization; rather they are leading a process, authorized by the organization, through which potential space, which had been collapsed by trauma, can be restored as a vital organizational resource.

In a sense, the consulting team created concentric playgrounds for this group. The outer circle was the consultation itself and the space opened for the task of understanding the organization's turmoil. The consultants created a tone of curiosity, empathy, and openness without judgment. The inner playground was that blank piece of paper, charged in the dual sense of that term—that is, both authorized as a field for real work and enlivened as a field in which personal expression is understood to be intimately and inevitably related to that work. Erikson (1977, p. 17) felt that the most simple and elegant definition of play was Plato's; at its essence, to play is to jump. This leadership team jumped. It put out the organization-in-their-minds for all to see and for whatever they might do with what they saw. The insight they took from this process led to gut-level learning that they could then bring back to their organization.

The consultation provided what Winnicott called a "holding environment" (1960a, p. 47) for the work of coming to terms with trauma. Very importantly, it facilitated the group's direct engagement with the risk implicit in that drawing. It allowed the group's "answering activity" (Milner, 1937, p. 184) to the "spontaneous gesture" (Winnicott, 1960b, p. 148) of the drawer, and it communicated a confidence that whatever was found in this potential space—even the image of a noose—could be faced and understood together. To do otherwise—to, presumably out of anxiety, avoid or downplay this "gesture"—would destroy the potential space and damage the organization as well. Trauma would continue to be enacted because testimony (Laub, 2018)—the testimony carried unconsciously by members of this group—had been censored.

Potential space has to do with the task of providing the conditions for a useful benign regression, a regression in the service of contacting feelings and thoughts that have been dissociated in an effort to avoid pain. Winnicott notes that “The person we are trying to help needs a new experience in a specialized setting. The experience … of a non-purposive state … [a state of] relaxation that belongs to trust and to the acceptance of the professional reliability of the … setting” (1971b, p. 55). The idea of potential space within an organization is an idea about how members join a difficult task with full creative resources. For this to happen, Winnicott would suggest that the organization's leadership must be able to contact—within itself or through consultation—elements of maternal authority, that is, elements having to do with setting the tone for potential space, managing the boundary around it, and interpreting the processes evolving within it.

Mother's helper

Here is another example of creating a potential space to deal with organizational trouble. The medical director of an urban mental health center requested help with confusions and morale problems accumulating in his clinic. He was the second in command, with a female executive director as his boss. The consulting team's conversations with both leaders suggested that the clinic was suffering from its success. It had begun not many years earlier as a volunteer hotline and had grown into a crisis center handling thousands of calls per year. Driven by this pool of clients, one new service after the other had been generated, including several residential treatment settings and outpatient clinics.

Along the way, roles had gotten confused for at least two reasons. The clinic had come to see part of its mission as direct service, actually meeting the needs of more impoverished clients. This charitable task had gotten confused with the treatment task, within which the reality of physical deprivation sometimes becomes intertwined with the client's earlier feelings of emotional deprivation, and then are played out in the transference to the therapist. Thus, two necessary forms of help—the need for actual food and for understanding emotional hunger—had gotten mixed up in this organization. Second, in the competitive financial environment in which the clinic now operated, the tail of grants was beginning to wag the dog of mission. Worse still, the language of business—with its survival-of-the-fittest tolerance for casualties—was invading the task of care, care for the very casualties the capitalist zeitgeist was implicated in creating.

Though it seemed clear in our conversations with the clinic's leadership that some reflection on these issues might be useful to the staff, their commitment to carrying out an organizational consultation seemed ambivalent. Instead, they opted to ask us for help with what they saw as a more pressing need, namely, training for their clinical leadership in basic ideas about the kinds of psychological troubles they were facing and their treatment. If we could include a way of helping them think organizationally, that would be fine, but it would not be the primary focus.

So, the Erikson Institute team did indeed design a Clinical Leadership Retreat, and thirty staff members from the clinic came for a weekend of meetings. The team supplied good food, some focused but informal instruction, a lot of time for discussion and, perhaps of equal importance, the opportunity for this group to meet and interact with each other, something they could have done at home, but, for whatever reasons, had not. A wide range of topics was covered, and on the last morning of the workshop, a subgroup of the consulting team led a brief consultation to the clinic system, beginning with a short presentation about organizational dynamics.

After the presentation, the team invited members to participate in an exercise designed to acquaint them with possible dynamics in their organization. We moved the chairs to the side of the conference room in which the retreat had taken place, creating a large open space. Then we invited members to gather in their administrative groups (e.g., this residence or that service), use drawing materials to signify, symbolically if they wished, who they were, and then gather some chairs and sit together. They were quite enthusiastic about this task and took to it energetically. Ten or so minutes later, they had assembled themselves in various parts of the room and had drawn colorful signs or pictures designating who they were. We then invited them to look around the room and to see their whole organization. They did so with pleasure but also with a new level of seriousness. Then we said to them: "This is Clinic X. What conversation would you like to have with each other?"

The first few comments had to do with the startling and gratifying experience of seeing the whole organization. Putting names to faces and knowing what people did throughout the system had gotten lost in the growth, but also the angst, of the organization. Then curiosity emerged: Why had each of the residence leaders put their signs on their chairs and left themselves standing behind the chairs? Did this unconsciously represent the current situation of the residences, so full with clients that the staff, who were supposed to interact as part of a home, actually had no space of their own within it?

Then, from the farthest reaches of these different seating groups came an outburst of pain. The director of the new Day Treatment Program was near tears: "Look where we are! As far away from the administration as it's possible to be. This is exactly where we are in this organization: so far away that we are forgotten. No wonder we can't get what we need to make this new service work." Indeed it was true that the administrative group was in the opposite part of the room, and the day treatment group was something of a tail to the loosely formed circle of other subgroups. In the middle of it all, true to its central place in the clinic's history and current operation, was the Hotline Team.

The Day Treatment director continued: "My staff is so angry at me. I feel like a mother who is supposed to do everything and can't do anything right." In the middle of this intense lament, one of the hotline staff loudly interrupted, "Bbbrrringg! Bbbrrringg!", then pretended to answer the phone with the standard hotline greeting: "You've reached …" "This is what happens at Clinic X," he said, and for a moment, all seemed to agree on the fragmenting and disorganizing effects of the task of emergency responsiveness to trauma. A minute later, when the former conversation resumed, he again interrupted with a pretend crisis call. This time we consulted to the defensive possibility within such interruption, the way that for all of us we may not only be exasperated by the phone's ringing, but often grateful for its having gotten us out of something we didn't want to be in in the first place.

This intervention led to a more textured discussion. The mother metaphor was taken up by the group, and what emerged was the status of the Day Treatment Program in the minds of the other services. It was seen as yet another new service, a new baby really, brought into the world prematurely, without full planning, by the clinic's leadership—not only because there was a client need but also because there was funding. It was also seen as unable to take care of itself and left to the other services, the older kids, to look after somehow. They, however, resented the attention and resources lavished initially on the newcomer and saw it as a foster child, not really one of them because it was not clearly mission-related, or at least they had not felt helped to see how. And besides, there were a lot of kids, each feeling their own needs. This line of interpretative thinking seemed confirmed when one service leader said: "Thank God your service came along. Last year we were the new baby that no one wanted to attend to. I'm sorry for you, but I'm glad it's not us anymore."

The conversation ended with ideas about how the group as a whole could help to manage the integration of new services. People felt that they had been present for each other in new, real, and creative ways. At dinner that night, this large group, each paying for his or her own meal individually, managed to spontaneously put together enough money for a hefty tip. The conversation could be seen as having major implications for the clinic's leadership as well. Indeed, the female Day Treatment director—the embattled mother who could never do enough for her own staff and who felt so alone in that task—could be seen as a displacement figure for the executive director, who had not been able to attend the retreat herself. The Day Treatment leader came to stand for the dynamics around the new, but needy and loosely related baby in a family of other competitive children. That the male medical director was tactfully opening this process for reflection suggested that a potential partnership was emerging at the directorial level through which these feelings might be held, engaged, and resolved.

Maternal authority

One result of this exercise was the group's astonishment that it had unconsciously created, in the here and now, the geographical relationships and attendant problems of the organization. Along with that came a sense of conviction about the power of unconscious processes within the system. The concrete space of the conference room had become a living potential space, and "maximally intense experience" had occurred. How did this happen? I want to suggest that it depended on the exercise of a certain kind of authority in the leadership of the institution and in the consultants, an authority that derives from the maternal authority intrinsic to the creation of potential space. By maternal authority, I am not referring to gender per se, but to a combination of management and interpretation in the service of deep play—and, as I have stated earlier, play involves both creativity and regression, and is therefore serious business.

The relationship between the medical director and the consulting staff, along with the members' accruing confidence in us throughout the weekend, had made for a feeling that we were "professionally reliable" and for the faith that something could be gained from their "relaxing" into an open conversation. The consulting team had asked everyone at the beginning of the weekend what they hoped for from the retreat. Given their frantic work lives, members felt this to be a new and deeply recognizing provision. They felt invited to join and they felt listened to. We then met their requests with specific clinical training related to their work. We brought ideas about tasks, roles, and boundaries to an understanding of their clinical dilemmas. We helped them resolve confusions, engage differences, and see context. We looked after their dependency needs, both physically and figuratively. In this context of reliable holding, the group could "jump," and that they did so implied their belief that they would land safely, with our help.

Management in the consultative part of the event meant not only the management of time, space, and task, though these boundaries are critical. It also meant self-management by the leadership and the consultants, which allowed the process within the play space to evolve. Often, organizations-in-the-minds of members and many organizations in fact tend toward a stereotypically "paternal" model of authority, an authority that is directive about what to do and what not to do, based on leadership's knowledge about how to accomplish the organization's task in the world. "Maternal" authority is different. At its foundation is what one might think of as the maternal "Yes," a faith in the child's developmental process. In organizations, this translates into a "How are they right?" stance (Shapiro, 2020) as a basis for understanding whatever is unfolding. Maternal authority is a protective authority insofar as it holds intrusion on the play space out; there are questions *not* to be asked. But it is also a generative authority in that it recognizes and legitimizes the subject's authority arising from within the developmental process. And it answers that authority with the sense emerging from its unconscious expression. Perhaps most importantly, it recognizes this sense as intrinsically linked to task—in earliest life, to the task of development; in work life, to the organization's mission.

In this example, we invited the group to move their bodies, to deal with objects, to create something, and to own the space. We invited them to see their whole organization, implicitly saying to them that we trusted their capacity to handle what they saw and ours to handle how they handled themselves. We invited the conversation they *wanted* to have with each other, trusting not only their and our capacities to handle the conversation but their *wish* to speak to each other as well. We interpreted only once: to address what Jaques (1955) called a social defense, meaning the way that a central structure of the organization—the crisis hotline—was being mobilized defensively to interrupt an emerging, unsettling dialogue. We then simply joined their evolving metaphor of the mother who couldn't deal with the needs and dynamics among her children. We helped them take the metaphor seriously and explore its meaning throughout the organization.

What emerged was not only their creative engagement with each other, revitalizing as that is to an organization's work life, but also an interpretation for the executive director. With the help of her partner, the medical director, the executive director might come to see the dynamic within the organization, how she in her role might be involved with it and how her staff might be ready to participate in its solution. This would help her take up her leadership role more fully. It might also allow the new Day Treatment director to join more freely because she would no longer have to represent the "mother" within the system who couldn't do anything right.

The executive director's absence from the retreat might have reflected her avoidance of encountering the staff's feelings and what, from a psychoanalytic perspective, could be their transference to her role. That is, the staff dynamic suggested that a maternal role was being projected onto the executive director. The staff's problems in dealing with the anger of their emotionally deprived clients might well mirror their anger about being deprived the attention and care a mother is "supposed" to provide. To the extent that the executive director was carrying this definition of "mother" and felt the staff's latent fury coming her way, she might have felt disinclined to engage with them. The competitive business model in which the clinic now found itself, with its psychic pull toward the paternal mode, might also have made it difficult for her as a female leader to contact aspects of maternal authority within herself and to distinguish its exercise from the transference demand for her care.

Maternal authority is not about the provision of directions or standards, though those have their place in any organization. Nor is it simply the provision of care. Rather, it's a provision of a space for a generative process. In an anxious system, this kind of provision, partly because it invites personal development in the staff, can be experienced as a demand and a deprivation. "Just tell me what to do" can seem so much easier. Fortunately in this system, the Executive Director's male partner was able to risk hearing the staff's painful experience, on behalf of his boss, and, in the way he participated, to allow it to unfold in the service of learning. In doing so, he came to represent the Third (Muller, 1996), the "other parent" so to speak, who could now help make sense of the organizational dynamic and the embattled executive director's place in it. This kind of creative pairing between paternal and maternal authority seemed essential to this organization's growth.

This example is not about trauma per se. Certainly there was great stress within this system, and cumulative stress can both lead to trauma and make it difficult to recover from it. And certainly the system was dealing with traumatized clients. Secondary traumatization within the staff may well have been a factor in the organization's need for "maternal" care. The place actual trauma made its appearance in this story, however, was in those pretend phone calls. Being regularly interrupted by trauma is indeed disorganizing, but, in this system, it had also become a defense against disturbing discussion. Trauma was used to limit what people were able to say to each other. To put this differently, a culture of emergency affected members' capacities to speak openly and think reflectively. But an emergency culture, because it fragments a sustained effort to deal with accumulated stress in a system, actually increases the risk of a genuine emergency. Building workable potential space reduces that risk.

After shock

One final example of trauma and potential space. The Psychoanalytic Institute of Northern California (PINC) suffered a major organizational trauma. (The name of the Institute can be used because several members of the Institute published, with the support of the Institute's board of directors, a paper (Burka et al., 2019) about the effects of the trauma on the organization and the Institute's work to repair it. The authors requested that I use the name of the Institute in this summary. The many responses to their courageous paper attest to how critical it is to openly discuss events like this.) PINC's trauma had to do with the fact that two senior analysts were found to have committed serious ethical violations. Though the exact nature of the violations could not be made public, it is hard to overstate how damaging such a violation is to the functioning of an analytic institute. It was experienced as a profound betrayal and understandably led to fractured collegial connections and a breakdown of normal committee work.

The Institute's leadership struggled with how best to handle the crisis, including the enormous distress felt by Institute members. An organizational consultant was brought in to work with the board and some key committees. Eventually the board created a task force, initially meant to review and make recommendations about the Institute's ethical guidelines. The task force realized, however, that they could not proceed without addressing the disturbance in the Institute. After a lengthy process, the board re-authorized the task force; the task now included offering individual interviews to Institute members to provide an opportunity to hear their reactions to the ethics investigations, in the hope that the interviews would contribute to rebuilding trust and openness in the organization. This healing gesture, undertaken with great care, was quite successful; a large percentage of members availed themselves of these personal interviews. Extremely painful feelings were shared with candor and passion. Once the interviews were completed, the task force added the task of sharing what they had learned with the Institute community. They organized a number of feedback sessions with subgroups of the community. The last and largest of these meetings, held in a town hall, was one which I was invited to help design, and to which I then consulted.

The program had three parts. First, the members of the task force presented what they had learned to the whole group of perhaps sixty people. Each member described one theme, abstracted from Institute members' various reactions to the trauma. The presenters used anonymous quotes to illustrate—in quite moving language—that particular theme. After questions, the large group broke into small groups to discuss the report in as much depth as possible. As consultant, I sat in briefly on each small group. Then the whole group reconvened, this time with the chairs in two large concentric circles, to digest what they had learned in the small group discussions and to think about the implications for the organization going forward.

It was an extremely moving event. Task force members had the task, tone, and structure of the meeting so fully "inside" themselves that it unfolded beautifully. During the first large-group session, Institute members listened intently, especially to quotes extracted with permission from the debriefing interviews. These verbatim comments were poignant and powerful. Some members had come hoping to learn more about what had actually happened. So, there was some frustration with the limits of what the task force leadership could say. Nevertheless, the task of processing intense feelings remained in the forefront. The small group sessions succeeded in giving space for everyone's voice; there were no silent members. In the second large-group session, the concentric circle seating arrangement allowed a more visual sense of the whole community, which the task force now rejoined as members among other members. In this context, members worked to sort out feelings and fantasies, to assess the damage to the Institute, and to reintegrate the community.

As I heard it, there was enormous anxiety about naming the two analysts. Despite the fact that many people were well aware of who had left the Institute, some members acted as though those names might not be known, and leadership felt a continuing obligation not to name names. Members' extreme caution about naming suggested to me a very basic, contagious anxiety, to which large organizations are especially prone. Naming makes things real, which may well have been felt as a reenactment of the trauma. Speaking these names seemed sacrilegious, something that might merit being struck by lightning, which was actually an image that came up in the course of discussion. Even without naming or discussion of the specifics of the violations, it became apparent that some members "knew" more than others, either as part of leadership or simply from what they had heard along the way. These differences between members were highly charged, as though any knowledge was carnal knowledge, both enticing and forbidden. Everybody or every group that "knew" something was caught up in the spreading guilt, and feared becoming a lightning rod for the rage in the system. In relation to this, the fear of legal action—also spoken about in the course of discussion—seemed to me not only a part of the real world, which indeed must be managed; it also represented the reified projection of this intense, large-group, persecutory anxiety: the lightning bolts of the law.

The brief concluding statements by task force leadership reflected the great care everyone had invested in the process. Members' earlier centrifugal explosiveness away from the organization—as though it had become Ground Zero in their minds—had left leadership alone to pick up the pieces, and also under attack, as some members vented their rage. This trauma-related dynamic could have become hugely problematic to members' willingness to take up leadership roles in the future, and thus to the organizational strength of the Institute. This is one reason that the individual interviews were such a critical and healing intervention; leadership representatives actually reached out and contacted members, thereby reversing the centrifugal process.

In situations like this, members' feelings toward the organization can have many sources, including as a displacement from those whose actions betrayed professional ethics. Another source can be the organization's seeming to hold secrets and to be silencing of its members. The dilemma for leadership is that it has an ethical and legal obligation to protect the privacy of the person accused of a violation but an obligation to the community as well. In this context, members sometimes find themselves asking for information from the administrative groups—for example, the ethics committee—who are legally required to keep it private. One way to appreciate this—in addition to understandable ambivalence about knowing—is that members may not actually be asking for information "from above," so to speak, but asking for leadership's help, and perhaps their authorization, in sorting out members' freedom to talk with each other about the bits and pieces—part fantasy, part rumor, part fact—already circulating within the system. This request too can be complicated for leadership, but at least this latter question can be discussed more openly, and a legally and ethically informed institutional stance can be worked toward.

At some point in the day's conversations, members began to reflect on why this violation might have happened in the first place. Rather than simply getting caught up in breast-beating or projecting, they realized that they needed a space—something like a community meeting—to reflect more broadly on the strains within their work, the vulnerabilities everyone has, and the "wellness" of the community. This gathering awareness about the need to attend to the care of the community—including who should be entrusted with leading that and how it might be carried out—was one outcome of the day's events. Like the rest of the day, it was an important step in the Institute's recovery from trauma.

A special difficulty psychoanalytic institutes face in their efforts to recover has to do with their basic task. The work with patients and the work of a training analysis bring to life parent–child relationships. Feelings and fantasies toward the analyst play out in the consulting room for the purpose of understanding them. As we have seen, potential space is an arena of deep play—in this case, the playing out of inner life so that it can be known experientially. But ethical violations are a form of "irreversible purpose" (Erikson, 1961, p. 156) that collapses potential space and breaches the boundary around it. Transference dynamics spread through the system even more than they might ordinarily, and leadership may well become caught up in them, both in terms of how they are reacted to and how they may be induced to act.

This half-day program, however, seemed to have rebuilt a safe-enough, even if still highly charged, potential space. Managed by task force leadership in partnership with consultation, it allowed for the expression of very difficult feelings, deeper understanding of how trauma was playing out in the organization, and the recognition of a communal need. The traumatic experiences that threatened the fabric of the organization were engaged, survived, and learned from. What a joy to discover, in the process of rebuilding it, the place for the community's "wellness" in all of this, the place for coming together as adult members of an organization—in different roles to be sure—to solve problems and share stresses. And what a source of resilience community is in the face of trauma!

CHAPTER 6

On the mantelpiece: organizational trauma in plain sight

The huge Pacific Rim area is known as the "Ring of Fire" because of the vast fault lines encircling it. Miraculously, however, the United States Pacific Northwest seems to have been spared a major quake. But ancient records in Japan noted an unusual event: more than a millennium ago, a tidal wave not associated with an earthquake. They called it a "ghost wave." Based on emergent science of the last twenty years, it turns out there *was* an earthquake associated with that wave, but it occurred thousands of miles away, in the Pacific Northwest (Schulz, 2015). In fact, the Cascadia fault has led to powerful earthquakes roughly every 250 years for millennia, the last one occurring 320 years ago. The seemingly charmed life of that area turns out to be potentially catastrophic wishful thinking. How was this not known? Simply because Native American residents left no written record of such quakes, and white settlers arrived 100 years after the last one. Geologic history, in this case, is longer than a part of human history—with potentially dire consequences. Future trauma might well occur because of a failure to grasp past, unremembered trauma.

Hot and bothered

The tale of the Cascadia fault occurred to me when I was invited to speak about the state of psychoanalytic education to a large psychoanalytic organization, comprised mainly of psychologists (Division 39 of the American Psychological Association). The title of the conference was "Hot and Bothered," and the title of my panel was "Passing the Torch." The metaphor of fire was clearly in circulation, but so, as I came to believe, was the metaphor of fault lines. There was much to be excited about with regard to this organization's programs of psychoanalytic education and training. In many places, creative efforts were being made to meet the next generation's longing for meaning, to deepen interdisciplinary connections, and to bring effective treatment to underserved groups. That said, as I approached the topic, I found myself concerned. In part, this had to do with various conversations and teaching experiences I've had with trainees, and in part with the evolution of this professional group, of which I've been a member since its beginning. I found myself wondering if my work on the transmission of trauma (Fromm, 2012a) might have been part of why the conference organizers had asked me to speak about educational transmission.

I also found myself reacting to some of the conference materials. Psychoanalytic listening—whether to a patient or to an organization—includes paying attention to these reactions. What a person—like me in this instance—experiences in his role, which can be easy to dismiss, may in fact be important information about what is happening in that particular organizational context. Bringing those reactions—what one might think of as a form of emotional intelligence—into dialogue with others can help a group see underlying issues they may have sensed but had not known how to, or were afraid to, address. My reactions to the conference materials could be seen as little "ghost waves," which had their effect on me but seemed without any objective counterpart in the external context that would have helped make sense of them. Nevertheless, I felt I had to take them seriously. Noticing my reactions and organizing my comments around them made my presentation less an academic one than a consultative inquiry about Division 39's current relationship to training.

What evoked these "ghost waves" in me? The conference materials, distributed to everyone, included, as I read them, unnoticed questions and unexplained comments. Lacan, in his study of Poe's *Purloined Letter*, made the point that the unconscious is often hidden in plain sight, right there on the mantelpiece, so to speak (Muller & Richardson, 1988). I've come to believe that putting the unconscious or at least unspoken aspects of an organization out there for all to see is a form of organizational leadership. It represents the hope—ambivalent to be sure—that someone will actually see the trouble and help make sense of it. It seems to me deeply psychoanalytic to notice what is on the mantelpiece, and to work with people toward a shared understanding of what it might mean. In fact, what could be more useful to trainees than learning how to understand their training context through a psychoanalytic method?

So, what did the conference organizers put on the mantelpiece? Three things struck me. First, the conference title: "Hot and Bothered." This seemed to have struck a chord with the membership; fourteen presentations had the word "sex" or a variant in the title. In their welcome note, the conference organizers wrote: "We do intend to get you 'hot and bothered' or at least engaged in exploring how psychoanalytic thought, theory and practice is an essential part of an examined and engaged life." The second half of that sentence doesn't quite measure up to the first or to some of the more provocative titles of presentations. It still leaves the question: really, why "Hot and Bothered"? And if the presenters rushed to take up the "Hot" theme, where was the "Bothered"?

In their welcome note, the conference organizers also asked playfully that we not "take to the streets" during our time together. They followed that with two stories. The first had to do with an early, eccentric psychoanalyst, Wilhelm Reich, who did take to the streets to lecture on sexuality while his girlfriend handed out condoms and watched for the police. The second told the story of one of the group's inspirational leaders, who suggested that a panel on feminism be disbanded in favor of "raising hell" on the streets about the continued inequality of women in our society. Both stories took us out into the world, the latter especially capturing the bothered-ness that can sometimes be transformed into social activism. Division 39's members had actually taken up that latter task successfully when they protested the American Psychological Association's role in the U. S. government's torture program.

But two other things on the mantelpiece raised further questions. First, the conference subtitle: "Coming Together without Falling Apart." Both the initial announcement of the conference and the welcome note used the phrase "Coming Together" or a variant several times. "Falling Apart" disappeared completely; in fact, only one presentation of dozens referred to it at all. Why? Was there a "falling apart" the organization felt at risk of, such that it called it to our attention, then seemingly repressed it? *Must* hot-and-bothered-ness be directed outward, for fear of internal fragmentation? And if falling apart was the anxiety, what were its fault lines?

One possible answer might relate to the third thing on the mantel, and to a question that brings us back to the main conference title: Who, exactly, is "Hot and Bothered?" The main conference image, on all of its materials, was a portrait of Freud, painted by a member in flaming colors. To my eye and I'm sure to others, Freud looked beyond bothered; he actually looked quite angry. But why? Had the organization done something to him? Given some of the presentations in the conference, a case could be made that Freud had become something of a straw man for parts of this group, someone to define itself against. These last two things on the mantelpiece raised important questions: Did this group risk falling apart if it seriously examined its relation to Freud? Had Freud perhaps been thrown out with the bathwater of whatever this group was defining itself against? And if so, at what cost?

What are we treating?

This is where I left a consultative line of thought and returned to the "passing the torch" theme. Briefly, my hypothesis, based on my training travels, was that this organization faced the serious risk of losing the "doctor" in throwing out the "medical." At Riggs case conferences, Senior Erikson Scholar Vamık Volkan invariably began his discussion by asking "What are we treating?" (Fromm, 2013). This question takes people aback. Isn't the question, "Who are we treating?" with that "Who" meant to recognize the person-as-subject, no matter how embattled? Doesn't the "What are we treating?" question objectify the patient?

But orienting ourselves as psychoanalytic therapists to *what* we are treating—along with the *who*—helps us center on certain things: the historical, often trauma-related tragedy the patient is struggling with, the phase-specific developmental anxieties associated with that tragedy, the defenses the patient has built to manage them, the regressive danger the patient fears falling into, and how all of this relates to the current crisis. In other words, to use Freud's language (1923b), the "What" question helps us think about the "It" with which the "I" is suffering. And in turn, this formulation of the trouble helps us hold an informed therapeutic stance and guides potentially useful interventions.

As I've let the what-are-we-treating question resonate with me over time, I've found myself thinking that we psychologist-psychoanalysts—who bring our own professional expertise and vantage point to the work—would do well to *locate the doctor in ourselves*. For all of the problems associated with Freud's metaphor of psychoanalysis as surgery, we are *treating*, and we are treating *something*—something with which the patient is *suffering*. In psychoanalysis, we set in motion—and stay with, each step of the way—a treatment process, an opening up of the self. We take the patient into psychoanalytic care, try to manage pain, make our interpretive intervention, attend to complications—in the patient and in ourselves—and, if things go well, facilitate a recovery process.

Fault lines

Is this view of treatment in unspoken tension with other views of treatment in this organization? My conversations with trainees suggest that it is, that one fault line has to do with the difficulty of integrating a doctor-like responsibility and doctor-like view of the process into more purely psychological or relational ways of working. Trainees are often left with a confusing or contradictory picture of what that treatment process is. How might this problem with integration have developed? One trainee said that he had no idea about the history of the organization, no idea about the tectonic plate, so to speak, on which his training was taking place, and no idea about the formative quake at the organization's beginning. But is it possible that something about that quake is affecting his training? As we have seen (Davoine & Gaudilliere, 2004), people *feel* the fallout of their parents' "cut-out" history. Might trainees feel the cut-out history of this organization and need a conversation that grapples with its traumatic origin and the theoretical and technical fallout?

Briefly, that traumatic origin begins with Nazi persecution, which led many European analysts to flee to the United States. Exiled from their countries, robbed of their possessions, narrowly escaping murder, and suffering horrific losses of other family members, many of these refugees arrived in this country in a state of profound shock, deprivation, and grief. Their adoption into American psychoanalytic institutes restored them in many ways and allowed institutes to build themselves around these prestigious newcomers. Psychiatric training at that time had already embraced psychoanalysis, while clinical psychology was just becoming its own field. Even though Freud explicitly stated that psychoanalysis was not a purely medical discipline (1926e)—in fact that it was a general science of psychology—the dynamics of American institutes, including financial dynamics, led to their offering training only to medical doctors and prohibiting clinical training to psychologists and other professionals.

So, a group that included Europe's excluded came to exclude another group. The first quake of existential anxiety and exile led to a second quake of marginalization, and created what the group in power deemed to be second-class citizens. This eventually led the latter group of psychologists to sue organized psychoanalysis. The outcome was a victory for psychology because there was clear evidence that institute admission policies had much more to do with restraint of trade than with qualifications. But this legal victory occurred without either group's coming to terms with the projections it had of the other or with how those projections—for example, of being second class—had been taken in. While many psychologists have since been admitted to the original training institutes, Division 39 continues on a somewhat parallel track to the national psychoanalytic organization. This is the trauma-influenced backstory, and it raises a number of questions. Was the conference organizers' admonition not to "take to the streets" a way of asking the group to put aside the organization's history of activism in favor of a focus on the psychoanalytic task? And was my encouragement to "locate the doctor within" an invitation to move away from the anger of the Freud portrait and reconsider the deeply clinical aspects of that task?

Finding oneself in the other and the other in oneself is not easy, even if it is enormously helpful in healing fault lines and avoiding future quakes. As I said, there was one—and only one—use of the phrase "falling apart" in the program, outside its never-to-be-seen-again place on the mantelpiece: a paper called "Coming Together *through* Falling Apart." The paper suggested that a process of opening up—of history, experiences, differences, and whatever else, with no guarantee about what will emerge, but toward the goal of learning—might lead to a stronger and deeper "coming together." This is, in fact, the process of a good psychotherapy. Psychoanalytic history does indeed suggest that this is a risky process; so many psychoanalytic groups have fallen apart over theoretical or technical differences. My consultation suggested, however, that there are risks for the next generation in not having this conversation. The primary risk is that trainees will, as I did, feel the "ghost waves" but not understand where they came from or how they were shaping their clinical learning.

How did we get here?

Unlike Division 39, the A. K. Rice Institute, the second organization for which I gave what turned out to be a consultative presentation, explicitly asked "How did we get here?" in the title of its national scientific meeting. Its planning committee also explicitly invited my thoughts on inter-generational trauma, "maybe even as [it] relates to [us]." The core activity of the Institute is the study of leadership and authority within groups and organizations. It does this by sponsoring Group Relations Conferences in various parts of the country. As discussed in Chapter 5, GRCs—unlike the national scientific meeting, which is a more presentation-oriented conference—focus on the here-and-now experiences of members as they engage with the tasks of various group events and as they relate to each other and the staff in that process. They are intensive experiences, the learning from which, particularly as it relates to the exercise of leadership and authority, is deep and lifelong for many, though it comes at a price in terms of anxiety and personal struggle. In a sense, GRC work has a high risk/high gain element to it, particularly as it engages not-fully-conscious group processes and allows members to see themselves or act in unfamiliar ways.

This new and relatively difficult methodology was coming into its own in the United States at the same time that issues of social justice, mistrust of institutional authority, and identity politics, in the aftermath of Vietnam and Watergate, were finding their way into the societal dynamic. GRCs, because they explicitly pay attention to, and bring to the surface, the interaction between system and context, were well positioned to understand these dynamics, but only with good-enough containment of the intensity of feeling aroused in the process. This strain, perhaps along with personal injuries encountered in the work, affected the A. K. Rice Institute profoundly. Within this context, a major leadership crisis occurred between the Institute and a senior leader, my friend and colleague, Dr. Edward Shapiro, who had been hired to direct the Institute's national GRC. This tension led to an even more highly charged conference and eventually to the termination of Dr. Shapiro's contract. To some degree, this was a crisis between the founding and next generations of practitioners, and the fallout of these events was intense and lasting. It became one factor in the Institute's nearly fragmenting in subsequent years.

Twenty-five years later, Ed Shapiro was rehired as the director of the national GRC, and invited to speak about his experience then and now at the Institute's more traditional national scientific meeting. I was invited to reflect on the organizational trauma. I did so by offering a set of thoughts, not simply about what had happened back then, but about how that past trauma—the issues that led to it and that flowed from it—may have played out and been communicated in the here and now of the current scientific meeting. In this sense, my keynote talk took up the invitation to consult to the organization from the perspective of the ongoing transmission of trauma.

Witnessing

Prior to the scientific meeting, a fascinating thing happened in my conversations with the colleague who had invited me to deliver this keynote. We both forgot a scheduled phone meeting. After we connected and had our discussion, I had a dream in which I needed a witness protection program! Taking up the invitation to present began to feel like a risky, even dangerous venture. So I reminded myself, and the Institute, of the importance trauma theorists place on witnessing. Indeed, Caruth in her book *Listening to Trauma* (2014) highlights the crucial role of witnessing in countering a person's or a group's deeply defensive tendency to disconnect traumatic experience from the painful testimony that might make sense of it. The psychoanalyst Jacques Lacan re-articulated Freud's "Where Id was, there Ego shall be" as "Where It was, there I must come to be" (1977, p. 129). Trauma is an "It" that overwhelms the "I." It assaults the basic human capacity to process experience. Caruth argues that testimony is the essential way that the "I" comes back into being, as it relates both to individual and collective trauma.

In a sense, my keynote was a form of testimony, not in the narrative sense of what happened when, but through my attempting to hear, explore, and reflect on what the organization might be saying now, through communications embedded in the meeting materials. As with the previous example of Division 39, a key assumption in this form of consultation is that an organization inevitably speaks through its delegated representatives—in this case the organizers of the A. K. Rice Institute's scientific meeting—and in that way, communicates aspects of its unresolved conflicts. Thus, my data and method were basically psychoanalytic: My job was to listen to what the organization might be saying, to reflect that back, and to help get thoughts and feelings into speech. As the psychoanalyst Adam Phillips said: "People are only ever as mad as the other person is deaf" (1996, p. 34). Whatever "madness" the organization was trying to recover from I was trying to hear in its current form.

Again, as with an individual, what an organization might be saying is often right there on the mantelpiece: staring us in the face but seemingly invisible. In this case, too, I began to see the meeting's materials themselves as a kind of quasi-dream put forward by the organization for the organization to see but resisting recognition as potentially meaningful. My data also included my experience of this quasi-dream—of what was told, how and when it was told, and what I thought and felt in the process. From a psychoanalytic consulting perspective, what happens in organizations all the time—the quirky bits of how things are done that everyone takes for granted but that strike and perplex someone fresh to the system—are entry points for curiosity and reflection.

But, very importantly, all of this is just projection unless it receives some validation from the person or organization the interpretation is for.

This was another preliminary point I stressed to the group. People trained in psychoanalysis have a certain power to interpret, but they don't necessarily have the authority to do so. That comes from negotiation with whoever is asking for the interpretation, and from whatever validation comes afterwards—not in conscious agreement but in the less conscious unfolding of a progressive process. If what I was about to say to this group was to be useful—apart from its potential interest at a conceptual or methodological level—that would have to come from them. In passing, it was interesting to me that the conference planners had scheduled a "What's on your mind?" discussion *before* my presentation and a Happy Hour immediately after it. That, along with the scheduling of the presentation relatively far along into the conference, made me wonder whether the keynote speaker for this group was a bit like the corpse at an Irish wake: You need one to have the party but you don't expect him to say very much! And, given human ambivalence about testimony, you worry that he might!

On the mantelpiece

So—with an invitation to the reader to continue to suspend disbelief for a bit as we move forward with this perhaps unfamiliar methodology—what did this organization put on the mantelpiece? The first thing that struck me was the title of the scientific meeting itself: *Authority: Yours, Mine, Ours, Theirs; How Did We Get Here and Where Do We Go Now?* That first question—"How did we get here"—as it resonated with other communications—had a slightly dazed ring to it. As though history had been lost, and as though the meeting represented an awakening in a slightly disoriented state, a state of mind—or loss of mind—not uncommon when there has been trauma. Also suggestive of a traumatic context, both questions conveyed an absence of agency. Not only might we not know how we got here, but "Where do we go now?" conveyed a feeling of being lost and a bit of desperation. The psychoanalyst Wilfred Bion—the founder of this group's methodology—put Freud's concept of free-floating attention in his own words: psychoanalysts were to approach the clinical situation "without memory or desire" (1967). The title of the scientific meeting suggested that the Institute was not only without memory but without desire as well. This is a good stance for clinical work or for consulting, but not for an organization's development.

That first question, "How did we get here?" also begged another: Where exactly is Here? Perhaps a hypothesis was in the full conference title: Here is a place where Authority is distributed among "Yours, Mine, Ours and Theirs." In 1968—a year that included the assassinations of Martin Luther King and Robert Kennedy, the Vietnam War, and the embattled demonstrations on the Chicago streets outside the Democratic National Convention—in that horrifically violent year, a film was made, the title of which includes three quarters of the meeting's title: *Your, Mine and Ours.* The plot was pure Hollywood. Two military people, both of whose spouses have died—one in war—strike up a relationship, fall in love, but initially keep from each other the fact that both have many children from their first marriages—ten for him, eight for her! Eventually, after various romantic misadventures, they determine to get married, unleashing huge resistance and major mischief from their kids. After another crisis or two—including importantly the children's horror at having to "re-bury" their lost parents in order to allow a new person into their lives—they make their peace with this "blended" family, accept cross-adoption, and rejoice in Mom's giving birth to a new baby. Hollywood indeed! The film ends, though, with the eldest son going off for his own stint in the Marines. A Hollywood ending it was certainly meant to be, but joining the Marines in 1968 could just as easily be seen as the story's coming full circle to the trauma of war and loss.

The A. K. Rice Institute was born one year later, and the title of this film was embedded in the title of this scientific meeting. Might this mean anything? One possibility would have to do with the organization's aspiration to transcend individual, personal authority and join it to collective authority: Yours and Mine becoming Ours, which is certainly one of any organization's tasks. But in the meeting title, there's a remainder: Theirs. Does this point toward something that resists integration into the collective, something not transcended, an irreducible Otherness of some sort? The film *Yours, Mine and Ours* begins with traumatic loss and may well end with loss, but, in between, differences are transcended and new life is born through dealing with loss, through mourning, through "re-burying" lost loved ones. Does that remainder hint at losses the organization has not mourned? Put differently, are there ghosts within the word "Theirs"? If so, who are these ghosts and how might the organization come to know them?

Both sides now

There were other bits of data on the mantelpiece that supported the hypothesis that the Institute was struggling with how to integrate its disparate parts into a "blended" group. For example, a set of word clouds meant to highlight the topics of various presentations obscured the meaning of the words completely. Instead, their intense, clashing colors and angularity of parts against parts suggested cacophony and conflict. Yet the images were oddly alike. For all of the shouting voices and associative bombardment, there were no real differences among them. It inevitably raised a question about what differences might have led to the intensity within these word clouds and why those differences had become so stereotyped.

Then there was the Call for Papers. Eight topics were suggested, with "Authority and its exercise" immediately followed by "Anti-authoritarian citizen uprisings," and ending with "Your other related interests." Room for everyone but also an immediacy of conflict. This was followed by eight "underlying questions to consider," three to five questions more than one tends to find in a Call for Papers in other conferences! The first question invited courage, the third referenced fear. Here is the fifth question:

> Question 5: *In conference life is the most appropriate use of the "authority of the director" to suppress challenges to authority so members can examine their projections into authority figures, or as an invitation to share interpretations among all members of the system so that the social construction underway can be examined?*

To my ear, this question creates an either/or where a "both sides now" is more appropriate. GRCs really are an opportunity to examine one's personal relationship to authority, including one's projections onto authority—after all, everyone grew up with parental figures and had strong reactions to them. But in the context of a GRC, conference directors explicitly invite shared sense-making about this. Question 5 seems to set up an "our" experience as members against the "theirs" of conference leadership and staff. Then there is that troubling verb, "suppress," as opposed to "meet," or even "greet," apparent challenges to authority for the learning potential within them. And those quotation marks around the "authority of the director." What happened to this organization such that quotation marks find their way into this question? Did whatever happened have to do with the distinctive authority of GRC directors? Does blurring that distinction—reducing or perhaps even mocking "their" authority—now seem like a solution? And in that leveling of authority, what is lost?

At the bottom of the Call for Papers, a symbol with the word "Authorized" was printed. Drivers in Europe recognize this symbol as signifying "Do Not Enter." Was the Institute putting on its mantelpiece its unconscious realization that the primary object of its study—the study of authority in organizational life—remained an extremely charged task? If it were to be entered into at all, "ghosts" from the traumatic past—perhaps a past in which authority was experienced as abusive or abandoning, the latter a particular danger given a methodology that focuses on the group rather than the individual—would still need to be encountered?

A Scarlet Letter

One last thing on the mantelpiece. Under that first word, "Authority," in the conference title, there was a question: "Is it the new Scarlet Letter?" The question was put in parentheses in the Call for Papers, then disappeared altogether from the online program, then reappeared without parentheses on the front page of the printed program. If "Authority" were the Institute's new Scarlet Letter, what would that mean? The novel (Hawthorne, 1850), of course, is about a relationship between two people, and therefore about the hope—at least in fantasy—that a loving pair can create for others. But the Scarlet Letter pair is deemed illicit by the conventional and, to be sure, male authority of the time. It's interesting that in Hawthorne's masterpiece—written in a "fever" (said his wife) in the six months after his mother died—Hester's A is never actually named as standing for "adultery." Rather she is called "able" for her ability to counsel other troubled women and "artist" for her beautiful embroidery (Fromm, 2014a; Mellow, 1980).

Quite stunningly, Hester's embroidered A was printed on the front page of the conference program and on all of the name badges. *Everyone at the conference wore the Scarlet Letter near their hearts!* Which raises a question: What was the Institute saying to itself? Was it perhaps saying something not only about authority as a Scarlet Letter, but about *pairing* with authority? Was the organization highlighting some illicit—or deemed illicit—boundary crossing, some dramatic joining with authority, which might seem transgressive in some way but also might potentially open possibilities for growth? I recall vividly a moment in a GRC when an African American female member took up with feeling and thoughtfulness a comment made by a white male staff member; it was a deep joining with the work, not with that particular staff member, but, from the group's reaction, it was experienced as a betrayal. Is this what warrants a Scarlet Letter? And was the Institute, in putting that A near our hearts, saying that grappling with the implications of *The Scarlet Letter*—of pairing with authority across highly charged boundaries in the service of a task—is the difficult but deeply hopeful way forward?

To step back for a moment, a bit of this organization's traumatic history had to do with broken pairs. About ten years before the scientific meeting, a major organizational change occurred. Regional groups, which made up the organization's membership and governance, were formally and unilaterally separated from the national organization and offered an optional affiliate status. The organization declared itself an educational organization, not a membership organization. This was experienced by regional groups as cataclysmic; while the organization may have been trying to deal with, among other things, the enormous strain of managing conflicts about training standards and who would be chosen for highly coveted staff roles in GRCs—an issue in the 1990 crisis—its solution to the traumatic past created a traumatized present. The fallout from the severing of long-standing pairing relationships was profound, as though a sudden divorce had occurred. But, by the time of this scientific meeting, the broken pairs of regional and national groups seemed to have developed a new interest in each other, a bit of a courtship. So, it was not surprising that references to hope and to pairs—illicit or not—were finding their way into the discourse.

An important part of this beginning rapprochement was a second keynote, in a certain sense paired with mine, given by Ed Shapiro, the director of that long-ago GRC, on "Learning from the Director's Role." A generation after that painful—indeed personally and organizationally traumatic—experience, he had found the courage, based on his devotion to the work, to take up the director's role again (Shapiro, 2020). And the Institute had come to a place where it could make this invitation to him. Indeed, his presentation seemed to me a progressive, even healing, full-circle opportunity for the organization to hear and work with his reflections, especially as they included something about the issues then and now. From the point of view of trauma, this is precisely how ghosts become ancestors, so to speak: through revisiting in words the heretofore un-worked-through experiences of an excruciating history.

Who are We?

The background of identity upheaval within the Institute raises the question of who is the "We" in the title of the scientific meeting. At this point in my reflections, a personal story occurred to me. Several years ago, one week before I was to direct my first GRC for one of the regional affiliates, I was writing a clinical note, as I always did immediately after a therapy session with a patient. As I dated it, I suddenly thought, "My sister's birthday," and I found myself with strong but confusing feelings. This sister was my parents' first child; she died at two weeks of age. A year and a half later, I was born and named for the obstetrician who delivered both of us. So, in its way, a story about parental trauma and its transmission had suddenly occurred to me. Perhaps most disconcerting was that I knew instantly that it had to do with the upcoming conference, though I had no idea how. When I told this story to a colleague, she said, matter-of-factly, "Oh, last year's conference died in its infancy." Indeed, the preceding year's GRC was the first in perhaps thirty years to have been cancelled for lack of membership. My colleague's interpretation felt absolutely true. I was astonished to realize that this personal and, to some degree formative, experience of my life had become so powerfully but unconsciously intertwined with the upcoming conference.

This experience led me to understand something about who "We" are. People involved in group relations have come to the work *in one way only*: through the experience of GR Conferences, and therefore through not only the traumatic experiences they might have encountered within them but also through the way those experiences may link—often quite unconsciously—to trauma in their own lives. Perhaps no other learning experience brings people so deeply into contact with this juncture of present and past. To take this seriously means that, in GRCs, people risk an encounter with the Other they don't fully know, both outside and inside. They risk an encounter with the legacy of historical trauma as much as of personal trauma. And, as in my story, they have to rely on others to help them make sense of their experience. Dependency and interdependency are inevitable and essential, even if they are also at times hated. These risks are taken in the service of learning, and in the hope that the "deep play" space of the conference will make such learning survivable, even transformative.

This is a critical aspect of who the "We" of this organization are. The Institute is the container for this potentially traumatic content, and for the rich, disconcerting links people make between the personal and the organizational in the service of learning. I came to feel that, in this national scientific meeting, the Institute's leadership had not only done the job of convening members and organizing a set of learning opportunities, but, more importantly, it had risked putting the organization's collective unconscious out there for all to see and make sense of, as my keynote attempted to do. My hope was that the questions I raised might open a conversation about how the organization got to where it was and where it might *want* to go.

Icarus

The psychoanalyst, Al Margulies (2013), notes a less discussed aspect of trauma in his consideration of Pieter Bruegel's remarkable 1565 *Landscape with the Fall of Icarus*. The painting depicts a hilly landscape sloping down toward a harbor and a ship near the shore. Various groups of people are carrying on the activities of their daily lives; many are busy with their daily work. As in other Bruegel paintings of community life, the viewer must work to find the protagonist—in this case Icarus, who has fallen from the sky into the water. In the moment this painting captures, only his legs are visible.

W. H. Auden (1940b), whom we met in an earlier chapter, reflected on this painting:

About suffering they were never wrong,
The old Masters: how well they understood
Its human position: how it takes place
While someone else is eating or opening a window or just walking dully along …
In Brueghel's Icarus, for instance: how everything turns away
Quite leisurely from the disaster; the ploughman may
Have heard the splash, the forsaken cry,
But for him it was not an important failure; the sun shone
As it had to on the white legs disappearing into the green
Water, and the expensive delicate ship that must have seen
Something amazing, a boy falling out of the sky,
Had somewhere to get to and sailed calmly on.

Like the "delicate ship" in Auden's poem and like all organizations, the two I have been discussing had "somewhere to get to." Recall that early question one of them asked, "Where do we go now?" What Bruegel shows us is that trauma is traumatic because it is suffered *alone.* People may see or hear something, but no one really notices, no one calls out, and no one rescues. In taking up the "human position" of carrying on their work, organizations risk an "important failure"; in the case of the A. K. Rice Institute, it may have missed—and missed a conversation about—some of the "forsaken cries" its members must have felt, at one moment or another, as they fell from their heights and took that deep dive into the organization's basic work, the work of Group Relations Conferences.

Icarus' aloneness is ours too. He is one of many figures in Bruegel's painting, all of whom, like all of us, take risks in our daily work, especially if that work touches people in personal ways. It's to the credit of Division 39's and the A. K. Rice Institute's leadership that it brought bits and pieces of that work, recovered from the depths of past trauma, to the surface, and put them on their conferences' mantelpiece for all of us to see. "Something amazing" to be sure. A set of questions from this dive, a set of questions about a fault line, and a way of listening to organizational trauma have been the subjects of this chapter. The goal of this listening is that trauma not be suffered alone.

Part III

Trauma in society

CHAPTER 7

National nightmare: the legacy of perpetrator trauma

In the last footnote to the Introduction of his magnificent *A German Generation* (2012), Thomas Kohut quotes his psychoanalyst father: "If the depth psychologist (or the historian, for that matter) is to make a contribution to the understanding of man's role in history and his control over his destiny, then he must try to extend his empathic observation not only to the victims but also to the persecutors, not only to the martyrs but also to the torturers. He must discover the human, the all-too-human, whether in the normal ... or in the psychopathological, in the good and in the evil" (H. Kohut, 1969–70, p. 119).

Thomas Kohut is a psychoanalytically trained historian but he is also a son who learned deeply from his father. Taking up the latter's encouragement to find the all-too-human within the horrific, Kohut proposed that the Austen Riggs Center's Erikson Institute—of which I was the director at that time and he a board member—convene an interdisciplinary conference, which came to be called "The Legacy of Perpetrator Trauma in Groups and Families." With the help of a number of German colleagues, Kohut invited the key participants from Germany and Austria, and I directed what turned out to be a profound, intellectually stimulating, and emotionally intense two days. This chapter is one outcome of that conference. It was written just as current societal dynamics were turning toward the populism and authoritarianism we have since seen develop more fully.

There was a history to the conference theme. For two consecutive years, the Erikson Institute's Fall Conference had studied the transmission of trauma, the clinical relevance of which was becoming increasingly clear. Papers from these conferences were published under the title *Lost in Transmission: Studies of Trauma across Generations* (Fromm, 2012a). They joined a literature that began with Selma Fraiberg's classic paper, "Ghosts in the Nursery" (Fraiberg et al., 1975) and expanded enormously as the suffering of second-generation Holocaust survivors became known and treated.

In succeeding years, we have learned that, as the French psychoanalysts Françoise Davoine and Jean-Max Gaudilliere argue in *History Beyond Trauma* (2004), paraphrasing Wittgenstein, "Whereof one cannot speak, thereof one cannot stay silent." What human beings cannot contain of their experience—what has been traumatically overwhelming, unbearable, unthinkable—falls out of social discourse, but onto and into the next generation, as an affective sensitivity, a strange symptom, a chaotic urgency, in the words of one of our presenters, Gerhard Wilke, "an encapsulated presence," and sometimes an unconscious mission.

The challenge of empathy

This new conference was radically different from the earlier two in the subjects of its focus. As Wilke pointed out in the conference brochure, "Psychoanalytic understanding of the working through of such traumatic material is largely based on work done with survivors, émigrés, refugees and their children. What we know less well are the trans-generational phenomena of children of perpetrators" (2012)—a generation not guilty by deed but so often caught up in feeling ashamed, guilty, responsible, and horrified by association. In this conference—that Kohut, and in some ways his father, proposed—we hoped to learn about the configuration and dynamics of this particular traumatic history.

In a clinical case conference some time ago, a young male patient told the staff that the hospital "is haunted by the forces of the dead." "They are here as much as there are helping people here," he said

(Fromm, 2012a, p. xx). To the degree that a person is unconsciously preoccupied with what may well be a haunting family history—who even at times may represent this hauntedness to and for his family—to that degree, the person's subjectivity is "lost in transmission," sometimes with tragic consequences: the German patient whose grandfather worked in the V-2 program at the beginning of World War II and who, years later, hurled himself from his dormitory balcony, thereby becoming a human missile; the Austrian patient whose suicide attempts always involved the products of his grandfather's pharmaceutical company, itself implicated in a horrific Holocaust history. Erikson Scholar and psychoanalyst Vamık Volkan has discussed this kind of uncanny but stunning intergenerational enactment in a remarkable case history published recently under the title *A Nazi Legacy* (2015).

The task of the Legacy of Perpetrator Trauma conference was to explore this phenomenon through the stories of post-war German and Austrian generations. We hoped to help clinicians and scholars revisit and understand more deeply the psychological aftermath of the Third Reich through a consideration of the inner conflicts of those who may carry this psychic burden, on behalf of their families, their society and, in fact, for the rest of us. What might we learn about individual, family, and group dynamics associated with the offspring of perpetrators, and what are the implications of this learning for society?

True to Erikson's conviction that learning occurs in the boundary areas between fields of study, the conference represented a range of disciplines: history, psychoanalysis, psychology, sociology, and others. The tradition of the Erikson Institute is to hold *working conferences*, by which we mean that the presenters do not have the answers to the questions of the conference, except perhaps for themselves; that learning occurs through active dialogue among presenters and members; and that sometimes how we talk about something—the process dimension of the conversation—illuminates more deeply what we are talking about. In this conference, that process dimension was inescapable. We were dealing with an extremely serious subject and highly charged material. Members' joining this conference represented an act of courage because it inevitably meant encountering genuinely disturbing feelings, and inevitably challenged us to think more deeply, more discerningly, and, as Heinz Kohut suggested, more empathically about those feelings.

Freud spoke about every family's "archaic heritage" (1939a, p. 38), and one task of transmission turns out to be the generational struggle to resist the dissociation of that heritage, to recognize, in Davoine and Gaudilliere's phrase, the "cut-out" unconscious (2004, p. 61)—cut out, that is, from the official narrative, whether that narrative is the family's or the society's—and to bring its full, tragic story into social discourse. How the unconscious gets "cut out"—and an astonishing 1930s dream journal kept by a woman named Charlotte Beradt (1968), to which I will return later, may open a window onto that process—leads to one set of questions. How it gets re-inscribed, if you will—the profound task of telling the story—is where the conference began.

The danger of love

The conference was structured around three presentations, with considerable time for general discussion. The first theme to emerge was a simple but powerful one: how to love when the object of that love is implicated in horrific crimes. Alexandra Senfft, a freelance journalist, whose personal story, *Silence Hurts: A German Family History* was published in 2007, put it in hypothetical form: "What if my grandfather had taken me onto his lap and I had begun to love him?" (This and other quotes come from the presentations and discussions at the conference.) Other similar, not at all hypothetical, statements spoke to the visceral experience of trying to contain the good and the bad at the same time, of vomiting out at the moment of taking in, of genuine love and horror at the feeling of loving.

It was as though it fell to the next generation to at least attempt to integrate what they experienced with their parents and what they also knew about them, an integration that the parents themselves seemed not to make at all (Covington, 2016). Rather the perpetrator generation, the generation of "knowing and not knowing," seemed essentially to be living out that old definition of schizophrenia, that is, the split personality, and living permanently in what Melanie Klein (1946) called the paranoid–schizoid position, the place where at all costs good and bad must be kept separate. The maturational effort toward what Klein called the depressive position, that is, the task of holding the good and bad in the same space and working toward some sort of integration, fell to the next generation. It was a profoundly difficult emotional assignment.

Part of the integrative task that fell to the children of perpetrators included feeling the guilt and shame of their parents' actions, which they themselves had warded off. Their children's responses took more than one form. We heard examples of essentially manic efforts at reparation, not necessarily directed to the victims of the Nazis, but to other suffering people in far-off countries. By "manic" I don't only mean frenetically active and obsessively preoccupied; I also mean what is termed a "manic defense" (Klein, 1940), that is, manic reparation in the service of keeping at bay the very feelings of guilt motivating it. We noted as well friction between this generation and their children when the latter did not want to continue the reparation project but rather hoped to go on with their own lives. That latter wish, understandable as it is, is of course not at all easy to accomplish, not only because of their parents' pressure to continue the reparative mission, but because of the larger task of individuating from the chaos of such immense family disaster (Scholz, 2020).

Another form this effort to process parental perpetration took, in the second and third generations, was identification with the victims, sometimes very literally and to a quasi-psychotic degree. Vamık Volkan in his recent book, *A Nazi Legacy* (2015), tells the story of a man who in his sleep leaves his bed to frantically open windows night after night. Though this man's troubles were many and complex, this particular stubborn and mysterious symptom was eventually understood in relation to his Nazi grandfather, who murdered Jews by gassing them inside a school bus. His victims—*like his grandson years later*—frantically tried to open windows.

Alexandra Senfft structured her presentation around two questions: her mother's question, "Why did they kill my father?" and her own, "Why did my mother die?" In the story, Ms. Senfft's mother loved her own father and was devastated when he was hanged for war crimes when she was fourteen. Over time, as she learned about his Nazi career and his role in deporting 65,000 Jews, she became increasingly depressed and alcoholic. In a family context where her own mother refused to believe, or to speak about, what had happened and who admitted no guilt or shame at all, Ms. Senfft's mother spiraled into madness.

Or perhaps into a mad sanity. In her alcoholic state, she would panic about being closed in and scream for help. Davoine and Gaudilliere, in *History beyond Trauma* (2004), report clinical work in which psychosis and trauma go hand in hand. They are convinced that the psychotic patient is madly conducting a research into the rupture between his family and the social fabric, a rupture brought about through trauma and betrayal. Beyond her screaming about the suffocating silence of her family, was Ms. Senfft's mother also living out her fragmented imagining of what her father's victims might have experienced? And was that part of her tragic death, self-inflicted while drunk, in scalding water?

One more thing Ms. Senfft's mother did while drunk, much more in the direction of an active transmission: She talked to her oldest child, and as Ms. Senfft said, "I let her." Frightened of "becoming" her, Ms. Senfft needed to know why her mother died, one year after her own mother did, and boxes of letters left to her became a way into that terrible story. Like another presenter, Marcus Carney, whose award-winning documentary, *The End of the Neubacher Project* (2007), tells the story of his mother's family and its involvement in Austrian National Socialism, Ms. Senfft took up the task of inscription of a cut-out history, the task of "how to give my mother a voice."

But she then encountered the same terror her mother felt, the terrifying dilemma of exploding the silence or sinking into it. In a sense, by taking the risk of learning and then speaking the truth of her family history, she found herself in another transmission role: destroying the family myth, she *became the perpetrator*, the one who inflicts on her family, *for the first time*, the horrific images and feelings that have been so strenuously split off and kept at bay. As we saw in Chapter 1, the psychoanalyst Donald Winnicott in a paper called "Fear of Breakdown" came to a remarkable intuition: "The patient needs to 'remember' … but it is not possible to remember something that has not yet happened, and this thing of the past has not happened yet because the patient was not there for it to happen to" (1974, p. 105). It's as though Ms. Senfft's family had dissociated themselves so thoroughly from their own lives that, in a very powerful sense, they were at risk of experiencing *in the future, at her hands* the trauma of what their family had already done.

Ms. Senfft experienced enormous and sustained family resistance to her writing her book. She was criticized, seen as having something terribly wrong with her, and shunned. "Drive carefully" after one such family meeting had a menacing ring to it. Ultimately she lost her family when her book came out, though, crucially, not her whole family: Her father supported her throughout the project. As she said, "I don't know what I would have done if he had turned against me." And, in a sense, her mother was there too, as the "open wound" of her family that "nobody treated." Until her daughter did by writing her story.

The word "therapist" has an ancient Greek root in the word "therapon" (Davoine & Gaudilliere, 2004, p. 153), the second-in-combat, the one who *attends to the burial ritual of the warrior*. In a sense, this is the role that Ms. Senfft served for her mother. In his enigmatic statement that the symbol is "the murder of the thing" (1977, p. 104), the psychoanalyst Jacques Lacan evokes the varying levels at which inscription—and the witnessing embedded in it—destroys something. He also refers to its role in a person's fundamentally separating from the traumatic context: the way that inscription on a tombstone allows leaving the dead—and the trauma leading to the death—because now one knows where to truly find them.

A delegated life

Another presenter, Gerhard Wilke, a sociologist and organizational consultant, referred to present-day Germany as a "post-traumatic society." Today's understanding of PTSD includes three major elements: overwhelming exposure to horror, manifested in the symptom triad of flashbacks, dissociation, and hyper-arousal; the experience of sudden serious loss; and what has come to be called "moral injury." Coined by the VA psychiatrist, Jonathan Shay (2014) and broadened by Brett Litz (2014), moral injury refers to a deep sense of betrayal of "what's right," committed by someone in legitimate authority or by oneself, in a high-stakes situation. It represents the devastating emotional legacy of witnessing or participating in something that fundamentally violates one's most basic sense of moral order. All three elements occur simultaneously and with extraordinary intensity in perpetrator families.

Wilke captures one aspect of the second and third generations' sense of themselves in the statement that "We live a delegated life." From his point of view, his generation is always representing someone to someone else, and, one way or the other, is implicated constantly in working out something for someone else. This is part of the perhaps naïve but urgent longing for "one's own life," expressed by the third generation. Wilke attempted to get some grasp on this phenomenon for himself personally by leaving Germany for London, from which vantage point, two things happened. First, he was constantly seen as a Nazi, which he actually found useful; in the safer, more playful context of London, he could dare to face the Nazi in himself. But his former countrymen did not have the luxury of this perspective from a distance, so the second thing that happened was Dr. Wilke's dedicating himself to helping them achieve it, as best he and they could. He did this through consulting to their work lives (Wilke et al., 2005) and helping them see—not an easy task, to be sure—the playing out of war trauma in their daily relation to authority, to ordinary assertiveness, to their need for order, and so on.

Following Wilke's presentation, we had set aside a considerable length of time for conference discussion. The first half of that time was to be a space for volunteer members to express freely what they had experienced in the conference—and where those experiences had led them in their associations—to which Wilke consulted; the second half was to be a more reflective and integrative conversation for everyone, to which both he and I were to consult. But first, the opportunity was to simply bring out whatever members were carrying emotionally from the presentations and discussions so far. This was obviously not an easy task, even if it promised some degree of relief, learning, and even intimacy. As I had from the very beginning of the conference, I told myself once again to try to "hold the whole thing," meaning that I was keenly aware of how critical it was for the staff to contain this process, to manage boundaries, and to be present as sensible authority.

In the first discussion, members were very attentive to the presence of two Holocaust survivors in their midst. Nevertheless—or perhaps because of this—the unfolding conversation was extraordinary in its emotional scope and detail. Stories about members' families came out, many associated with wartime experiences. References to the conference material included very personal reactions, sometimes of feeling things from both sides. Anxiety ebbed and flowed, and, at one point, in the midst of the unstructured opening up of experiences, one of the Holocaust survivors spoke with feeling about "needing a framework" for what was happening. Not long thereafter, a second Holocaust survivor began to speak at some length and rather theoretically about trauma. Interesting as his comments were, the effect was to interrupt the expression of what members were carrying and how it linked to their personal experiences.

Wilke consulted to what might be the group's need, via this member's discourse, to protect itself from the intensity of feeling that had been emerging. Despite this intervention, members seemed to defer to the Holocaust survivor who had been speaking, and indeed his comments, again very astute but conveyed almost as a lecture, continued at some length, limiting the opportunity for other members to speak about their experiences. Eventually, one German member and Wilke again intervened with the speaker in ways that some members felt to be too confrontational. And suddenly, just as this part of the group discussion was coming to an end, we were back to the old roles of German perpetrator and Jewish victim. Sadly, a framework of sorts had indeed fallen into place, and the flow of conversation—if not of history, to pick up on one of Thomas Kohut's (2012) concepts—had stopped.

In the broader reflective discussion that followed, the group tried to process what had happened, with only partial success. Feelings were still running high and tended toward polarized positions. The group did its best to reflect on the events of the first discussion and at least allowed members' different perspectives to be articulated. The hypothesis I found myself with, and offered to the group, was that, as this powerful conversation was coming to a close—and therefore as we were all about *to be silenced permanently* (this discussion group being the last conference event)—there was something unbearable about, in Heinz Kohut's terms, the effort to "extend [our] empathic observation" (1969–70, p. 119). The anxiety about ending up on the wrong moral side of history, not to mention being stuck with horrifying identifications, was enormous. The old roles—and the sense of being back to square one—disappointing as they were, were nevertheless reassuring. We knew where, in a projective sense, to leave the good and the bad. Though it was hard to know what members did with my intervention and indeed how they actually understood what had happened, it seemed to me that the potential learning from and about the group's process was invaluable.

The destruction of dream life

"What haunts are not the dead, but the gaps left within us by the secrets of others." This quote from the Hungarian psychoanalyst, Nicholas Abraham, begins a recent book—part legal treatise, part Holocaust history, part family study—by Philippe Sands (2016). As we have seen so far, one generation's secrets become the next generation's gaps, and also their hauntedness. But a remarkable dream journal from the 1930s suggests the ways that, in the context of terror and destructive group processes, the earlier generation attempted to keep secrets from itself, leading to profound, collective dissociation and the licensing of horrific destructiveness. A natural experiment in what Gordon Lawrence (1991) called "social dreaming," the journal illuminates the steady assault on a person's inner life and the way that massive social trauma and malignant authoritarianism turn an essential privacy into dangerous secrecy, even from oneself.

In his remarkable analysis of Freud's Irma dream—the foundational dream in psychoanalytic dream theory—Erik Erikson (1954) noticed a group process. Freud's intellectual ambition for his new science of psychoanalysis—an ambition that was the "cornerstone of his identity" and "almost an obligation to his people" (p. 169)—came up against something having gone dangerously wrong in his patient's treatment. In the face of this set of anxieties—guilt for harming his patient, fear of failing to meet the internalized aspirations of his ethnic group, fear of persecution by jealous colleagues—Freud, in his dream, defensively joins his professional group and blames someone else for the trouble. Erikson notes how "infantile wishes to belong to and believe in organizations providing for collective reassurance against individual anxiety … easily join other repressed childhood temptations—and force their way into dreams" (p. 158).

As I have argued elsewhere,

> Adaptation requires that we "see" the Other on whom we depend so fully throughout development, and psychic change relies to some extent on our seeing the Other whose conflicts speak to and through us. In certain contexts … envisioning the Other may move beyond the familial environment to larger social realities …

> [E]ach dreamer is potentially a "seer" of his or her "people" and of the relationship to that Other. This has been described (Lawrence, 1991) as "social dreaming." In my own terms, I consider it an aspect of unconscious citizenship. (Fromm, 2000, p. 289)

But what if the Other is all-powerful and ruthlessly dangerous? And what if that Other sees that you see it?

This is the framework from which I would like to reflect on the earlier question about how the unconscious may become "cut out" and on the remarkable journal mentioned above. Throughout the 1930s, the journalist, Charlotte Beradt, kept a notebook, published in 1968 with the title, *The Third Reich of Dreams*, in which she recorded the dreams of ordinary, "non-political" German citizens, just after National Socialism came into power. Here is one of those dreams:

> It was about nine in the evening. My consultations were over, and I was stretching out on the couch to relax with a book, when suddenly the walls of my room and then my apartment disappeared. I looked around and discovered to my horror that as far as the eye could see no apartment had walls anymore. Then I heard a loudspeaker boom, "According to the decree of the 17th of this month on the Abolition of Walls …" (Beradt, 1968, p. 21)

This is the dream of a middle-aged doctor, who that day, in response to the block warden's apparently casual, half-joking observation that he had no flag outside his apartment, thought to himself, "Not on my four walls" (p. 22). The consequence in his dream is that his walls and all others are abolished. The physical boundary between private and public life no longer exists, just as, during the day, the boundary between private thought ("Not on my four walls") and public communication (no flag) did not exist either. Stunned by this experience, the doctor wrote his dream down, only to be accused of writing his dreams in the next night's dream.

Beradt thus documents the penetration of the totalitarian Other into private life, including the private life of dreaming. She thereby raises for us questions about the effect of such serious boundary disturbance, and presumably both sleep and dream deprivation (R. Friedman, 2019a), on a terrorized group. From a different context, the psychoanalyst, Christopher Bollas (1989), considering the problem of sexual abuse, argues that the invading Other "electrifies the dream process" itself (p. 175), rendering it too charged with anxiety to be at all useful in the processing of wishes and the development of symbolic functioning. In this vein, the epigram to Bruno Bettelheim's Afterword to Beradt's book is: "Sleep no more. Macbeth doth murder sleep" (Beradt, 1968, p. 149).

Here is another dream on this theme: "I dreamt I was talking in my sleep and to be on the safe side was speaking Russian (which I don't know, and anyway I never talk in my sleep). I was speaking so that I would not even understand myself and so no one else could understand me" (Fromm, 2000, p. 52). The dreamer dreams in a language that not only those around her but she herself cannot understand. As I wrote elsewhere: "If dreaming represents an effort, albeit ambivalent, to process important inner and outer life events, what does it mean to dream in order not to understand yourself?" (2000, p. 292).

What I believe we see here is "a desperate effort not only at safety but at anything that would feel like a boundary; the dreamer's demand that she have a private life is paid for by her keeping that private life from herself" (Fromm, 2000, p. 292). Beradt is remarkably attuned to the humor and the profound absurdity in these dreams, which she also sees in the dreams of many young Germans in which they express shame and horror at having the wrong color hair or the wrong kind of nose. Beradt is astonished and also amused by the utter silliness and arbitrariness of these physical ideals, bought into, however, with a teenager's deadly seriousness and enforced with brutality, either by the state or one's peers.

A third dream on the theme of the public and the private: "In place of the street signs which had been abolished, posters had been set up on every corner, proclaiming in white letters on a black background the twenty words people were not allowed to say. The first was 'Lord,' the last was 'I'" (2000, p. 23). In this dream of an educated young woman, reference points, represented by street signs, are abolished. Given the words that have been censured, the more fundamental reference points of "Lord," representing a higher power or a moral order, and of "I," that is, personal subjectivity, are forbidden as well. The disoriented dreamer is left in a terrorized dyadic relationship with the unseen authority behind the posters. So, this woman's comments, to some degree like the previous dreamer, that "To be on the safe side, I must have dreamt this dream in English" (p. 23).

Jacques Lacan returned Freud's foundational description of the trajectory of clinical psychoanalysis—"Where Id was, there Ego shall be" (1933a, p. 80)—to its original German: "Where It was, there I must come to be" (1977). This last dream suggests that the totalitarian process perversely reverses this trajectory: Where I was, only It will be, It referring to the dominant-submissive pairing between the state and its subjects. There is no Third (Muller, 1996), through which to ground the pair in a larger symbolic and moral order. As Beradt puts it, these dreams were "dictated … by a dictatorship." She suggests that this "[D]ream imagery might thus help to describe the structure of a reality that was just on the verge of becoming a nightmare" (p. 9).

Beradt adds that:

> The dreams we are concerned with were not produced by conflicts arising in their authors' private realm, and certainly not by some past conflict that had left a psychological wound. Instead they arose from conflicts into which these people had been driven by a public realm in which half-truths, vague notions, and a combination of fact, rumor, and conjecture had produced a general feeling of uncertainty and unrest. These dreams may deal with disturbed human relations, but it was the environment that had disturbed them. (p. 15)

She records many dreams in which this social dimension of fear, uncertainty, and miscommunication plays out with predictable results. In several dreams, she observes a "chorus" who intone statements like "There's not a thing one can do" (p. 72), or whose silence accuses the dreamer of a costly and misguided refusal to join.

Indeed, so many dreams include, to the dreamer's shock, "silent and expressionless faces" (p. 25), no human response at all when the dreamer expects and desperately needs one. In a sense, these dreams foreshadow the child development research of many years later having to do with the "still-face experiment" (Tronick, 2007), in which the mother is instructed to break the communicative rhythm of looks, smiles, and sounds with her infant, and instead present a "still face" for a short time. After efforts to re-engage mother—to restore what Erikson would call "basic trust" in this intimate social process—the infant invariably withdraws into what looks like hopelessness and reflexive shame.

If one essential function of the dream-work is overcoming trauma-induced helplessness, Beradt shows us dreams in which the collapse analogous to that in the still-face experiment occurs, and terrorized helplessness is recurrently justified. In one dream, the dreamer is "no longer able to speak except in chorus with my group" (p. 87), and another person dreams "I was saying, 'I don't *have* to always say *no* anymore'" (p. 119). About this last quasi-delusional contortion seemingly in the direction of freedom, Beradt comments: "Amid all the 'musts' of life under totalitarian rule, this almost touching magic formula, 'don't have to,' demonstrates once again what effort it costs to be against the state when freedom is a burden and bondage comes as a relief" (p. 119).

Beradt calls this group process the "imperceptible and undramatic … transition from suggestion to autosuggestion" (p. 119), as insidious as it is terrifying. As we have noted earlier, Erikson (1959) writes that: "Where the human being despairs of an essential wholeness, he re-structures himself and the world by taking refuge in totalism" (p. 133). He emphasized the person's insisting on an "absolute boundary": "Nothing that belongs inside must be left outside; nothing that must be outside should be tolerated inside" (p. 133). In its extreme, this leads to a societal process of purification (Volkan, 1997, 2013). Beradt's book documents this despair of an essential wholeness and the subsequent disastrous splitting and restructuring. Elsewhere I wrote that, "[R]elentlessly, we see the ethno-syntonic but ego-dystonic conflict resolved in favor of membership rather than identity or conscience. The totalitarian outcome is the self-alienated subject rather than the citizen, and the destruction of dream life—one space for self-other confrontation—is at the heart of the totalitarian method" (Fromm, 2000, p. 293).

In the Name of the Father

The title of the volume for which this chapter was originally written, *History Flows through Us* (Frie, 2018) comes from the final chapter of Thomas Kohut's *A German Generation* (2012). My goal was to illuminate some of the inter-generational, dream, and group processes by which this flow works to shape individual feelings, attitudes, and behaviors. The title of Kohut's concluding chapter is "The Authority of Historical Experience," with the word "authority" connoting, to my mind, not only the power historical experience unconsciously exercises over people but also the set of rights or claims one generation makes on the other. It seems to me, as I have argued elsewhere (Fromm, 2012a), that the transmission of trauma from one generation to the next reflects a complex authority issue. To some degree, the experience of the next generation has been "authored," if you will, by the unspoken, indeed unspeakable, traumas in their parents' histories, and some of these children—Ms. Senfft's mother perhaps—are lost in this transmission.

Others, like Ms. Senfft herself, may have been especially, if unconsciously, "authorized" to carry the parent's trauma into the future. "She talked to me, and I let her." This may take the form of a symptom, of an "unthought known," in Christopher Bollas' apt phrase (1987), or of an urgent question: for example, "Why did my mother die?" One way or the other, such transgenerational experience "must come into being as emotional understanding if the [person] is ultimately to take authority for his or her own life as distinct from that of the traumatized parent" (Fromm, 2012a1, p. 113). Ms. Senfft's story suggests that the authority of one generation's historical experience—and its raw, if unconscious power over the next—can be mitigated by that next generation's finding the authority—and to be sure, the courage (Covington, 2020)—to become its author, and to somehow inscribe this "archaic heritage" (Freud, 1939a, p. 38) into the larger human discourse.

Ms. Senfft needed her father to find this authority, and fathers are a major part of the story Kohut tells in *A German Generation*. He argues that the defeated, humiliated, and lost fathers of World War I—from the PTSD perspective, a set of acute losses, horrific shocks, and moral injuries—set the experiential stage for the next generation's profoundly powerful peer relationships—indeed their driven merger with the collective—which in turn made them vulnerable to, indeed hungry for, the return of a powerful, idealized father. Beradt reports a dream in which the phrase "In the Name of …" is proclaimed over the radio repeatedly, but its last word is "Fuhrer" (1968, p. 40). In this dream, Hitler supplants all fathers, including the Heavenly One.

As we noted in Chapter 3, in the Preface to *Young Man Luther* (1958), Erikson—the son of a German Jewish woman and a Danish Gentile father whom, to his great pain, he never knew—concludes with:

> … a memory which had been utterly covered by the rubble of the cities and by the bleached bones of men of my kind in Europe. In my youth, as a wandering artist, I stayed one night with a friend in a small village by the upper Rhine. His father was a Protestant Pastor; and in the morning, as the family sat down to breakfast, the old man said the Lord's Prayer in Luther's German. Never having "knowingly" heard it, I had the experience, as seldom before or after, of a wholeness captured in a few simple words, of poetry fusing the aesthetic and the moral … (1958, p. 10)

Once again, the longing for wholeness and its being found, however temporarily, through a father.

Thomas Kohut concludes his introductory chapter with a memory too:

> My own interest in history can be traced back to fishing trips with my father in rural Wisconsin when I was very little. I do not recall us ever catching anything, but I vividly remember listening with rapt attention as my father told me stories of the Persian and Peloponnesian wars as we sat in a little rowboat in the hot sun on a lake … (2012, p. 18)

Barely fifteen years after his own escape from Vienna, Heinz Kohut is with his son, alone on a boat, safely separate from other people, warmed by the sun, waiting for nature to offer something special from its depths, passing along stories of long ago and far away wars. From which comes that son's life's vocation, a story of too close a war, the specter of lost and nearly lost fathers, and a profoundly generative transmission.

CHAPTER 8

The cure for depression is jihad: a case study

"The cure for depression is jihad." So declares a young man, speaking perfect English, in an ISIS recruitment video. Mental health professionals might wonder about the nature of this depression and what kind of cure jihad is. Perhaps a clue can be found in another assertion, this one from an American man speaking of his jihadist experience: "*This* is the real Disneyland." How can this almost comical, even oddly sweet, oxymoron relate to something so deadly? Disneyland is the playing out on a grand scale of a child's fantasy. Is that true of jihad as well?

The first quote about the cure for depression speaks to what Jessica Stern (2014) calls a "push factor," that which drives someone into something; the second about Disneyland speaks to a "pull factor." In her in-depth interview with Mr. X, a convicted Swedish Neo-Nazi terrorist and mercenary in Bosnia, Dr. Stern, whom I came to know when she was an Erikson Scholar at the Austen Riggs Center, sets herself the task of "thick description" (2014, p. 1) of a single terrorist. "To reintegrate violent extremists or prevent them from turning to violence, we need to understand their motivations … And to understand their motivations, we need to talk to them" (p. 11). In this chapter, which builds upon my discussion of her work at a meeting of the American Psychoanalytic Association, I will try to say something about what a psychoanalytic listener might think about on hearing this brave and fascinating encounter. I will follow the content and process of Dr. Stern's interview (2014) as it unfolds, in the service of furthering her task of understanding more deeply a very troubled person, one who represents a very troubling societal dynamic.

Why me?

In the interview, Mr. X first insists that Dr. Stern use his real name, but then changes his mind about that. More than once, he declares his wish to kill people, then claims to have been misunderstood by Dr. Stern and asks to have that statement deleted. Seemingly before our eyes, this man of violent certainty vacillates. What might be happening in his mind? From a clinical point of view, could we be seeing the beginnings of shame in Mr. X, a moment of re-socialization or of feeling that how he is seen by Dr. Stern—and through her, by others—is starting to matter to him? If so, this would be a very good sign, and allowing him to back away from premature declarations would support his taking a crucial developmental step toward socialization. As we shall see later, premature declarations, intolerance of shame, and what Erikson would think of as identity foreclosure can be enormously problematic for a young adult (Erikson, 1959).

Another apparent contradiction: Mr. X steadfastly refuses to give interviews, but then agrees to one with Dr. Stern. Why? It was Dr. Stern's intuition that her books—one on her experience of interviewing other terrorists (2003) and one on her experience as the victim of terror (2010)—had something to do with his saying "Yes" to her. Indeed she felt quite certain that the latter book did. In *Denial* (2010), Dr. Stern tells the excruciating story of her having been raped at gunpoint as an adolescent. She describes this trauma in the context of her life history and, eventually, of the rapist's. Perhaps most strikingly, she tells us about her father's inability to be there for her at this tragic moment, a wound she found the courage to address with him much later in her life. When she did, she, and he too, learned why: horrific trauma in his own childhood in Nazi Germany.

If Dr. Stern's intuition is correct, why was this story compelling to Mr. X? Did it give him an opportunity to play out Nazi-like sadism? Did he take pleasure in being a threatening presence or was he moved toward remorse? Might Mr. X have unconsciously imagined Dr. Stern as his victim, but now alive and interested in him? Or did he see in her the victim he himself had once been? And perhaps something else as well: At a crucial moment in both their stories, a father abandoned his child. For Dr. Stern, her father returned, but Mr. X's did not. Might this relationship with fathers also have been critical to what developed between these two people—both to Dr. Stern's feeling "safe enough" with Mr. X and to his relating to her essentially as his analyst, with "a determination to make some sense out of his experience" (p. 6)?

Breaking bad

From this analytic point of view, what might we make of the bits of Mr. X's history that come through in the interview? Around age eleven, Mr. X became fascinated with World War II and especially with Nazis. He was drawn to their black uniforms, the marching, and the fact that it was all forbidden. How one wants to say to Mr. X, "Something happened to you then!" These critical turning points in a child's life mean something; when they come up in a personal encounter, they invite both empathy and curiosity. Sometimes they point to a broader narrative about what happened in the family. How might his parents and grandparents—it turns out that there were two sets, one biological and one adopted—have been affected by WWII? Might Mr. X as a child have been taking up something from their histories? This line of thought—illustrated by earlier stories in this volume—is described convincingly by Françoise Davoine and Jean-Max Gaudilliere in their book, *History beyond Trauma* (2004).

From a developmental perspective, rather than a family historical perspective, this eleven-year-old boy's preoccupation with black/marching/forbidden suggests that he was heading toward reorganizing his sense of himself around a *negative identity*. This term—like the terms "identity crisis," "alienation," and "father figure," all of which come into this story—are vulnerable to easy overuse. But the emotional power bound up and so often released in this adolescent reorganization is enormous. Here is Erikson (1959) on this subject:

> Such vindictive choices of a negative identity represent … a desperate attempt at regaining some mastery in a situation in which the available positive identity elements cancel each other out … [I]t is easier to derive a sense of identity out of a *total* identification with that which one is *least* supposed to be than to struggle for a feeling of reality in acceptable roles which are unattainable … Many a late adolescent, if faced with continuing diffusion, would rather be *nobody*, or *somebody bad*, or *indeed dead*—and this totally and by free choice—than not quite somebody. (p. 132)

Erikson, writing in a totalitarian era, uses the word "total" advisedly. He goes on to a remarkable statement, one that I have referred to often in this volume: "Where the human being despairs of an essential wholeness, he restructures himself and the world by taking refuge in totalism … an absolute boundary is emphasized … nothing that belongs inside must be left outside, nothing that must be outside should be tolerated inside" (p. 133). To which he adds:

> Psychoanalysis reveals how strong … man's unconscious proclivities … are for total realignments … and, on the other hand, how much energy is employed in inner defenses against [this kind of] threatening total reorientation in which black may turn into white and vice versa. Only the affect released in sudden [spiritual] conversions testifies to the quantity of this energy. (p. 133)

Torture

If Erikson is right, something very powerful was going on inside Mr. X as a little boy. Another chilling detail from his history supports that conjecture. In his childhood, Mr. X tortured animals "to see how they would respond" (Stern, 2014, p. 6). When we as clinicians hear this in a developmental history, we freeze for a moment; our attention sharpens and an inner alarm sounds. This is not a good sign. This behavior may not only be about emergent sadism, however, though it certainly is that too. It can also be about morbid curiosity. The animals represent a split-off part of the disturbed child. As all parents know, children identify with animals from a very early age. So, Mr. X's action suggests childhood questions *about himself*: Do I still feel pain? What's going on inside me? Ironically—given his playing this out with animals—am I still human? And, of course, the child both hopes that he is and hopes that he isn't, so as to finally free himself from intense inner pain. This, like the Nazi fascination, is a form of acting-out, that is, it's a dramatization in action of what the child unconsciously hopes an important adult will see and thereby help the child bring into language.

Years later, at one of those crucial late adolescent moments, Mr. X joined the Swedish Rangers, but he was soon discharged because there was no war. Speaking of his intense frustration at that time, he comments to Dr. Stern that his education was wasted: "It was like training to be a doctor and never getting to operate" (p. 6). From a psychoanalytic point of view, what an interesting association between a military impulse and a healing profession! And, of course, it may also be an association to those earlier "operations" on animals. Like so many troubled young men of his age, Mr. X longs for a workable identity pathway as a *healing solution*—in this case, one that provides a licensed outlet for rage, but also one that orders, contains, and redirects his chaotic aggressive impulses under the leadership of a father figure.

With this pathway closed off, ironically by Sweden's being in a phase of peace, Mr. X becomes a mercenary in the Bosnian war. "I wanted to participate in a real fight and kill the enemy" (p. 6)—perhaps the real Disneyland of playing out violent fantasies, no longer channeled and legitimized by authorized military leadership. He then describes the orgasmic, addictive, even binge aspects of his and others' violence—the process of giving oneself over to the momentum of it. "It was like a drug ... You always want more," says Mr. X (p. 6). Like most binges, continuing the violent eruption postpones the dimly perceived dread of encountering the wreckage. Mr. X accents in this part of the interview the pleasure he settles into, seemingly on the other side of civilization or of belonging to the human race. Now he tortures people.

At this point, Dr. Stern's interview takes us, for the first time, to a simple but powerful group dynamic. Why did Mr. X torture people? His initial response was a macho "Because I could!" But that quickly became: "If I didn't, they'd tease me for being a pussy" (p. 7). In this statement, Mr. X highlights the power of the group's shaming to enforce a grotesque of masculinity, defined as the killing of weakness, in oneself and the other. It's also the killing off of any empathic response to the other, which, in the perverse value system of the disturbed warrior, is felt as a hated feminization. As if to confirm the psychological equation between empathy and "being a pussy," Mr. X later says, "Now I feel such a distance from violence that I sometimes feel castrated" (p. 8).

Like Dr. Stern, Lydia Wilson, a research fellow at the Centre for the Resolution of Intractable Conflict at Oxford University, has also interviewed returning or captured militants in an effort to map the pathways in and out of jihadism and to explore points of decision-making (Wilson, 2017). Her data suggest that cold-blooded killing is used, for example by ISIS, as an initiation rite for new members. The recruit is forced or cajoled into setting his horror aside and venting his righteous rage, thereby finding himself feeling free but no longer human. In the either/or world of jihad, the actions taken to join one group cut the young person off from their other groups, indeed from the human world itself, and leave him no one to return to. By design, bonding becomes bondage.

The first bite

Killing empathy—like continuing the binge—closes off the possibility of what the psychoanalyst Melanie Klein calls the depressive position (1946), that phase of development in which love and hate coexist and mature into feelings of concern and guilt. Killing empathy keeps the person on the other side of that maturational divide, in a place Klein calls the paranoid–schizoid position, a place of primitive anxieties and all good versus all bad. In clinical work, one sometimes encounters a patient who experiences a violent impulse at the moment when he sees vulnerability in the other's eyes, that is, when he sees that she has already been wounded by him. Paradoxically, it's the threat of unbearable guilt that must be eliminated. In Mr. X's story, he searches for a real war, but eventually comes to another reality; he *realizes* with horror what he has done when he faces his victims' families. Horror for him seems to be the beginning of near unbearable empathy.

It's at this moment in Dr. Stern's report—the moment when Mr. X speaks of a group-enforced murder of empathy—that she herself speaks of empathy, and that something fascinating is enacted between these two people. This man and woman, alone in what turns out to be the conjugal visiting room of the prison where this long interview was taking place, have lunch! Hesitating for an instant to accept his offer of food, Dr. Stern tells us that: "It was essential to remain utterly present … I had to try to imagine myself … in his shoes. This kind of empathy takes energy, and I found myself wanting to partake of the food and drink" (p. 7).

Then she notices that one of the two sandwiches on the plate between them—the one nearest her—already has had a bite taken out of it. She hesitates again. Was he trying to invade her, to contaminate her, she wonders? Whatever he might consciously have been doing—if anything—it's worth realizing that empathy *is* a kind of invasion, a mutual invasion in some ways. One person feels her way into another person, who may be very anxious about that and whose protective defenses may lead to his own version of empathy: "What is she up to? What do I know about her? How can I use that to protect myself?" And to empathize with someone on that violent other side of civilized norms *does* mean—probably to both parties—the willingness to risk contamination.

Dr. Stern generally does not use her middle name on her publications. But she did on the one containing this interview. Her middle name is Eve, and how striking it is that, at this moment in the story, Eve is asked to take the second bite! As if this lone-wolf Adam is unconsciously saying (and she is unconsciously registering): "Will you really join me in eating from the tree of such forbidden and horrific knowledge?" Dr. Stern's work suggests that no one can come back from the other side without someone's being willing to take that bite. The former Neo-Nazi who runs a rehabilitation program called Exit Sweden agrees; these men must be met by someone who *knows* deep down, or is willing to come to know, what they did and who they are, if they are ever to make it back.

Erikson reminds us that, in *Genesis*, paradise was lost via a bite (1950, p. 79)! But this child analyst, of course, hears that story of our origins developmentally; when the infant acquires teeth—and the ability to bite the breast—the loss of paradise we call weaning may be set in motion. This too echoes in Mr. X's early history. His biological mother "couldn't take care of him" (Stern, 2014, p. 8), and gave him up for adoption sometime in his infancy. As a baby, he experienced a very early loss, though we don't know when in the attachment process this occurred and what its consequences were at that time. But might Mr. X, in this dramatic moment of sharing a meal with a woman, be putting before her, from the depths of his unconscious, a crime he feels he committed against his mother: the bite that lost her? The psychoanalyst Harry Guntrip (1968) described schizoid anxiety, the kind that leads people to seal themselves off from relationships, as "*love made hungry*" (p. 24), a phrase meant to describe a child's terror that his hunger for the other leads him to behave in ways that destroy her. About Exit Sweden, Mr. X says: "My greatest fear was that [they] would not want … me. I hesitated for almost a year before I dared to make contact. It was better not to do it than to be rejected" (p. 10). Wanting people was dangerous for Mr. X, and he worried that others would feel it was dangerous for them as well. Better to withdraw and to violently seal himself off from others.

Doing unto others

We learn about Mr. X's adoption relatively far along in the interview. The early childhood information is rather sparse, but what does come through is quite striking. This man who kills immigrants to Sweden was of mixed race! We learn that Mr. X was conceived while his biological father, a British citizen, was on government assignment in Sweden. He returned to England after completing his work, but promised to return for his wife and son. He never did. Mr. X's mother could not raise her son alone, so she gave him up for adoption. A Swedish farming couple, who were unable to conceive, took him in when he was two years old.

This information raises many questions, the answers to which might help develop a deeper psychological understanding of Mr. X. What races were his biological mother and father? How did they meet? Who were these people? What are their stories, including the story of the father's assignment and failure to return? Was the child two years old when he was given up by his mother, or was he in care? What happened to his biological parents? Who told Mr. X about all of this? And about his adoptive parents, we learn that they beat him. Why? Who did it? For what behavior? And what about the brother who comes into the story? Was he too adopted, or, as sometimes happens after an adoption, was he their biological son? If so, how did this complicated sibling relationship play out? All of these questions and many others would help construct the full story of this family and of their developing, but troubled child, which in turn would generate more powerful hypotheses about his later behavior. Dr. Stern's method of in-depth interviews, leading to in-depth formulation of a person's life-in-context, is immensely promising for our understanding of society's troubled individuals, whether or not they ever declare themselves to be "patients."

We do learn that Mr. X grew up in a community where there were no other mixed-race children, and that, not only was he beaten by his parents, but, from ages five to eleven (interestingly, eleven being the age he developed his fascination with Nazis) he was tortured—constantly and cruelly teased—by the local kids. So, later on, beginning around that pre-adolescent moment, he identifies with the aggressor. He does unto others—and unto his weakened victimized self—as has been done unto him, finally feeling, one imagines, a sense of mastery. In this process, the process of learning to become violent, he transfers his split-off experience of weakness and pain into the other person; they feel, through his doing, what he is trying desperately not to feel. This is not only a psychological defense; it is a form of communication, one that Dr. Stern is trying to hear. This crucial turn in Mr. X's development leads to the triumph and the tragedy of "I don't feel connected to anyone. I don't belong anywhere" (p. 8).

Revering the irreversible

Dr. Stern then takes us into the fascinating world of de-radicalization programs and the enormous, very real difficulties of leaving radical groups. Five hundred people work for Exit Sweden's parent organization, known as "*Fryhuset*," named for the cold storage building where the organization was first housed. How amazingly appropriate a name! These men certainly need a cooling off period, but the psychoanalyst Donald Winnicott also contributes a temperature-related concept from his understanding of child development. He refers to "the freezing of the failure situation" (1954, p. 281). This has to do with a child's capacity to shut down in the face of trauma, and to carry on with part of the self dissociated until the child's human circumstances are such that re-integration as a full human being becomes possible.

What are those circumstances? Dr. Stern's empathy project, and the empathy project—along with massive practical help, to be sure—of the former Neo-Nazi who started the Exit Sweden program. "I know what they've been through [and] they know that I know," he says. "They join because they're searching for a father-figure, or an identity, or a way to give their lives purpose and meaning" (Stern, 2014, pp. 9–10). The outlines of this man's own story may oversimplify things but they are compelling; throughout his childhood, "I felt like a failure. I needed glasses, and nobody noticed that … I was bullied and I thought that being part of the movement would protect me" (p. 9). The plight of a child who can't see in a context of adults who can't see either. Ostracized by one group, he finds another. Erikson (1959) writes that: "Group identity harnesses a young person's aggressive energies in the service of its ideology. [It] encompasses the individual's identity as it also completes it. Thus identity and ideology are two aspects of the same process" (p. 157).

Dr. Wilson's observations are fully consistent with this (2017). She tried to determine how "fused" militants were with the ISIS ideology: that is, how fully self-identity had become large-group identity, such that an insult to one was an insult to the other. She heard from these young men about their deep anxiety and isolation before joining ISIS. Their sense of lost adolescence and lost opportunities had led them to ask their families and community, "What is there to hope for?" Receiving no answer, they found themselves drawn to an ideology that promised to "take complete care" of their lives. Essentially, group ideology replaced failed leadership in the young person's life. It promised to restore something precious that had been lost—a paradise of some sort—and it rationalized vengeance as justice. One of Dr. Wilson's conclusions was that jihad had "hijacked the dreams of troubled young people."

The comment by Exit Sweden's founder about "giving their lives purpose" also brings to mind another comment by Erikson: that it is the family's job to help the child "make the distinction between play and irreversible purpose" (1961, p. 156). From this angle, de-radicalization programs, like Exit Sweden, could be seen as taking up the task of reversing the irreversible. From Erikson's point of view, a child's acting out is not only in the service of discharging inner tensions; it is also in the hope that someone will see the trouble and help make sense of it. For example, the boy failing in school hopes that someone will see that he actually needs glasses, or the boy torturing animals hopes someone will see that he is being tortured by his classmates. In these circumstances, it's critical that the consequences of the action in the real world, both to others and to oneself, be more or less reversible; one might say more or less survivable by everyone. But when a Disneyland of violent fantasies becomes a *real* Disneyland, the person has taken himself to some psychologically and existentially different place, from which it is much harder to return.

Passage into action

One of Dr. Stern's research questions about radicalization is whether it is a step-by-step process or a discontinuous one. Certainly there are individual variations, all worth studying. Dr. Stern uses the word "edge" to describe a moment in the trajectory of a person's radicalization. That, along with the language of being on one side or the other, and of burning bridges, also suggests a discontinuity in the process. The psychoanalyst Jacques Lacan (1962–63) may have contributed an evocative concept to this conversation. Acting out, because it is the dramatization of a message, exists in what he calls the Symbolic Order. In contrast is the "passage to the act." This is an idea from early French psychiatry, which described those impulsive, often violent acts that marked the beginning of an acute psychotic episode.

Understood in this latter way, radicalization into a group may sometimes be a person's defense against individual psychotic breakdown. That first reference to the cure for depression links the societal action of joining jihad with psychopathology, and the life phase in which these young people are vulnerable to radicalization is also the one in which they are most vulnerable to psychotic or profoundly depressive breakdowns. Erikson's idea of identity diffusion (1959) gives this danger a rather benign name, but his case studies make the seriousness of the crisis clear, even if there is hope in how transitory and responsive to human contact it is.

For Lacan, however, the passage to the act has a different significance. It is not acting out in the usual sense. The person as a subject, holding on to an unconscious hope that the message-in-action will be seen by the other, no longer exists. Instead, in the act—perhaps in the instant of despair preceding the act—the person exits the social and symbolic world altogether. Life is lived now as if as an object in what Lacan calls the Real, as other and alien to oneself. From this perspective, how did Mr. X make the fateful decision to become a mercenary and leave for Bosnia? What happened, when, where, with whom? In the study of these discontinuous moments in the arc of a person's radicalization, it is crucial to understand the precipitating context, or, better, the context of the precipice.

Clinical vignettes about the passage to the act almost always depict an impulsive throwing oneself away: not just burning a bridge but jumping from it. For example, a patient who had been sexually abused in her family was doing well in her treatment. After considerable hesitation and reflection, and after years of no contact, she opened a line of communication with the person who abused her. Then one day, on her way to an appointment, she walked through the reception area of the clinic. To her shock, he was sitting there. Their eyes met, and he winked at her. She immediately left the building and attempted suicide. No thought. No pause. No cry for help. Simply horror, hatred, and self-hatred becoming action. Fortunately the patient survived, but the disaster of that moment had hugely damaging consequences, which she and the clinic staff attempted to work through as best they could.

In his effort to come back from the other side, Mr. X says: "I needed people willing to meet me; they [Exit Sweden] regard me as a human being" (Stern, 2014, p. 10). Once they did, perhaps he could as well. That is, he could begin his own crossing back over to personhood—from killing object to feeling subject—by way of the other's seeing him as a person. Importantly, from Mr. X's point of view, this also included their willingness to fight with him, to meet a former killer's larger-than-life aggression without fear. This is part of what the psychiatrist Harry Stack Sullivan called the process of a person's "shrinking to life size" (1940, p. 33). As Dr. Wilson (2017) notes, the narratives offered to these young people, for ill or for good, may be considerably less important than the quality of the relationships through which they are offered. Her stories indicate that restorative relationships do not view the recruit as a victim, but rather as determined to be "faithful" to something. Whatever that something is needs to be understood on a deeper and very personal level, often related to great pain within the recruit's family of origin.

Societal dynamics

Mr. X, like many other terrorists, whether from the nationalist or fundamentalist side, is sometimes regarded as a "lone wolf." But, while his personal and family dynamics may have led to what the psychoanalyst Wilfred Bion (1961) called a *valency* for such action, we have also learned in recent years that these men are representing something. There's a politics in this, which raises questions about how to understand Mr. X in societal terms. After all, the goal of Mr. X's group was to bring down the Swedish government; the attacks were not only on immigrants but on the government's immigration policy. A government spokesperson dismisses these groups as "not a threat to the democracy" (Stern, 2014, p. 1), but we are told that they have "thousands of adherents." They are therefore a force *in* the democracy, but using actions instead of words or votes. Why? What are they saying? Can it be heard? How might we understand this in psycho-political terms?

Something a bit bizarre and potentially maddening is reported at the end of Dr. Stern's paper: Swedish law prohibits Exit Sweden, presumably for privacy reasons, from keeping a data base of former clients. So, no follow-up outcome research is possible—despite the fact that other societies manage this, despite the fact that funding for these programs might depend on this research, and despite the common good that might come to similarly troubled men. This policy may well make sense somehow, and, whether it does or not, presumably it has been arrived at via due process. But for some people, this kind of policy could be felt as an over-the-top political correctness and be reacted to with feelings stemming from personal trauma.

What might this governmental policy have triggered in Mr. X? We know that Mr. X's father was part of a government. Did Mr. X come to feel that this governmental representative had victimized his mother? Or did he feel that government had taken his father away from his son? Wouldn't such confused feelings be a potential source of rage at government? On the other hand, the policy described above could also feel to Mr. X like the action of a rigid Mommy State, one that feels she must adopt every child that comes along, but *won't take care of me!* Both of these speculations relate to the phenomenon of transference: the deep relational patterns we carry around from early life and react to powerfully but unconsciously. In a societal context, transference is not only one person's idiosyncratic distortion; it may also reflect an acute sensitivity to deep emotion—to deep hurt, humiliation, and loss—potentially shared by others.

In 2004, at a Group Relations Conference in the Netherlands—in which Dutch and English were "official" conference languages—Dutch members spoke perfect English throughout, seemingly an effort to be gracious and inclusive to international members. At the same conference in 2006, Dutch was spoken with a vengeance. What happened? In retrospect, that seemed clear: the murder of Theo Van Gogh in late 2004 by militant Islamists shockingly dramatized the rage and alienation within this determinedly tolerant but now increasingly conflicted country. Resurgent nationalism had found its way naturally but unconsciously into the conference.

GRCs, as we have seen, are intensive here-and-now experiences of learning about authority, groups, and organizations. In my experience, they also function as societal MRIs. They are one source of learning about the radicalizing or integrative group dynamics that mediate between a society and its members, some of whom, like Mr. X, carry from their histories serious vulnerabilities. These vulnerabilities may well be triggered by societal dynamics, and then ignite their own societal dynamic. Terrible as these reactions are—and of course they need to be managed by society in the service of protecting its members—they can and should also be viewed through an interpretive lens.

Dr. Stern's in-depth interviews and Dr. Wilson's "appreciative inquiry" method lead to similar conclusions. These men think they know their own stories, but, over time, a deeper, remarkably consistent story emerges. Betrayal by someone in authority in the young person's life creates a vulnerability to, and leads to exploitation by, terrorist narratives that promise to set the world right. Often, the young person seems to be enacting a transgenerational transmission of trauma, specifically the trauma of displacement and humiliation that happened to his parents. Jihadis in Europe, who tend to be second generation immigrants, are reacting against the difficulties their parents faced in integrating into European societies; jihadis from the Middle East feel the trauma of colonialism, despite never having experienced it themselves. For both, the humiliation of their parents, leading to feelings of anger and betrayal at both the societal oppressor and at their parents, is a major factor in their radicalization. The previous generation's narratives, therefore, are extremely important to understanding the younger generation's actions. We will see in Chapter 10 that betrayal, and sometimes catastrophic disillusionment, by someone in authority is the critical factor in "moral injury" (Shay, 2014), now considered to be central to war-related trauma. As we learn from Dr. Stern and Dr. Wilson, it is also a major part of the trajectory from trauma to terrorism.

CHAPTER 9

Sky of tears: clinical work after 9/11

On the ninth day of the eleventh month of 2002, a few hundred people, mostly mental health clinicians, gathered at the New York University Medical Center for a conference on the theme, *September 11th: Psychoanalytic Reflections in the Second Year*. A mile from Ground Zero, various presentations took up the learning emerging from clinical work with so many traumatized patients one year after the attack on the World Trade Center. At the invitation of two psychoanalytic colleagues from New York, I took up the role of discussant for a panel of three presentations reflecting on this work. I felt both honored and surprised by this request, since, at that time, I worked in a small psychiatric hospital (the Austen Riggs Center) three hours by car north of the city. After I read the presentations, I felt admiring, even in awe, of the presenters' work, but I also felt like one of those people, mentioned in the presentations, who had not come to work that day, that is, who had accidentally escaped the disaster. I began my assignment feeling the shame and guilt of the survivor. From my insulated spot in the Berkshire Hills of Western Massachusetts, I hesitated to discuss this work. Not having been there, I felt inclined to de-authorize myself from speaking.

But then again, I was invited, and this must have meant something, perhaps relating directly to where I was coming from: a small hospital-based psychotherapy practice with severely troubled psychiatric patients, a long experience of directing the hospital's open therapeutic community program on Norman Rockwell's Main Street, and at that time a role directing its Erikson Institute for Education and Research. The task of the Institute is discovering and learning about the connections between the intensive psychological treatment done at the hospital and the larger social context of our patients' and our own lives. Perhaps my place of work—a hospital treating many traumatized people, its functioning as a community, my having been that community's doctor for many years, its location in the rural environment in which many New Yorker's vacation or have second homes—was seen by those in New York as a place of refuge. And perhaps my invitation was also addressed to that wandering, benevolent, cross-cultural sense-maker for whom my Institute was named.

"I didn't think the glass would break"

On September 11, 2001, at one in the afternoon, we at Riggs held a special All-Center Meeting to which all patients, clinical staff, and support staff were invited. The hospital is a completely open psychiatric facility for patients—most of them with trauma in their backgrounds—who have not benefited from other forms of treatment. By open, I mean that there are no locked doors, restraints, or privileging systems in the treatment program. Patients take up their own authority to join the treatment enterprise. They accept the responsibility for keeping themselves safe with our support and for helping us manage the hospital. In the process, they examine the ways in which they engage with these tasks in the service of understanding the problems that brought them to the hospital.

All-Center Meetings are held monthly, co-chaired by the medical director and a patient elected to lead the community for a period of time. This particular emergency meeting was called by the medical director to inform the total community of whatever was known so far about the external crisis—it literally began with his giving a news summary of the attacks and their aftermath—and to be with each other as we tried to take that information in. I remember the hastily written, but beautiful and moving prayer offered to the group by a newer male patient who, up to that time, had been regarded warily as potentially explosive himself. Whatever anxiety about aggression might have been projected into him by others was quietly re-owned as ours, or perhaps was displaced further onto the attackers. This man was suddenly a known and valued member of the community.

I also remember the actual explosion of glass three days later, when an angry young woman struck the large plate glass window in the stairwell outside her preoccupied and impatient therapist's office, creating a hole in the building and potentially endangering anyone who might have been walking below. It was as though her behavior was saying unconsciously, "Terrorism is here: face it, deal with it." We did deal with it by seeing her action in the interpretive context of that particular week and raising the question as to what it meant that one of our patients, on a microcosmic scale, had mirrored the New York attack on a building. But, in taking up the primary task of making sense of our patient's behavior, we had to simultaneously attend to this patient's citizenship in our community as well. So we also insisted that she address the community about her action. One of the things she said to the community was: "I didn't think the glass would break." It struck me again that the "borderline" patient (Fromm, 2012b3)—like all of us to some degree—lives in what Lacan (1977) calls the Imaginary Order: inside a bubble of wishfulness. She both takes for granted that the glass will not break and yet needs to know that it will—in fact needs, if she is going to live in the only world we have, to find the "borderline" between wishfulness and reality.

Two months later, after the broken glass of 9/11, we held an open meeting for people in the local community to talk with each other about the impact of terrorism on their daily lives. To our surprise, fifty-five people came on a bleak November evening and spoke without pause for two hours. It began with a young woman who had guiltily fled New York with her children and who sobbed about her fear and her sense of disloyalty. It continued with the World War II generation, despondent about the world they had hoped to make safe for their grandchildren. It included teachers who saw their young students' efforts to process the disaster but didn't feel authorized within the politicized climate of their school systems to facilitate or even observe that, thereby leaving the children alone with their anxiety.

And two months later, a patient of mine discharged himself from the hospital roughly according to plan. What had not been planned was the shift within his family. In the spring of 2001, this college student said "goodnight" to his roommate and jumped from his seventh floor apartment. Amazingly, because of a recent snowfall, he lived, and was taken by ambulance to the hospital of which his father was CEO. His father reacted to this horror with a stiffening of his defensive remoteness and rigidity—until 9/11, until the unforgettable images of people leaping from those towers, at which point this powerful man broke down into a life-changing depression and asked for his son's help. My patient discharged himself for the purpose of giving it—to his long-term gain or cost, I don't know.

Even in the Berkshires, 9/11 reverberated. Two long-time friends of the hospital, the psychoanalysts, Françoise Davoine and Jean-Max Gaudilliere, are convinced that psychosis and trauma go hand-in-hand, and that the psychotic patient is madly conducting a research into the rupture between his family and the social fabric, a rupture brought about through trauma and betrayal. As we have seen in earlier chapters, this work, published in *History beyond Trauma* (2004), powerfully links the clinical arena with the historical and the political. After 9/11, one of their patients said, referring to her actual traumatic experience with the Middle Eastern Mafia and her psychotic experience as a Middle Eastern goddess: "I was in hell; now the United States is."

The inner and outer worlds

One theme in the conference, presented by Dr. Martha Bragin (2002), was the dangerous resonance between the inner world and the outer world in the face of trauma. To oversimplify, a frustrated toddler sometimes wants to topple those towering figures who seem to rule his life; how many times have parents heard the angry retort "You're not the boss of me!" So, what happens for this child when real towers topple, and topple as the result of rage? Is there a symbolic resonance that adds to the upset child's reaction? Therapists were reminded that people often come to treatment for problems that begin early in life and that we do well to hear the ways in which actual traumatic events touch upon developmental trauma and lead to complex reactions.

But, of course, actual trauma also has its effects independent of early life events. Freud's major theoretical shift in *Beyond the Pleasure Principle* (1920g) was to some degree in response to patients traumatized by World War I. To his credit, given his momentous discoveries in *The Interpretation of Dreams* (1900a), he recognized that not all dreams are exclusively about the inner world, indeed that there were genuinely distinctive trauma dreams, primarily related to terrible events in the outer world. This recognition opened a new path in Freud's theoretical development.

There is, of course, an interplay between the inner and outer worlds. In a paper called "The Trauma of Incest," Bollas hypothesizes about the horrifying situation of a girl's dreaming about the future man in her life and waking to find an abusive father in her bed. He imagined that a "topographic reversal" must occur, meaning that the child's mind would be shocked into undoing its ordinary ways of processing feelings and fantasies—which is what we do while dreaming—in the face of something having become real in this concrete way. Trauma "electrifies the dream process" (1989, p. 175), says Bollas, and therefore terrifies the person about sleep, about letting one's mind go, and about playing out scenarios in fantasy. Volkan (2004a) adds that the actualization of an unconscious fantasy—for example, the actual loss of a parent the child was seriously in conflict with—creates, among other things, the challenge of sorting out the terrible question: Did I cause this or not? That last question speaks to the fragile boundary that sometimes exists between the inner and outer worlds, and one thing that makes trauma traumatic is that it assaults this boundary. What actually happened is one thing; how it meets individual psychology is another, and sometimes that is very hard to sort out.

The 9/11 attacks violated boundaries on many levels, including the sociocultural one. For example, it assaulted the sense of invulnerability—part of American exceptionalism—we in the U.S. have felt for so long, given the oceans that separate us from foreign threats. We might also wonder about boundary strains prior to the attacks, including the strain on people's ordinary need for repression to get on with daily life. For example, how much of the Catholic Church's problems with sexual abuse by priests has to do with strain on sexual repression in today's Western culture? In the same way that a culture of violence can assault our defenses against safely repressed aggressive impulses, a sexualized culture may well act traumatically upon the sexual repression necessary for a priest's celibacy. Indeed the attacks themselves reflected, among other things, Middle Eastern rage at what they perceived to be an assault by American culture on their religious and sexual boundaries.

One story in this conference presentation clearly illustrated the loss of boundaries of a traumatized person. A young man felt he was "breathing in the bodies" in the post-9/11 New York air, literally taking the remains of others into himself. An angry African American teenager before 9/11, he broke down emotionally after the attacks; he could neither eat nor sleep, became obsessed with the "evil" of the attackers and repeatedly declared that these terrorist-avengers were "not me." As it turned out, this feverish disavowing of vengeful rage—clearly an effort at a boundary—had links to historical trauma within his family, and to a role he had unconsciously taken up, or perhaps been unconsciously assigned, in response. Decades before, a beloved grandfather had been the victim of a racist mob who nearly lynched him. His children watched in horror, and over time, this young man indeed "breathed in" their furious longing for justice. One loss of boundaries was between the part of him who wanted to take up that unconscious task and the foreign avengers in those planes who actually had. Hence, his frantic need to declare that they were "not me."

The psychologically adaptive effort in this young man's obsession with the terrorists—mirroring emotional work the nation itself had to do—was how to turn rage into outrage and vengeful impulses into justice-seeking actions. From a societal angle, this was the quest of the civil rights movement. This young man's trouble, should he become able to see the history and relational meaning behind it, made him, in effect, a member of that movement. But to the extent that he had not come to understand this intertwining of two traumas, to the extent that his family history was simply being enacted, he was vulnerable to the unconscious resonance between the trauma of 9/11 and that earlier tragedy. This story is an example of the inter-generational transmission of trauma, coming to the fore in a young man's 9/11 breakdown and in the context of a new national trauma.

Help

Another theme in the conference, presented by Dr. Laura Silverman (Silverman & Hirky, 2002), focused on what holds a person's sense of internal cohesion and stability after trauma. Psychotherapy work across cultures highlights the challenge of providing structures and processes that are responsive and containing in different crisis situations. The idea of differential "tiers" of victimization, based on something like geography (how close or distant one is from the "center" of the trauma) rather than on more individualized subjective variables (like the meaning of the traumatic experience within one's own life history) was thought to be illusory. More important is developing the capacity for narrative coherence, the ability of the survivor to tell his or her story clearly and with feeling. This turns out to be a marker of the traumatized person's psychological recovery.

But this ideal of recovery—a survivor's coming to a place of integration and mastery over the traumatic experience—can also be a bit illusory. Recovery is an individualized process. After his mother's death, Roland Barthes (1981) wrote:

> It is said that mourning, by its gradual labor, slowly erases pain; I could not, I cannot believe this; because for me, Time eliminates the emotion of loss … that is all. For the rest, everything has remained motionless. For what I have lost is not a Figure (the Mother), but a being, and not a being, but a quality (a soul): not the indispensable but the irreplaceable. (p. 75)

Barthes could seem like one of those traumatized people who, on the surface, look like they need help and yet resist it fiercely. But people not only make ego-preservative efforts in the face of trauma, some of which may look like resistance—for example, a person's effort to maintain some basic psychological equilibrium by refusing to talk about trauma—they also make other-preservative efforts. With Barthes, we see a person's effort to hold onto the person he has lost, and to do so fully, with as much individualized meaning as possible.

Some traumatized people were described in this conference presentation as in a trance-like state, as though they were channeling something from their histories. To be sure, this may well represent massive dissociation as a psychological defense against unbearable emotional pain, especially the pain of irretrievable loss. But channeling implies being in contact with the dead, and, as Barthes' story illustrates, that is often more important than getting on with the living. This perhaps transitory fact raises the profound question of what help means to a traumatized person. If it means enforced separation in the name of recovery, it won't work. In a Group Relations Conference, about which we have heard a lot in this volume, a consultant once said to the Large Study Group, "I don't know why you're angry with me. I'm not trying to help you." In my experience, people know intuitively what that means.

Consider another Group Relations Conference, four months after 9/11, in which a group formed to study how that disaster was affecting the conference. One of its members was of Middle Eastern origin. In the course of this study, he allowed himself to be "profiled" by other members—that is, to be imagined, projected into, and related to as containing dangerous and alien characteristics. Later, in a Review Group, other members were shocked that he had permitted this with such equanimity. Someone asked him what his name meant. With a shy smile, he said it meant "Resurrection." He realized that he could allow himself to be buried by the projective fantasies of others because his lineage would save him. He was securely in touch with his deep emotional connection to those "others" from preceding generations, and that in-touch-ness helped him withstand what others were doing to him now.

Respecting both the life-saving ego-preservative and other-preservative efforts of the traumatized person means that therapists need some kind of a "Yes" from those they want to help. This is, in fact, always true. Otherwise, without negotiating the task and getting to that Yes, we risk "doing to" rather than "doing or being with." Having been "done to"—and being helpless in the face of action from outside—is one of the things that makes trauma traumatic. Getting to "Yes" involves, to use another set of Winnicottian ideas, a "period of hesitation" in a context of proximity (1941, p. 53). This is a time dimension in which an available but not intrusive therapist makes an offering, and the other person, no matter how much he or she may be in objective need, authorizes the contact, or at least recognizes the possibility of future help, and thereby the possibility of the future. To paraphrase Winnicott (1974), a person can't be helped before being there to be helped.

Clinicians may well face a disappointing amount of rejection from the traumatized people they hope to help, but it's worth their noticing forms of help that people actually do use. For example, we heard about a program for East African trauma survivors, which took place in New York and included a psychotherapy service, but also provided ordinary communal activities (eating meals together) and time for experiencing oneself as a tourist rather than only as a victim. A sense of community and of being able to take up roles other than that of patient actually helped, even when the psychotherapy service was not used. Clinicians too need something like a therapeutic community because they too are exposed to the trauma of their clients. With regard to 9/11, clients in New York expose their therapists to trauma in their home city and potentially to trauma they themselves have suffered. This intermixing of experiences and potential identification between client and clinician can compromise the latter's capacity to contain strong emotions. Self-awareness is extremely important and must be sustained by one's own professional community. Otherwise, we risk losing our boundaries, losing our ability to manage our own feelings, and potentially pushing our own needs for cure into our patients.

"Your daughter is drawing your dreams"

Another theme in the conference presentations comes from the title of a book by Dr. Susan Coates and her colleagues called *Trauma and Human Bonds* (Coates et al., 2003). From their work with children and families in temporary clinics organized after the attacks, they argue that what makes trauma traumatic is that it is suffered alone. A 1943 study by Anna Freud and Dorothy Burlingham called *War and Children* came to the same conclusion. Children sent to the countryside to escape the Blitz were more traumatized than those who stayed in London with their mothers. And in the bomb shelters, children whose mothers said "Don't worry; we'll be alright" survived the experience with far less trauma than those children whose mothers could not contain anxiety enough to be convincingly reassuring. From one angle, that reassurance sounds delusional. From another, it makes perfect Winnicottian sense;

what Sigmund Freud called the "protective shield" (1920g) became for Winnicott the child's necessary illusion of safety and power within a responsive maternal environment, a creative experience essential to the developmental challenge of bearing the strain between the inner and outer worlds (1951).

Dr. Coates reported a heart-wrenching story of a little girl whose father had died on the 104th floor of the World Trade Center and who said that her grandmother "saw something in her room. She saw an angel. It looked like a butterfly. So that's what made me want to draw a butterfly. I think I will call it a butterfly angel. I think the butterfly was Dad" (2003, p. 35). A Daddy-butterfly-angel—alive, innocent, and able to fly: the creativity of a child keeping her father alive and with her, in the context of a loving grandmother. It reminded me of an image that sustained me after 9/11. Another little girl, whose across-the-river kindergarten class was doing a Statue of Liberty project, made a drawing two days after 9/11: Liberty holding two baby twin towers in her arms—a Winnicottian Madonna whom I will never forget. It is this sense of restored union that protects and cures.

In their work with children, Dr. Coates and her colleagues emphasize normalizing the child's reactions, containment of the child's feelings rather than exploring them, and, at the right time, promoting identification with the lost loved one. She and her colleagues saw frequently how a child knows about the reality of a lost parent and doesn't know at the same time. This seemed like the child's natural creation of an intermediate area between the objective fact of loss and her subjective experience of possible presence. This is what Winnicott called a transitional space (1951) for a child—and sometimes for an adult too—who cannot yet bear the pain of what has happened. In Chapter 1, we noted Winnicott's paradoxical comment: "This thing of the past has not happened yet because the patient was not there for it to happen to" (1974, p. 105). Can we modify this to suggest that the child's actually experiencing what she, at a different psychic level, knows to be true and to already have happened depends on the emotional presence of the other person, and, until that time, the potential experience is held by the child in trust, as it were—not only the trust that a parental figure will arrive as a facilitating developmental presence for the child, but also that, if that person has not arrived yet, then he or she too must need a person with whom to experience what the child is holding.

As noted earlier, the story of Maria illustrates so clearly the way a child holds for her parents, not only her own terrifying experience, but theirs too. This three-year-old, suffering through nightly nightmares, scrawled bright reds, yellows, and blacks on the drawing pad, as she described the buildings that had burned and fallen. The family had seen the destruction on TV and initially were horrified to think that they were watching Maria's father's death. But her father turned out to be alive, and Maria emphasized how he had escaped the disaster, inhaling smoke and having pieces of the fiery building fall on him. "He has marks from the fire on his arms," she said. In fact, Maria's father had not been at the World Trade Center that day. He indeed was employed as a cook in its top floor restaurant, but he had exchanged shifts with a colleague so that he could run errands. The burn marks on his arm were old ones from splattered grease. His agonizing survivor guilt had led him to withdraw from his family and ruminate about how his friend had died, images that found their way into his own nightmares. On seeing Maria's drawings, he was shocked by her belief that he had nearly died in the disaster, and he realized how much he had lost touch with his daughter.

"So your daughter is drawing your dreams," his therapist said to him (2003, p. 42), thereby putting father and daughter back into emotional contact with each other. At a simple but profound level, the therapist functioned as a "Third" to a parent–child couple in unconscious resonance with, but dangerous isolation from, each other. In Chapter 3, we discussed the Fifth Avenue sidewalk Santa and the change in attitude he noticed during the 2001 festive season: "The normality is not there. The parents will not let the hands of their children go. The kids sense that. It's like water seeping down, and the kids feel it. Their reactions to Santa are not natural. There is an anxiety, but the kids can't make the connections" (Leduff, 2001). This astute man was noticing a powerful double message in the parents' action. Consciously and verbally, the message was "Here's Santa; love him"; unconsciously and physically, it was "Here's Santa; fear him." The unnamed trauma of September 11th was communicated to the next generation by the squeeze of a hand, and it took someone in the position of the "Third," like this Santa, to see and name the trouble.

Unconscious attunement between child and parent is powerful. Children naturally and irresistibly synthesize the information that matters, as Maria did. Sometimes the aftermath of trauma is lived out by the child's identifying with what the distressed parent projects onto the child. For example, a parent may not be able to bear the feeling of having failed to protect his child, and so unconsciously insists that the child doesn't really know what happened, indeed that the child is still the embodiment of innocence. Or the parent who looks at her child, sees her dead husband's eyes and can't bear this reminder of loss, so reflexively looks away. These intimate exchanges show us how trauma is transmitted from one generation to the other, in both directions.

Coates and her colleagues report the results of a simple study conducted soon after 9/11. Parents were asked how their children were responding to the tragedy. Their answers were organized into two categories: those who said they did know and those who said they didn't. The scale of the finding was astonishing, even if its conclusion wasn't: Children whose parents said they didn't know how their child was responding after 9/11 were eleven times more likely to have behavior problems at ages 6–11 and four times more likely at ages 12–17. One way to understand this is that parents "mind" children. But when parents lose their minds under circumstances of extreme distress, children play out their uncontained distress. Sometimes, as Maria did, they find ways to mind their parents. That is, they bring to their parents in one way or another, something crucial that requires understanding, something related to the child's *and* the parents' traumatic context. The critical question is whether the parents can hear the child's effort at making sense of what is happening, even if that effort is communicated, as kids do, in a drawing, a nightmare, or disruptive behavior.

Fonagy and his colleagues at the Anna Freud Center (2002) have developed the concept of mentalization to describe this minding function. Their research shows the relationship between a parent's capacity to sense what is going on in the mind of the child and the child's proneness toward, or resilience in the face of, traumatization. Mentalization sometimes fails because of a parent's own unbearable traumatic experience. As with the sidewalk Santa, what we see instead is the parent's panic-driven, nonverbal gesture, registered and made sense of unconsciously by the child. The therapist's role, as a Third—perhaps replacing another

Third if the second parent has been lost—is to help the parent see what his child might be carrying on his behalf, however that is being imagined or even taken personally by the child. Speaking with a child about this, as Maria's father did, restores everyone and strengthens the family as a holding environment.

A dream of life

The word "therapist," as Davoine and Gaudilliere point out in *History Beyond Trauma*, comes from the Greek; it means "the second in combat" (2004, p. 153), the one not on the front line who takes care of the one who is. They note the work of a WWI military psychiatrist, Dr. Thomas Salmon (p. 114), who outlined four principles for the therapist's treatment of traumatized soldiers: simplicity (no jargon), proximity (being with the traumatized person's raw experience), immediacy (depending on intuition), and expectancy (the dimension of hope). As a soldier, you get better because those back at the front need you. Davoine's psychotic patient, at the close of her successful treatment, said to her: "What cured me was your ferocity." Trauma from intentional human actions differs in significant ways from trauma as the consequence of natural disasters, not the least of which is that it is the result of the other's driven ferocity. Along with the containing and nurturing capacities we bring as therapists, we also need our own ferocity to be in a working commonality with—to be the "second" for—traumatized people.

Psychological trauma assaults the organism, overwhelming the mind's capacity to process reality. Psychic numbing occurs immediately as a massive organismic defense against the experience of overwhelming pain. Societal trauma ruptures the "skin" around a culture and throws the collective into pain-driven mindlessness. If sudden helplessness is at the heart of the traumatic experience, the natural tendency of the mind is to turn this passive imprinting of the horrific into something active. Thus, trauma begets trauma as vengeance is sought as a form of recovery.

Recovery does indeed involve an active relation to the traumatic experience, though not necessarily a vengeful one. Trauma dreams return the person to the scene of the disaster as part of the mind's effort to face and master, bit by bit, what happened before, as Winnicott argued, the person could "be there for it to happen to" (1974, p. 105). Trauma needs to be re-experienced in manageable doses; otherwise, a part of the self is missing. The wisdom of those clinicians working in New York after 9/11 was to understand that such a return has the best chance of success if done in the company of another person. But a return to the front lines, to the scene of war, to the horror of a hole in the social fabric, requires the company of a warrior. Ferocity has to do with the courage and determination to go there fully, with all of one's capacity to witness (Laub, 2018), and yet to insist on the possibility of making it through as a whole person.

As we saw in Chapter 1, sometimes an artist can provide this kind of company for a society, through a work that "goes to the front" and finds the human experience of what it is like to be there. In doing so, the artist contains and makes bearable the painful experiences of so many people, providing a collective sense of togetherness and binding the rupture to the Symbolic Order (Lacan, 1977). To be sure, this requires the artist's sustained empathic imagination, but it also requires a ferocity, and an ability to work from it. A major example of an artist's ability to put traumatic emotion fully into both language and music—leading to a post-9/11 cultural phenomenon and illustrating how culture, even popular culture, can provide a structure that holds people through trauma—is Bruce Springsteen's 2002 CD, "The Rising."

The enormous success of "The Rising" speaks, I believe, to its being used on a massive scale to process the trauma. It is an astonishing set of stories—emotional narratives—of 9/11. Springsteen takes us into the feelings of an accidental hero who cannot bear that "everybody acts like nothing's changed; the sky's still the same unbelievable blue," and is going to kill himself. Into stark, intense, contradictory emotions: "I want a kiss from your lips, I want an eye for an eye, I woke up this morning to an empty sky." Into the quiet grief of a spouse: "The evening falls, I got too much room in my bed, too many phone calls. You're missing." Into an anguished plea that "My City of Ruins" will "rise up" again. Even into the mind of a confused child/suicide bomber exploited by visions of paradise.

And amazingly, the straightforward rock-and-roll songs metamorphose into litanies that build to emotional outpouring. The title song, "Come On Up for the Rising," refers to the duty of rescue and the adrenaline of going up the stairs of those towers together. Here is part of that song's prayerful call and response: "Sky of blackness and sorrow (a dream of life); sky of love, sky of tears (a dream of life); sky of glory and sadness (a dream of life); sky of mercy, sky of fear (a dream of life)." This song occurred to me in listening to the presenters at the "A Year Later" conference. In their passionate, thoughtful, grief-filled clinical work with their patients, they too had "come on up for the rising," and had held ferociously and lovingly for all of us "a dream of life."

CHAPTER 10

The day I died: combat trauma and moral injury

August 8, 1918, Wilfred Bion, twenty years old and already an experienced World War I tank commander, was forced to take cover in the midst of a raging battle. With him was one of his troops, a young runner named Corporal Sweeting, whose brother had just been killed. In the shell crater, Bion saw to his horror that Sweeting himself had been hit and his chest blown open. Sweeting was dying and, panicked, he pleaded incessantly to Bion: "Mother, mother, write to my mother, Sir, won't you? You'll remember her address, Sir, won't you?" Bion too was panicked as well as repulsed by the dying young man's gaping wound and abject dependency. "Oh, for Christ's sake, shut up," he shouted back. Sweeting, rejected in his desperation, turned to the inner mother, quietly calling to her as he died. Bion vomited uncontrollably (Bion, 1997, p. 255).

Wilfred Bion went on to become a creative and influential psychoanalyst, whose autobiographical writings repeatedly returned to this terrible incident. He recounted it three times: first in a letter to his own mother, second in an autobiography called *The Long Week-End*, and finally in the late-life piece, "Amiens," written almost exactly forty years later. As Souter (2009) notes: "[Bion] never seems to have overcome the feeling that his continued existence was a betrayal of his dead comrades, and the resulting self-loathing permeates much of his work. His autobiographies have the quality of survivor testimony, with the associated emotional numbing, low self-esteem, grief and guilt" (p. 797).

Bion's theoretical writings too, as Souter points out, can be read through the lens of his effort to rework this traumatic experience. His treatment of psychotic patients taught him the critical importance of the analyst's capacity to contain and metabolize, rather than vomit back, the patient's horrific experience. His masterpiece, *Experiences in Groups* (1961), illuminates the critical importance of truly examining what leadership is, where authority comes from, and how it can be so terribly misused. In this way, he was part of the sweeping societal post-war disillusionment with the monarchical authority that had sent so many young men off to a futile war and the institutional authority that had supported it. To take one example, in a time of immense grief, church attendance in England decreased markedly after the War, as though clerical authority had to be rejected along with political leadership (Newcombe & Lerner, 1982).

Wilfred Bion referred to the incident in the shell crater as the day he died (Souter, 2009; Gaudilliere, 2020). His final account in "Amiens" (1970) ends in mid-sentence. Both actions suggest something about trauma: the sudden cutting off of emotional life in the service of survival, a dissociation from horror and also from empathy, but then the death of oneself in identification with, and perhaps as reparation for, the death of another. Another feature of trauma—in fact one of the things that makes trauma traumatic—is the response of the other. When Bion, after Sweeting's death, begins to pour out his horror and rage, an older officer dismisses it as not "much to worry about … the kind of thing one would expect" (1997, p. 298). Just as Bion dismissed Sweeting's "I'm done for" with "It was nothing," even as "his eyes were already glazing over" (1997, p. 127). As the psychoanalyst Adam Phillips put it: "People are only ever as mad as other people are deaf" (1996, p. 34). In other words, madness is about leadership's and society's sustained denial of trauma.

Afterlife

Wilfred Bion lived another sixty-one years after the day he died in 1918. To some degree, his life from that day forward was what many returning soldiers feel—as we heard in the Erikson Institute Conference "Untold Stories, Hidden Wounds: War Trauma and its Treatment"—to be an afterlife (Sherman, 2010). As in the dream of the upside-down world, mentioned in the Introduction—in which the patient was a real-life military commander—war experiences turn the world upside-down, thereby revealing a truth about the "real" world and a falsity about the "normal" world, to which the discharged soldier is returning. Indeed, the problems of post-deployment re-entry can be enormous. Loved ones back home are eager for the returning soldier to leave the war behind and to embrace the joys of everyday life—as though nothing has changed.

But for the traumatized soldier, everything has changed in at least two ways, one at the level of ego functioning and one at the level of identity. As we saw with Bion, the organismic reaction to trauma is dissociation; one automatically cuts off horrific experience in order to survive. But the organismic tendency after trauma is to revisit it—that's what traumatic dreams do—in order to become a whole person again. We see this in ordinary life: How often after a near-miss car accident, in which the driver calmly manages a dire situation, does he go through a terrifying scene-by-scene replay in that night's dreams? As though to be able now to feel what he couldn't in the moment and learn from it as best he can. This is a natural effort of the ego to be there, to be present, and to be whole, to encompass emotionally and manage now what one could not feel or manage in the moment. The irony of traumatic dreams—and of flashbacks in general—is that they are in the service of healing, but the person experiencing them—and those around them—feel they are destructive to the return to "normal" life. A related irony is that "normal" life—like the older officer's response to Bion—functions as a denial of precisely the traumatic experiences the soldier is trying to recover from.

In the play, *Equus* (Shaffer, 1973), the psychiatrist-protagonist muses out loud about normality; "It is the Ordinary made beautiful … the Average made lethal," he says (p. 65). In their afterlife, returning soldiers long for, and their families plead for, their rejoining normal life as the "ordinary made beautiful." But what is often ignored, or effortfully set aside, is how normal life is also the "average made lethal," in terms of the soldier's profound loss of the sometimes addictive intensity of wartime experience, the loss of the forged-through-fire emotional bonds with buddies, and the loss of taken-for-granted beliefs about oneself. This latter disturbance to identity is the second way in which the returning soldier can feel that everything has changed.

In *Childhood and Society,* Erik Erikson reflects on a story of a young Marine medical officer whose platoon was pinned down by enemy fire on a Pacific beach. He was a mild-mannered man who saw himself as absolutely without hatred for anyone and who had actually joined the medical corps because he could not bring himself to carry a gun. But then, in the dark of a nighttime firefight, as well as in the platoon's growing panic that they were considered expendable by those above them, someone put a submachine gun in the Marine's hands, at which point he lost memory for what happened next and thereafter suffered psychosomatic symptoms. As it turned out, there was a family history to this young man's refusal of guns, such that when one was forced on him—in the context of collective anger and fear, not only at the enemy but also at perceived abandonment by those in authority—he broke down into dissociation and an acute identity crisis. Erikson notes that, for soldiers like this, "… it was as if, subjectively, their lives no longer hung together—and never would again." For this Marine, the gun was "a symbol of evil, which endangered the principles by which [he] had attempted to safeguard personal integrity and social status in his life at home" (1950, p. 42). Experiences in war so often force a soldier to face the question, "Who am I now?" which becomes another profound demand for psychic work in the "afterlife."

Moral injury

A few years ago, the University of Pennsylvania Law School's innovative Center for Ethics and the Rule of Law hosted a conference called "Preventing and Treating the Invisible Wounds of War: Combat Trauma and Psychological Injury." It was an unusual conference in at least two ways. First, it brought together people from the military, law, philosophy, psychology, and other fields; in that sense, it was a fully interdisciplinary conference, something that would have been dear to the heart of Erik Erikson. And it was a working conference. No papers were presented; only themes introduced briefly by moderators who then presided over very lively discussions. The fact that so many different professions were involved promoted genuine learning across disciplines, but it also required a sustained effort to grapple with different languages, basic assumptions, and perspectives. This is the kind of effort the complex problems of our time require; it reminded me of a remark by the theologian and friend of Erikson, Reinhold Niebuhr: "Nothing we do … can be accomplished alone. Therefore we are saved by love" (1952, p. 63). In this conference, love meant actively listening in order to help soldiers.

One theme stood out in the conference: its focus on "moral injury" as a powerful if less considered component of war trauma. Moral injury is a term coined by Jonathan Shay (2014) and expanded by Brett Litz (2014), both participants in the Erikson Institute Conference on war trauma. Moral injury refers to the kind of identity crisis discussed above, particularly to the way in which a person may experience a deep sense of having witnessed or participated in actions that profoundly violate his core sense of "what's right." This very personal experience may refer to one's own action or to that of someone in authority, in which case feelings of betrayal intermix with feelings of violation. Moral injury tends to occur in a high-stakes situation, when physical and psychic survival are on the line.

Current thinking about PTSD tends to emphasize three precipitants: sudden exposure to horror—like Wilfred Bion's seeing the hole in Sweeting's chest—sudden loss, and moral injury. Both of these latter components are also part of Bion's story—not so much distinct phenomena but highly interrelated. Bion's reflexive vomiting interweaves with a faraway mother's imminent loss, and with his, as he felt it, cruel rejection of Sweeting's pleas. The word, "injury," is important; there is a current debate about whether PTSD—post-traumatic stress disorder—is more properly PTSI (Ochberg, 2013). The word "disorder" suggests that something is wrong with the person, as though he is defective in some way. "Injury" suggests that something happened to that person; a story lay behind his symptoms. Moral injury and sudden loss are not as responsive to the "exposure therapies" that are somewhat effective with the symptom triad of flashbacks, dissociation, and hyperarousal associated with sudden horror. Instead, those who attempt to treat moral injury and sudden loss take up the disturbing but also healing and humanizing power of stories.

My dad

One thing missing from CERL's "Wounds of War" conference was discussion of the relational underpinning implicit in some combat trauma stories. Fathers and mothers, buddies and girlfriends were central to these stories, including to the context for some suicides, but how those relationships figured in the soldiers' psychology and in their self-destructive actions was left to be spelled out. Trauma always has a background because we all carry around a psychology: an internalized pattern of relationships from our growing up, narratives about what happened and why, and a pattern of feelings, motivations, and defenses shaped over time. Erikson's Marine, for very good reasons from childhood, grew up to be a man who could not stand to feel angry, and then, in war, found himself with a gun in his hand.

In the stories veterans tell, fathers and father figures emerge as crucial to understanding the impact and background of war trauma. Particularly in a boy's development, his relationship with his father is part of his developing view of himself. If we think about this along the lines of normal narcissistic development (Kohut, 1971), a child gets off to a good start in life through a phase of normal grandiosity, the phase of being a superhero who can do anything in this world. But, of course, life doesn't always play along with this fantasy and in fact a child often feels quite helpless. So, the next normal phase in this development is: "Maybe I can't but my dad can!" This is the phase in which the child's shaky self-esteem and imaginary grandiosity leans on the idealized father for support.

Along this father-related narcissistic axis, a boy's sense of pride and confidence in himself depends on measuring up to the standards set, directly or indirectly, by his father. His ambitions and aspirations, his sense of ideals and honor, are grounded in this relationship. As is the negative side of this emotional picture. Not living up to ideals the child locates in his father is cause for immense shame. And being humiliated by the other, be it the actual father of childhood or a male in later life, threatens disqualification as a valued man and often leads to terrible rage. Then too, when the idealized other turns out to be deeply flawed—as we saw in Chapter 2—traumatic disillusionment (Wolf, 1995) occurs, with its own devastating, even suicidal, consequences.

The story of Terry (as told by Dr. Frank Ochberg) speaks to this dynamic (Fromm, 2014b). Terry was wounded in action in Vietnam in 1970. This could have meant transfer out and the end of his time in the war. But he decided to return to combat, and four months later, his platoon was ambushed. Most of the men were killed, including, horrifyingly, Terry's best friend, who died in his arms. In the ensuing chaos, the commanding officer ordered a retreat, even at the expense of leaving casualties behind. Generally a mild-mannered person, Terry burst into rage at his commander for abandoning his buddy and pointed his gun at him with intent to kill. Intervention by others stopped further disaster.

Terry suffered serious PTSD for a number of years after returning home. In addition to flashbacks and emotional numbing, survivor guilt—in the form of obsessive thoughts—haunted him; he was convinced that his buddy would not have been where he was—and therefore would not have been killed—if Terry had not decided to return to the front. His brother-in-arms died because of him. Why did Terry return to the war? Because he had the thought—"Isn't that a stupid thing? But that's what I thought" (Fromm, 2014b)—that if *he* had gotten killed, his father would have been proud of him. Giving up his life in order for the idealized father to be proud of his son. What a powerful statement of the life-and-death importance of a father's approval! And what fury it can unleash! In combat chaos, a commanding officer/father figure is willing to leave his troops/sons behind—not only an abandonment but, to Terry, a denigration of his brother, his love, and himself—and nearly pays for it with his own life.

Terry never had a close relationship with his father, even though he longed for one. There were many children in the family and perhaps other strains as well. Terry's father was a veteran himself, and while that may have become one standard—the honor of military service—for his son to emulate, perhaps in the service of earning his father's approval, it also opens up another possibility. Terry's father, like so many of those who return from war, did not speak about his experiences in combat. But, as we saw earlier, a parent's trauma tends to play out unconsciously in the family. What happened to Terry's father in his own combat experience? What needs to prove himself did he feel? What did he witness or participate in? What losses or remorse might he have experienced? And how might this have affected the relationship between father and son? Might his son's wartime experience have brought his father's buried experience back to life? Given whatever those experiences might have been, could the father stand his son's idealization? And could the son's decision to return to the front have been enacting, not only his own need to make the past work out differently, but his father's as well? These are some of the relational and inter-generational questions that emerge from a deeper exploration of combat trauma stories as they relate to the family a soldier grew up in.

Mother

Are there potentially similar relational issues for boys and their mothers? The answer to this question is less obvious than it is for father and son. But Wilfred Bion first told the story of the day he died to his mother, not his father: a story of another son's dying wish to reach his mother. In a moving article, Dave Phillipps (2015) reports on the 2nd Battalion, 7th Marine Regiment, "one of the hardest hit military units in Afghanistan" (p. 1). The title of the article tells the story: "In a Unit Stalked by Suicide, Veterans Try to Save One Another." Tragically, at the time of its writing, soldiers were more likely to die by suicide than in combat. The suicide rate in the 2/7, as it was called, was four times the rate for other young veterans and fourteen times the rate for all Americans. In the vignettes about the 2/7 members who killed themselves after returning home, for some a triggering event was the breakup with a girlfriend or a fight with a spouse. For a few vets, their deaths had a strange staging to them—sometimes after putting on his dress uniform, and sometimes shooting himself in front of his mother or girlfriend.

What might this mean? Certainly, one could imagine anger building up in the back-home relationship with girlfriends and spouses, along with dangerously low frustration tolerance, guilt for not being able to leave the war behind, and ambivalent dependence on one's family for help. With regard to the latter, traumatized veterans are desperate not to be left alone with their memories and also desperate to protect their loved ones from them. The resulting conflict is unbearable, for some literally so. But why shoot oneself in dress uniform? And why shoot oneself in front of one's mother, the mother who, in dire combat circumstances, a soldier might desperately call out for?

When asked about the meaning of life, Freud reportedly gave a very non-psychoanalytic answer: Life is about love and work. To some degree and speaking quite schematically, a boy's relationship to his father is about work: What can I do in this world and how well can I do it? And a boy's relationship to his mother is about love: How much do you love me and how well can I love others? Whereas in the relationship with father, competence is a defining value, with mother, goodness is. Failure along the paternal axis of self-love results in shame and humiliation; failure in the task of other-love along the maternal axis results in guilt and self-condemnation.

From this perspective, what is enacted by shooting oneself in front of one's mother? Is something unspeakable being communicated? Might the suicidal soldier be saying: "Mom, I killed someone. I'm so sorry. I can't be forgiven"? Might he be leaving his mother with the unbearable feelings—for example, of helplessly witnessing death right in front of her—that he could not contain inside himself, as though she must once again take up that very early childhood task of emotional containment for him. Is his dress uniform a kind of apology: "No matter where I ended up, Mom, here is where I started—in a place where I thought that honor mattered"?

One critical dimension of a child's relationship with his mother is that he was inside her once. Being born is a first separation, to be followed by many more, some of which move toward the father. The adolescent boy's becoming inspired toward the male culture of war represents a major separation, from home and from the maternal environment it represents. Killing someone can feel like a permanent and irreparable separation from the maternal circle of love and goodness (Covington, 2020; Sherman, 2014). Returning soldiers sometimes feel like monsters, like they could never tell their mothers what happened, and like they are forever now outside the human community. As one veteran put it, "Something happens over there. You wake up a primal part of your brain you are not supposed to listen to, and it becomes part of you. I shot an old woman. I shot her on purpose because she was running at us with an RPG. You see someone blown in half … You can try but it is hard to get away from that" (Phillipps, 2015, p. 5). As the poet, T. S. Eliot, wrote at the end of WWI, "After such knowledge, what forgiveness?" (1920). A soldier's belief in the utter impossibility of reunion with the source of love may well be another major factor in combat trauma.

Counting

One feature of Terry's treatment was a form of exposure therapy invented by his therapist, Dr. Frank Ochberg, which Dr. Ochberg calls the Counting Method (1996; Miller & Ochberg, 2012). Rather than simply ask the patient to tell him about the traumatic event, Dr. Ochberg, at the right moment, invites him to re-experience the event, but to do so in silence and in his therapist's presence. While the patient does this, Dr. Ochberg counts out loud from 1 to 100. He tells the patient that, as he is re-experiencing the unwanted memory or flashback, he will hear Dr. Ochberg counting. Dr. Ochberg hopes that in the middle of the counting, the patient will be dealing with the worst part of that event, and be past it—and feeling safer—as Dr. Ochberg gets closer to 100. Then patient and therapist talk about what the patient just experienced, while Dr. Ochberg takes notes about it. Dr. Ochberg makes clear that this is "an elective surgery. We don't have to rush into it. We'll do it when you're ready for it. But it will expose you and me together to what actually happened" (Fromm, 2014b, p. 211).

The Counting Method worked well for many of Dr. Ochberg's patients. Its intuitive brilliance, as I heard it, is not only as an exposure therapy per se. Rather, Dr. Ochberg establishes a therapeutic context and relationship, designed, in a sense, to undo the traumatic experience in a number of ways. First, he says, "When you're ready," which means that the traumatized person now has agency over the core traumatic experience of helplessness. And Dr. Ochberg says, "We together" to a person who has experienced the terrible aloneness of trauma. And he brings time into the timelessness of trauma. In any experience of overwhelming anxiety, time collapses and the person is caught in an endless now. The counting method introduces time—a beginning, middle, and end—to what has felt endless.

In trauma, the person automatically suspends unbearable experience. As we have seen, Donald Winnicott (1974) noted that trauma—in his practice, trauma in early childhood—had to do with events that, though they had indeed occurred, had not actually *happened yet to that person* because he was not there as a functioning ego for them to happen to. The experience had been cut off at its start. One consequence that surprised Winnicott was the person's searching for the trauma in the future as a way of trying to experience it for the first time, so as to master this already-having-happened but dissociated disaster. Dr. Ochberg notes that young therapists may be afraid of this process, for fear of not being able to contain the horror and thereby re-traumatizing the patient. Another of Winnicott's key notions is the importance of the therapist's survival (1969), meaning her capacity to remain present to the intensity of the patient's feeling and the truth of the story, both of which the patient feels he can't survive himself.

Dr. Ochberg provided his patient, Terry, with what Nancy Sherman called a "compassionate witness" (2014). Transferentially, he was a caring father figure in the context of a troubled relationship between the actual son and father. The text that he produces from these sessions documents the patient's traumatic experience, and becomes a "thing" out there that the patient no longer has to carry nonverbally inside himself. This speaks to the importance of inscription (Lacan, 1977): for example, the importance of a name on a tombstone. Paradoxically, the lost person can be forgotten—he need not be forever present in the mind—*because* the grieving person knows where to find him. Dr. Ochberg brings the patient into and through a process, the end point of which is a text. That text opens a path to forgetting the terrible event because it has a place—and a new relational context—in which it can be remembered.

Dr. Ochberg reads these texts to the patient, if the patient wants him to, then keeps them on file. "They're giving me their precious story," he said. "I'm taking the time to write it longhand on these yellow pads, not recording it. This is old fashioned work. I take dictation and then I read it back to them" (Fromm, 2014b, p. 212). At this point in our conversation, Dr. Ochberg was startled by an association. "You know, I just thought of something … When I was learning how to write essays, my Dad would take dictation. He would let me talk it out. He'd write it down, then he'd show me what he had written. That became the basis for my writing a term paper when I was in the 8th grade" (p. 212). That's what Dr. Ochberg provides to his patients now. From his up-until-then unconscious experience with his father, he gives that same experience to a wounded young man, who couldn't find the narrative he had already lived, including the one with his own father. The origin of the word "therapist," as noted in Chapter 9, comes from ancient Greece; it means the second-in-combat, the one who attends to those on the front line

(Davoine & Gaudilliere, 2004, p. 153). Dr. Ochberg took up the role of the second-in-combat for Terry and, as the ancient Greeks did, helped produce an essential text.

In fact, those ancient texts have proved to be enormously useful in the treatment of combat trauma. In his book, *Achilles in Vietnam*, Jonathan Shay (1995) reports how he treats traumatized veterans by reading them *The Iliad*, and he notes, as a major factor in the warrior's traumatization—something we also see in Terry's story—abandonment and betrayal by the authority on whom the troops depend. Similarly, his book, *Odysseus in America* (2002) speaks to *Combat Trauma and the Trials of Homecoming*, its subtitle, and uses an ancient text to articulate the deeply embedded but unarticulated feelings returning soldiers have. This method of treatment, and Brian Doerries' use of the play, *Ajax*, reported in *The Theater of War* (2016), suggest that the traumatized soldier might be able to rediscover self-empathy by reliving his experience, once removed, through the stories of past warriors.

The box

What happens before self-empathy can be achieved? What happens to experience that is coming back from dissociation but is still too hot to touch? What happens to loss that can't yet be mourned? Sometimes the traumatized person finds a way to put experience in cold storage, so to speak, or in a state of suspended animation. Indeed, post-combat life for many soldiers is itself a state of suspended animation: suspended between past and present, between feeling too intensely and not feeling at all, between the dead and the living.

"Oh, there's no keeping him from the box," Terry's wife said. "If he was going to go to the box, you didn't get in his way" (Fromm, 2014b, p. 215). Terry's box contained a collection of objects brought back from Vietnam, something of a hodge-podge but meaningful for their evocative links to people and events. The psychoanalyst, Vamık Volkan (1981), has written extensively about what he calls "linking objects"—concrete objects emotionally connected to profound loss the traumatized person is not yet able to mourn. These objects—like the trauma itself—are set aside on the return home, awaiting enough healing and a good-enough relational context through which to approach the experiences they contain. Terry tried to set aside trauma, contain it in his box, and keep it in the closet. In what came to seem to his family like a private ritual, he would recurrently go to the box, sort through its contents, stay with them for a while, then return the box to the closet. One critical aspect of this experience was that he could *smell* Vietnam, and it soothed him.

This to and fro process is exactly what happens in mourning. The representations of the lost loved one must be returned to in the mind over and over—and the memories and range of feelings associated with that person felt again—as part of the goodbye process. In traumatic loss, those feelings and memories are intense to the point of being unbearable, and so the normal mourning process is aborted. Instead, there is the box, a kind of miniature coffin that can't be buried because, while there has been acute grief, there has been no true mourning. A ritual, like the one that Terry performed, develops a drawn-out wake with "linking objects," which may over time become what Donald Winnicott called "transitional objects." That is, in the right circumstances, these objects that freeze time and feeling may warm up, as the person slowly becomes able to reconcile internal and external reality. What's needed for this to happen is a "holding environment," temporarily a box and a closet but eventually a person. In Terry's case, his family saw what he was doing, repeatedly asked about it, and finally insisted that he bring the box to his therapist. He did, and he also brought his family to that session. A private emotional process became public, with people who cared deeply about him, and, through this process—and Terry's therapy in general—the box was no longer necessary. Instead, Terry's medals could now be hung on the wall of his home, rather than buried in his closet.

Françoise Davoine and Jean-Max Gaudilliere, whose book, *History beyond Trauma* (2004) reports on their decades-long experience of working with psychotic and traumatized patients, sometimes ask the patient to bring something into the office from the context of trauma. This is not necessarily for its symbolic meaning; in fact, the traumatized person is generally not yet able to make meaning of the experience such that it can take symbolic form. Rather, it is the concreteness of the object, its physical link to the trauma that must come physically into the therapeutic space and be held there until it comes to have meaning. Trauma acts first of all on the body; like Terry's absolute need to smell Vietnam, it is a sensory experience temporarily de-sensitized for self-protection.

One aspect of the transition we saw in Terry's story is the movement from sensory experience to the mental and emotional work of processing what happened. Sometimes, a crucial step is bringing the actual linking object into the therapist's office.

Not counting

Earlier in this chapter, we saw how the emotional dynamics of home, and of peacetime itself, may function to reinforce the returning soldiers' dissociation. After war, society understandably wants to forget; in 1919, it wanted a Roaring Twenties to wipe away the horror of WWI (and also of the pandemic). This all too human societal dynamic is also costly. It erases the lessons that combat trauma has so painfully taught. As General Braceland said, paraphrasing Hegel, "Men learn from history only that men learn nothing from history" (1946, p. 587). Forgetting history also contributes to denying the truth of what happened, which further alienates the traumatized soldier. This denial is one of the things that makes trauma traumatic, and we might wonder how it affects the institutions meant to treat it.

In 2015, when the dire situation of 2/7 vets was first reported by *The New York Times*, the Veterans Administration did not know about their story because it did not track data about suicide trends in pre-discharge military units, nor did the Marine Corps track data about suicides of post-discharge service members. A unit that came to call itself "The Forgotten Battalion" (Phillipps, 2015, p. 4) during the war—because of its extended, under-resourced combat in a remote province of Afghanistan—began to think of itself as forgotten on their return home, by both the Corps they had fought with and the treatment services of the VA. Members of the 2/7 were killing themselves in record numbers, and no one seemed to be responding or even noticing. Intense feelings of abandonment and betrayal developed in 2/7 vets, exactly the feelings toward leadership that, for some, are part of moral injury in combat. This is an example of the way that traumatic feelings can be triggered back home, in relation to the systems meant to treat them. But is this phenomenon simply transference—the soldier's projection onto authority now what he suffered back then—or is this partly a systemic enactment?

Vets of the 2/7 report major difficulties navigating the VA system and long waits for appointments. Given such long-lasting wars and the redeployments necessary to fight them, there is, of course, an enormous need for treatment services. The VA's resources—not only the number of therapists available, but the resources to train and support them as they risk secondary traumatization—must be seriously strained. And the time it takes to treat wounded vets, especially in relationship-based treatments, must also be severely limited; after all, the longer a treatment takes, the longer the wait for other vets. These factors must surely be part of the reason that some 2/7 vets report maddeningly out-of-touch encounters with therapists: one vet is slipped a bottle of pills at the end of a session, after making it clear that he did not want medications; another is told that he should think of the death of his blown-up buddy as like a bad breakup and "get over it." This patient became so enraged he threw a chair across the room.

Therapists generally are doing the best they can, and there may well have been treatment reasons for both therapists' actions and dynamic reasons for both patients' reactions. But are there other questions—beyond the question of resources—that arise if we take these two vignettes as potentially representative of something systemic? One question begins with noticing how the therapists' actions made their patients feel. Therapists, especially under-resourced therapists treating intractable problems, are always at risk of unconscious reactions. They deeply want to help their patients, and their frustration about not being able to challenges their identity at its core. Any helper in these circumstances may subtly withdraw from or even unconsciously blame the patient. The troubled vets in these vignettes seemed to have taken in messages like: "I can't give you what you need, so take these meds instead," or "If you can't do what I'm suggesting, I can't help." At some basic level, they felt unheard and sent away.

This is in profound contrast to treatments like those of Drs. Ochberg and Shay, which, using different methods, are directed toward helping the traumatized vet get in touch with himself through their getting in touch with him. These are empathy-based treatment *relationships* for soldiers who have lost empathy for themselves and are terrified of losing it for their loved ones. Davoine and Gaudilliere (2004, p. 116) realized that their psychotherapeutic work with traumatized patients drew on principles discovered by a WWI military psychiatrist, Thomas Salmon, as he treated "shell-shocked" patients. These principles are: simplicity (no jargon, no manuals), proximity (experientially going to the front with the traumatized soldier), immediacy (relying on intuition and even coincidences in the lives of patient and therapist, like Dr. Ochberg's writing the story, just as his father did), and expectancy (getting better because those back at the front—in war or in peace—need you). How do treatment organizations support this raw, human work? How much do resource limitations, and perhaps even problematic organizational dynamics, interfere with it and trickle down to therapists on this new front line?

As mentioned, the Marine Corps did not track suicides of former members; the job of looking after those discharged from the Corps was delegated to the VA, which did not know in advance about tragic events in active units. If this were a health care system and we considered the system as a whole, we would see a built-in discontinuity of care. Of course, only half of this system has to do with health care; the other has to do with the capacity to fight a war. The organizational structure of the Corps and the VA, and their working relationship, was designed, no doubt, as a rational division of labor. But, as in any system, problems that arise can be viewed as opportunities to understand why the system functions one way and not another, and what might help it function better. Some vets feel that they have fallen into a gap between the Corps and the VA, which leads to a question: Is there meaning in this potentially re-traumatizing gap, re-traumatizing to the degree that it makes vets feel once again forgotten or left behind, as Terry's buddy was about to be?

Reportedly, one way this gap plays out is in a soldier's routine screening for PTSD at discharge. In the emotional climate of a hero's return, very often no symptoms are found. When they show up later—as the glow wears off, the challenges of home life mount, and triggering events occur—the official record shows no PTSD at discharge, raising questions about the authenticity of the trouble. In addition, symptom checklists, used to assess PTSD, are not constructed to capture moral injury. So the clean bill of health a discharging soldier receives does not assess core problems, but becomes an official document. The re-traumatizing outcome for some vets is that a system of care—which, in a certain sense, also stands for the care of one's buddies—seems to have broken ranks with them or suspects that they have broken ranks with it. Disillusionment and cynicism infiltrate the relationship, and the essential trust soldiers rely on is thrown into doubt.

To the extent that there is a problematic organizational gap between the Corps and the VA—reflecting the different ways those on active duty and those discharged are held in mind—we might think of this gap as a social defense for the overall system. Social defenses (Jaques, 1955) are ways work comes to be structured—through its organization, policies, procedures, resource allocation, and so on—such that it unconsciously protects the system from anxiety. This anxiety is sometimes about the organization's task itself and what it takes to carry that out. Over time, outside of anyone's awareness or intention, the organization of work evolves in such a way as to prioritize protecting the organization from anxiety, with potentially problematic fallout. For example, being a vet is felt to be a continuation of being a soldier. It's part of identity: the repair or healing phase following the all-out effort. An organizational gap between active duty and the VA—lived out, for example, in the PTSD procedure—challenges that identity. It may come to feel like the system itself is dissociating vets from their former role and status, and also from memory. As though the warrior can be valued, but the wounded cannot. As we saw in Terry's enraged outburst, there is intense feeling across this gap, and a potentially new moral injury.

A systems analysis asks: Why might this system be functioning in this way? What might be the nature of the anxiety that is taken care of by the gap between one part and the other? Can that anxiety be explored and understood for the betterment of all? These are very big questions, and, of course, I have no answers for them. But one path for that exploration would begin with the vet's experience of being unheard, and raises the question of what is so difficult for the system to hear? Could it be the vets' mortal vulnerability in a system that relies on its fighters' sense of invulnerability? Or do stories of moral injury in combat threaten to expose problematic decision-making? From this angle—perhaps a way of looking at things from the upside-down world (see the Introduction)—the work of the VA, rather than representing a critical part of the Corps' task (i.e. the restoration of its warriors and learning from their experience), might, deep down, be felt as a threat to it. Hence, the organizational gap between them.

Treatment with medications and CBT—and even the diagnosis of PTS *Disorder*—can be seen as playing out this gap and the system's anxiety as well. They reflect a mechanistic mind-set, embedded in the treatment, which dissociates the wounded from the rest of us, as though that person is somehow defective: chemically imbalanced or unable to think straight. The feeling of being sent away, which these vets seemed to take from their treatment encounters, may not be a misunderstanding, but an *accurate* understanding of the system's anxiety about listening seriously to its wounded. Moral *injury* forces all to see that the trouble, from the soldier's point of view, is about what I did for you, what happened in that process, and what you may or may not have done for me. As Tom Voss (2019b), an Iraq veteran and author of *Where War Ends* (2019a), writes, "Moral injury is a wound to the soul and psyche." Medications don't treat that; in fact, they are often felt as denying it. Instead, treating moral injury requires a therapist's getting in touch with the wounded person, committing to the truth, and being able to bear that together. Sometimes, systems evolve—in the service of defending against profound anxiety—in exactly the opposite direction, at a cost to those they serve and to their own learning.

CHAPTER 11

We don't speak of fear: large-group identity and chosen trauma

A few years ago, three colleagues, two from Israel and one from Palestine, met informally with a senior American government official who was working with the Israel–Palestine negotiating team. One colleague asked the official what happened in the formal negotiating conversation when people on either side talked about their fears. The American official seemed surprised. "We don't speak of fear," he said, later adding that he could see the sense in trying to address fear during negotiations, but that the team did not know how to do this.

How might we understand the absence of discussion about fear during these conversations, beyond the negotiating team's inability to lead it? After all, fear is one of the emotions at the heart of the conflict: fear for one's survival, fear of the mortal harm another group wants to inflict on one's own group, fear that disasters from the past will happen again. One answer to this question is tactical: the concern that the acknowledgment of fear weakens one's bargaining position. From this perspective, a posture of strength, or even machismo, may seem to promise better results. One consequence of such fear-denying posturing, however, is that the other group is likely to mirror it. In a group context where acknowledging fear is considered a weakness, "toughness" becomes an attractive fallback position. The risk, of course, in this enactment of what my colleague, Robi Friedman, calls the "soldier's matrix" (2019b) is of escalation: tit-for-tat positions, each in response to the other side. There are other consequences as well; this type of posturing, and embeddedness in the soldier's matrix, conflates fear with weakness, as though the two are the same. It thereby closes the opportunity to connect with the fear of others at a more human level—indeed as a shared and sensible emotion in a context of danger.

Chosen trauma

Peace talks between Israeli and Palestinian leaders seem forever stuck in limbo, effectively leaving the Israeli and Palestinian people, and generations to come, in limbo as well. Considering events as of this writing in late 2020—especially the recent specter of Israeli annexation of parts of the West Bank—stalled or broken-off talks seem like a tragedy waiting to happen. Young people may succumb to apathy temporarily but a return to rage is always a possibility, in part as a vitalizing alternative to helplessness or despair.

My three colleagues—one a psychologist and group analyst, another a lawyer working with the Palestinian team, and the third a former Israeli ambassador—are members of the International Dialogue Initiative. Established in 2007, the IDI is a nonprofit organization, which brings together unofficial representatives from various parts of the world. It works toward developing a common language among psychoanalysts who have studied the psychology of ethnic, national, or religious groups, and professionals from other disciplines who are involved in diplomacy, politics, or other forms of societal study and intervention. The IDI also functions as a conceptual sounding board and support group for those members currently engaged in consulting with societal groups and governmental authorities. Among other topics, the IDI examines mounting tensions in Israel and Palestine, in the hope of contributing to an understanding of, and a way of working differently with, this and other intractable conflicts. Central to that understanding is that emotions—like fear—are at the heart of such conflicts and learning how to speak about them safely prepares the ground for future negotiation (Rifkind, 2019).

Israelis and Palestinians have suffered enormous trauma. The Holocaust for Israelis and the Nakba for Palestinians condense into two words a multitude of horrific experiences suffered by millions of people. They constitute an unimaginable level of trauma for those who suffered them directly and also for their descendants. Beyond the reality of such trauma, we might also consider them in terms of what Volkan (2013, 2020) calls "chosen trauma." Chosen traumas are traumatic experiences that over time have come to represent and to organize the collective identities of the large groups who suffered the historical trauma. They become part of what characterizes and distinguishes each group of people as who they are, and they sometimes anchor those identities in a definition of the "Other" as the enemy. The historical catastrophes behind the Israeli–Palestinian conflict are still within living memory, and so not yet what Volkan means by chosen trauma. But negotiations that do not speak about fear may well reflect large-group identities that have been hardened by the collective memory of emotional trauma, and, in a basic sense, constructed by it as well. "Never again" constructs Israeli identity at some level. "Never surrender" does the same for Palestinian identity. Both sides know who they are, both sides feel their membership in something larger, and both sides do so through knowing who the "Other" is. In crises, leaders may perpetuate mutually antagonistic narratives and, consciously or unconsciously, use them to build identity cohesion and garner popular support. Large-group identity (Volkan, 2013, 2020) becomes a key factor in intractable conflicts.

Large-group identity is not a conscious, thought-through process. Nor does it begin in the late adolescent phase of identity formation—crucial as that phase is to the individual's embracing or differentiating from his large group. Rather, large-group identity is an emotional phenomenon beginning in early life, when a toddler is, both excitedly and fearfully, experimenting with leaving the home base of mother to explore his brand new world. In the course of this exploration, the child quickly takes in messages of "Here, with me, is safe. There is dangerous." And "here" soon generalizes from mother to family to home to village to religion to nationality. It also generalizes from safety to pride and morality. Things that belong "here" are good. Things that belong "there" are dirty or bad. "There" generalizes too, especially as the child takes in messages about the "Other." Erikson (1959) noted "the subtler methods by which children are induced to accept … prototypes of good and evil" (p. 27); the way that "minute displays of emotion … transmit to the human child the outlines of what really counts" (p. 28). "Every neurosis," he says, is a "*shared* panic" (p. 28).

Large-group identity has meanings related to one's own group—of sameness, safety, goodness, and belonging—and meanings related to those outside the group as well. If group anxiety is low, those meanings may include curiosity, generosity, and other emotions. But if group anxiety is high, for one reason or another, latent meanings of the other group as alien, threatening, or dirty may become prominent. And fear of the "Other" may be expressed in different forms, for example, as scorn or entitlement or a lack of curiosity. Large-group identity is fundamentally about security, and history may be read as a story of large-group insecurity, based on collective trauma, leading to that group's traumatizing another group.

The concept of "chosen trauma" refers to a powerful psychological process shared by members of a large societal group and taking place over many years. Devastating events at the hands of an "Other" in the history of any group must be mentally and emotionally processed over time. When members of the victimized group are unable to bear the humiliation, reverse their helplessness, or mourn their losses, they pass on to their children powerful, emotionally charged images of their injured selves. In the process, they bind the next generation to them, and pass along psychologically restorative tasks that the next generation is implicitly charged with taking up—for example, avenging humiliation, restoring pride, honoring the dead, and grieving their loss.

All these images and tasks contain references to the same historical event, and as decades pass, the representation of this event in the minds of thousands of people links them together, emerging virulently in times of crisis. A chosen trauma, in a sense, reflects the infection of a group's mourning process—an interference with efforts to come to terms with, and move beyond, the actual trauma. Its reactivation in times of crisis links group members to a shared, endangered sense of identity, which can be used by political leadership to promote new large-group movements, some of which may turn deadly. Fear—along with grievance and rage—can be mobilized in the service of polarizing "Who we are" and "Who they are."

Who are we?

Nation-states are born differently. Israel is what the historian-psychoanalyst Peter Loewenberg (1995) calls a "synthetic nation." Jewish people with different experiences, different investments in religion, and from different places—Europe, the Middle East, Russia, and Africa—came to Israel to live in relative peace and free from persecution. To do so, they needed to create a synthesis of their disparate influences. But the effort to unify distinct groups inevitably involves great internal strain, and differences within such a group can begin to feel persecutory to the group as a whole. For Israel, the major internal tension, though by no means the only one, is between religious and secular groups. These internal tensions tend to increase a group's need to externalize problematic narratives and project unacceptable ideas and feelings onto the "Other." The word "unacceptable" has a double meaning here: Not only may one Israeli group find the other Israeli group unacceptable in, for example, their particular religious practices, but they also may find their animosity toward that group unacceptable because it threatens a more secure societal integration.

For Israel, Palestine is not only the "Other" they hate, but also the "Other" they need, as a target for these animosities, so that some semblance of internal peace can be maintained. The same holds true for Palestine, which has become a flag bearer for the suffering of Arab peoples. Palestine not only has its own terrible problems to deal with—for example, the internal tension between Hamas and Fatah—but it also has problems that *stand for* something to Palestinians and to others. Such an identity—for example, as a victimized people or a dishonored people or an occupied people—is not "wanted" by the members of a society, at least at a conscious level. Nor do Israelis want to think of themselves as either victims or aggressors. But dialogues with the other group—necessary as they may be to work toward peaceful solutions—can also feel like threats to the broadly shared sense of who each group is. Struggle coheres and supports identity. In recent years, it has seemed that, when the world's eyes are diverted to other crises—for example, to ISIS—conflict erupts in Jerusalem or is provoked along the Gaza border. Attention once again returns to the Israel–Palestine conflict, which has the effect of reinforcing both groups' fundamental understanding of who they are, while also saying that some kind of genuinely helpful attention is needed.

A societal MRI

Earlier in this volume, we saw how the methodology of Group Relations Conferences can lead to powerful experiential learning about authority, leadership, group and inter-group dynamics and other important issues. At the heart of these conferences is the task of speaking to what is being experienced in the moment. Thus, they are one way to learn how to speak about fear, and about other emotions as well. They also function, in my experience, as societal MRIs. They tend to capture what the membership has taken in of national anxiety and to show, in the microcosm of the conference, how large-group identity plays out among members and staff. Here is an example from an international conference held in Israel.

In Chapter 5, we learned about one of the events of a GRC, something called the Institutional Event, the task of which has to do with members using their authority to decide which aspects of the conference they want to study further (e.g. how leadership is being enacted in the conference) and with what other groups they want to engage in that study (for example, a group studying leadership may want to engage the staff about their leadership, or may want to engage a group studying gender differences about the interrelatedness of gender and leadership). After the task of the IE is spelled out and questions are responded to, the director leaves, and two staff members stay behind to consult to how the group is taking up its task. Generally, because this large group is unnerved about being left on its own, a relatively tumultuous period follows, as this now unguided group works through phases of confusion, excitement, frustration, and whatever else. Eventually, after a few fits and starts, emergent leaders persuade enough members to join them in studying a given topic, and off they go to one of the rooms the staff has made available.

In the Israel conference, however, within five minutes of the director's setting out the task, the large-group room was empty. People fled the public space as though a bomb were going to explode, as they indeed had during the Intifada. The only other time in my experience the opening session of the IE played out this way was at a conference four months after 9/11. Seemingly driven by pervasive fearfulness, small groups in the Israel conference formed impulsively without a sense of identity or purpose. Then, quite startlingly, members of these nascent groups came to the staff to request two things: a room, even though rooms had already been made available to them, and a consultant, even though they had not yet met as a group, didn't know who they were, and didn't know what they wanted consultation about. But want one they did, with an insistence that betrayed the intensity of anxiety they were carrying. On reflection, it seemed to the staff that this was Israel in a microcosm, desperate for territory of its own and for the security of being with whoever was identified as in authority.

Once these smaller groups actually got to their spaces, they preferred not to speak to other groups. Or, if they had to carry out the second part of their task—which was relating to other groups in the service of learning (for example about leadership and gender)—perhaps they could do it without ever having to leave what they came to call "home." When they eventually did venture out for inter-group work, tensions erupted as members encountered conflicting aspects of Israeli identity. For example, a group who came to identify itself as "chosen"—and who in their "home" group explored that part of what they felt deeply to be their large-group identity—found it unbearable to sustain a meeting with a group who saw themselves as representing "vulnerability." Passions intensified, dialogue ceased, and participants fled the room. In retrospect, the actual explosion people feared in the opening of the IE seemed to have everything to do with parts of the Israeli psyche that were extremely difficult to hold together. These two groups felt powerfully the impossibility of containing Israel's dream and its nightmare within the same room.

In the closing plenary of a similar conference, a member reported a dream.

> There was a hospital that looked like a lighthouse. Ariel Sharon, gravely ill, was being wheeled in on a gurney. But the treatment in this hospital was unusual. People were hung upside-down for a while, and that seemed to help them get better.

As noted in the Introduction, the group's work on this dream—taken up for its potential collective meaning (Friedman, 2019a; Fromm, 2000; Lawrence, 1991)—quickly led to a startling understanding. The conference had turned members' understanding of their home organizations, and in some instances their home identities, upside-down. They had seen through to core dysfunction and hugely problematic dynamics.

While this learning was potentially transformative for their personal, organizational, and political lives, they now had the problem of re-entry. What were they to do with what they had learned? How dangerous would it be to bring this new learning back to their home groups? They were going back to the so-called right-side-up world and they were frightened! As were the members of the Israel conference.

Leaders

The Israeli leader in this dream was very ill, and his treatment attempted to show him something from a perspective diametrically opposed to his own. But seeing things from the other side, so to speak, can indeed be dangerous. Many years ago, two things happened in the life of the psychoanalyst, Vamık Volkan, that brought him to the study of international relations. The first was the death of his medical school roommate in the civil war between Greek and Turkish Cypriots. The second occurred when Anwar Sadat, the president of Egypt, took the extraordinary step of speaking to the Israeli Knesset and said that 70% of the trouble between Arabs and Israelis was psychological (Volkan, 2013, p. 23). These two events launched Volkan into a second career; while continuing his clinical psychoanalytic practice, he took up the task of trying to understand the psychological dimension of international conflicts. The Center for the Study of Mind and Human Interaction carried out that work for many years. The International Dialogue Initiative represents his most recent effort in that direction.

Anwar Sadat and his later Israeli counterpart, Yitzhak Rabin, were both assassinated *by their own people*. Their challenge to both sides' large-group identities—and the vested interests that accrue in relation to them—led to their deaths. Their societies, faced with external danger, internal fragmentation, and a context of massive historical trauma, were too vulnerable to allow real negotiation with the "Other." As we have seen throughout this volume, Erik Erikson described this regressive process as one in which "an absolute boundary is emphasized. Nothing that belongs inside must be left outside; nothing that must be outside should be tolerated inside" (1959, p. 133). Both Sadat and Rabin had created holes in that boundary at their own peril. The basic idea of talking with and hearing from the other side—and potentially of compromise, which is essential to the self-government of a diverse democracy—had taken on the risk of contamination. In the regressive mind-set (Volkan, 2004b), to compromise is to be compromised, in the sense of being dishonored and debased.

In psychological terms, this is an extreme splitting dynamic, in which all good is here, all bad is there, and no mixing of these absolutes can occur. Within this mind-set, which the psychoanalyst Melanie Klein (1946) called the "paranoid–schizoid" position, any questioning of one's own virtue and the other's vices—a questioning that would actually reflect a mature capacity to own one's shortcomings and to see the actions of both sides as making sense somehow—is unacceptable. For Erikson, a group's "tak[ing] refuge in totalism" has to do with their "despair of an essential wholeness" (1959, p. 133). He thus linked the splitting/purification dynamic to a longing for wholeness, as well as to defensive refuge-taking and to despair. Societal trauma may well lead to profound despair about a group's "essential wholeness," because so many people have been irreparably lost in the conflict. Large-group identity may be felt to be deeply damaged, weakened, helpless, humiliated, and grief-struck. Despair implies hopelessness about ever being made whole again.

In this context, it is no surprise that a society would want, and be vulnerable to, a leader who promises to restore collective self-esteem, a leader who could, in a sense, "treat" profound narcissistic injury. The narcissistic leader's projection of power and pride will be taken in by his people, who feel a kind of quickening that all might not be lost and who look to the leader as a savior (Volkan, 2004b). A mirroring dynamic ensues between leader and follower, each thriving on the image the other offers them. This is analogous to the fundamental mirroring a parent offers a child (Kohut, 1971), part of a healthy process in which the child comes to feel a positive sense of self and a belief that he can thrive in the world. But, at a societal level, the narcissistic leader is dealing with a deeply damaged large group, damaged not only by massive losses but by profound humiliation (Alderdice, 2012) as well. The regressed society's efforts toward repair too often attempt to bypass the losses in favor of reversing the humiliation.

Essential as some version of narcissistic repair is to the restoration of the group's identity, it is profoundly risky. The mirroring dynamic between leader and followers creates collective illusions about both sides, which have a life apart from reality. One's own side is idealized and the other denigrated. Intense emotions are catalyzed and acted out upon the group seen as causing the damage. Retaliatory violence seems to promise relief from despair, as though this crude form of justice will bring back all that has been lost. Even within societies, this kind of mirroring and splitting dynamic takes place, leading to the polarization we have seen in the United States under President Trump.

The psychoanalyst Jacques Lacan (1977) studied the mirroring process, which at its heart begins with the loving gaze of mother to child. Lacan argued that what the child sees in his mother's eyes, and later in the mirror, offers an illusory sense of wholeness, which offsets, but only to a degree, the child's everyday feelings of incompetence, frustration, and being new to the world. For Lacan, the mirror and the gaze were a seduction, a partial truth that vulnerable people wanted to believe as the whole truth. The mirroring dynamic defines what he called the Imaginary Order, in which narcissistic needs are gratified, but simultaneously an inevitable paranoia develops. Deep down, people know that the image in the mirror—or in the adulatory gaze of followers—is not the whole truth; indeed they know that that truth, whatever it might be, cannot be seen in the mirror. For the wishful-thinking narcissist, seeing is believing. For the paranoid, what is *not seen* is believed. And for Lacan, they are two sides of the same person. Again, witness the conspiracy theories of Trump's followers.

Narcissistic leaders, and the mirroring dynamic they mobilize, present a major risk to the societal self-esteem they are meant to restore. Mirroring is an imaginary process—one involving people's emotionally driven, wishful fantasies about themselves and their leaders. It thereby denies the truths it doesn't want to see and increasingly separates itself from reality. Illusions become more like delusions. The process of restoring a traumatized society takes a paranoid turn toward purification, as what is not seen threatens to invade what is seen. One need not look further than Hitler's Germany to see this process in its most extreme form—from its beginnings in an outraged effort to overcome deep humiliation and massive loss to a paranoid megalomania about purity (Volkan et al., 2002).

The psychological alternative to the paranoid–schizoid position is what Klein (1946) called the "depressive position," from which the whole problem—in the case of politicians, the whole country and its history—is taken in as one's own to deal with. It implies seeing the other as a person, rather than a stereotype, and being able to take responsibility for one's own aggressive actions. Finding the other in oneself and vice versa is the psychological difficulty of the work, and, as we have seen, it is dangerous in the context of societal trauma. Barack Obama might be described as an example of a "depressive position" president: that is, a president hoping to lead the whole country from an ethic of bipartisanship while taking responsibility for American aggression. His childhood experience of being the only child of a black-white, American African marriage may well have given him both the aspiration and the capacity to bridge seemingly unbridgeable differences.

In 2016, Obama became the first sitting U.S. president to visit the Hiroshima Peace Memorial. While recognizing both sides' aggression, his capacity for empathy exemplified the depressive position. Listen to President Obama's words in Hiroshima: "Why do we come to this place? … To force ourselves to imagine the moment when the bomb fell … to feel the dread of children … [to] listen to a silent cry … [to] remember all the innocents killed … to mourn the dead … Their souls speak to us." After his address, he embraced survivors of the bomb—the bomb his country had dropped—one of whom wept in his arms. This is the work of mourning that depressive-position leaders can help societies achieve. Crucially, it includes the leader's being willing to bear guilt and shame, associated with aggression, on behalf of his own group, no matter how justified that aggression might have been.

The Japanese man who wept in President Obama's arms survived because, as an eight-year-old boy walking to school on August 6, 1945, the force of the blast blew him into the river where he escaped the firestorm. So many of his friends and family simply disappeared in that moment, and for decades, Japan has worked to include all of their names in the Peace Memorial. This survivor, however, Mr. Shigeaki Mori, devoted himself to finding the names of the American airmen—prisoners of war in Hiroshima—who had also disappeared that day at the hands of their own countrymen. Both governments seemed content to keep those names among the disappeared, but Mr. Mori persisted and in 2009, sixty-four years after the bomb, those names too were added to the Peace Memorial (Soble, 2016). A "cut out" history (Davoine & Gaudilliere, 2004, p. 61) had been restored by a man who, like President Obama, was willing and able to feel for both sides. This is the great task of leadership.

Who are we now?

The kind and degree of anxiety suffered by some societies, including Israel and Palestine, reaches the level of what the psychoanalyst Donald Winnicott (1974) called a "*primitive agony*": for example, a group's fear of "disappearing from the face of the earth." Such levels of anxiety make it extremely difficult for people and their leadership to think clearly and contain emotional reactions. But a leader's answering the "Who are we?" question with that society's "chosen trauma" neglects another, at times more pressing, question: "Who are we now?" There is evidence that the next generation on both sides of the Israel–Palestine conflict struggles with this question and does not fully buy into prevailing narratives, even the "chosen trauma" scenario.

Palestinian youth feel stuck in an endless present and alienated from their own leadership. As in other parts of the Arab world, a young person's wish to work to his potential, especially for those well-educated, comes up against the enforced dependency so common in the patriarchal cultures of the Middle East. But identity based on dependency seems no longer sustainable without unbearable humiliation within one's own society. In one IDI meeting, the word most used to describe this phenomenon was "awakening," as though huge groups of people are no longer satisfied living passively in their dream lives and are ready to face reality. "They think they can have an impact," one person said.

Israeli youth struggle with disgust at the excesses, disparities, and corruptions of capitalism as it is playing out in their country; during the Arab Spring, their mantra was "Walk like an Egyptian," a formerly unthinkable identification with the other side. Added to this is resentment about political concessions to the ultra-orthodox minority, which impinge on their ordinary lives. And over all of this hovers the most critical "Who are we now?" question: If Israel annexes Palestine and suddenly has millions more Arab citizens, how can it remain simultaneously a Jewish state and a democratic state? Will it be a country that denies a huge number of Israeli Arab citizens the right to vote? Will it allow that vote and risk its disappearance as a Jewish state? Will it have to go on thinking of itself as an occupier or as living out a de facto apartheid? This is a large-group identity crisis in the making.

All of this is amplified by social media on both sides. The technological revolution has flattened the vertical hierarchy and broadened horizontal connections. Everyone has more information available than was formerly handed down to them from above. They are no longer dependent on government to understand the world. At the same time, they can communicate with colleagues and other groups instantly and take confidence from the sheer numbers they can mobilize. In Western Europe, the Reformation followed the invention of the printing press; are we seeing a correspondingly immense social movement facilitated by the invention of smart phones? And like the decades of religious wars that followed the Reformation, how much social turbulence and destructiveness will be encountered in this new journey on the road to a different relation toward authority?

For the endless time being, however, Prime Minister Netanyahu's stance promises security and territory—the two things the members of that Group Relations Conference were so desperate for—and so even progressive youth movements succumb to inertia. At an IDI meeting in Israel, a visiting Israeli official quipped, "Once I was young and promising. Now I'm just promising." Time has indeed passed, and undelivered promises have left the younger generation in both groups floundering. In response to this malaise, the potential for action, neither focused nor coherent but desperate for some sense of agency and catharsis, is real.

More fear

Meanwhile, both sides' relentless insistence on making sure that history does not repeat itself gravitates frighteningly in that direction. Mutual fear stimulates mutual hatred, which makes retributive justice appear reasonable. In July 2015, a few young ultra-orthodox settlers, in retaliation for a shooting that killed a settler, fire-bombed a random Palestinian home in the West Bank village of Duma. Two adults and their eighteen-month-old baby burned to death, as the attackers watched from a distance. About this carefully planned assault, the group's leader explained why they had taken the risk of sneaking through an olive grove to the center of Duma, bypassing several Palestinian homes on the outskirts: "When the attack is in the heart of the village, there is more fear."

By all reports, people on both sides of the conflict were "horrified" by this attack, and certainly the image of a burning baby is cause for horror. But perhaps something else too. As many have noted, we either remember or repeat history. The idea that a person whose society's history and large-group identity is fundamentally shaped by the Holocaust would plan and carry out a holocaust-in-microcosm is unthinkable. And yet it happened, with this repetition of history now reversing the roles of victim and aggressor. "Never again," a grief- and love-driven determination we can all understand in our bones, became, in this instance, "Actually, yes, it will happen again, but to them and at our hands." Cause for horror indeed! Fortunately an Israeli court recently ruled that, in the words of the chief prosecutor, "Terrorism is terrorism regardless of the identity of the perpetrators" (Halbfinger & Rasgon, 2020).

"We don't speak of fear," and yet creating "more fear" was one goal of this attack. Powerful emotions drive group action but, for various reasons, are excluded from the conversations in which these groups are represented. The capacity to speak feelings—a deceptively simple but actually quite difficult task—remains undeveloped, even as both groups struggle with a range of intense feelings. As human beings, we face many choices in life. A basic one, raised to a critical level in the midst of group conflict, is to speak or to act. At the very least, as the American official we met at the beginning of this chapter suggested, it would be good to know how to do the former.

CHAPTER 12

The stones speak: historical trauma and cultural healing

A few years ago, Professor Diane O'Donoghue, of the Tisch College of Citizenship and Public Service at Tufts University, spent several months at the Austen Riggs Center's Erikson Institute as an Erikson Scholar. In a lecture entitled "A Cemetery's Lament" (2014), she told an astonishing story, deeply related to citizenship and public service but also to trauma and healing. Diane is trained in art history and archaeology. Within these disciplines, the phrase, *saxa loquuntur*—"the stones speak"—refers to the study of ancient inscriptions and, more generally, to the meaning of ruins. But Freud extended the use of this Latin phrase by describing, in *Studies on Hysteria* (1895d), the psychoanalytic process as a kind of archaeological exploration of early childhood trauma. Diane included a psychological perspective in her presentation, and this chapter is based on my discussion of her paper.

The story

The *Währinger Friedhof* is Vienna's oldest surviving Jewish cemetery and the second oldest—after St. Marx cemetery, where Mozart is buried—in the city. It was established in the 1780s and expanded in the nineteenth century, as the progressive government of Emperor Franz Josef welcomed subjects of the Habsburg Empire—including the Freud family—to the imperial city. By the end of the century, having outgrown the Währinger space, the Jewish community established a new cemetery farther away. The Währinger was closed to new burials, but remained open and well maintained, a memorial space in a quiet, garden-like enclosure. This lasted until 1938, when, after the Nazi *Anschluss* and the reunification of Germany and Austria, the Währinger, like so many other Jewish sites, became the object of anti-Semitic hatred. Attacked by Nazis during the war, it was neglected by the city after the war, except for the occasional effort to protect it from desecration by local vandals.

Professor O'Donoghue noticed the cemetery quite by accident, on her daily trips into the city for her research. What struck her first was the anomaly of a derelict property in a city that prides itself on its grand architecture. The Währinger occupies five acres—twice the size of the land on which the original World Trade Center stood in New York—not far from the center of Vienna and along a route to the famed Vienna Woods. She soon learned that the Währinger was an old Jewish cemetery and that a local Jewish historian offered periodic tours. That tour turned out to be an "overwhelming," life-changing experience. (All quotes attributed to her come from her 2014 presentation.)

The cemetery gate opened onto "8,000 broken headstones, desecrated graves, graffiti and seventy years of overgrown trees and greenery." The first grave Diane came across was that of a man who was born in Odessa and died in Vienna in the middle of the nineteenth century. His monument, like Mozart's and others of that era, was a tall, neoclassical column, intentionally broken in the middle to signify a fallen hero. Because he was an assimilated Jew, his family had chosen not to place Jewish symbols on the headstone and used German for the inscription, which included a poem by the German-Jewish poet, Heinrich Heine. Diane speculated that the Nazis who destroyed the cemetery made a crucial "misreading," one that became central to how this story unfolded: The attackers must have thought that the grave was not that of a Jewish person, and so they did not reduce the stone to rubble or rub out the name of the person buried there, as was the fate of so many other graves.

Diane would come to realize that she was a descendant of this man. She had known about the family's lineage in Odessa but not that this ancestor had died in Vienna. In a further incredible twist to the story, she learned that because she had a relative buried in the Währinger and because, on her father's side, she was an EU, and therefore Austrian, citizen, she could join the tour guide—one of the increasingly rare surviving relatives of those buried in the cemetery—to legitimately petition the Austrian government to form a descendants' organization. This they did, leading to a completely unexpected turn of events.

A secret

The psychoanalyst Adam Phillips writes:

> People come for psychoanalysis … when they find that they can no longer keep a secret. What was once private has become, in spite of oneself, unbearable. A symptom is always the breaking of a confidence … From a psychoanalytic point of view, a symptom is a (secret) way of asking for something (forbidden) … a sign of a wish to make something known, but by disguising it … Freud presented [us] with [a] paradox … You can only tell yourself a secret by telling someone else. (1996, pp. 33–34)

Professor O'Donoghue notes that the Währinger cemetery "is operating within the political psyche of Vienna." Assuming that we can think in these terms, might the Währinger represent a secret that has now become unbearable to the Viennese psyche? Traveling between the outer world and the inner world of Vienna—literally in geographical terms but figuratively in psychological terms—we see the Währinger cemetery, a silent "public blight" in a city devoted to appearances. The stones within the cemetery—Diane reminded her audience of Freud's *saxa loquuntur* quote—are supposed to speak, to remind us of people who have been lost. But most of the stones in the Währinger have been actively or passively destroyed and the inscriptions effaced, one critical exception being that marking the grave of her ancestor. In general, though, this set of potentially speaking stones has been silenced.

And yet, it has been allowed to stand. Might we therefore think of it as an *unconscious monument*, and if these stones are speaking collectively, what might they be saying? Given the glaring incongruity of blight in the midst of grandeur, is the Währinger a symptom, and if so, of what? Diane uses the word *obliterated* to describe the fate of these stones. Etymologically, *obliterate* means *against the letter* and indeed many of the letters on those gravestones have been rubbed out. But the Währinger cemetery itself has not been obliterated, the way that, for example, the bones of Richard III were paved over—albeit accidentally—for the construction of a parking lot in Leicester. Rather, might the Währinger stones be read, as we have done earlier in this volume, through the lens of Poe's *The Purloined Letter* (Muller & Richardson, 1988): the envelope has been torn to shreds, but it's *still on the mantelpiece*. Why?

Professor O'Donoghue writes, "How is it that this place has been allowed to remain in this condition?" Or, at least, that's what she intended to write. What she actually wrote was, "How is it that this place has been allowed to *remind* in this condition?" As though an example of unconscious to unconscious communication Freud spoke about (1913i), her slip suggests an answer to her own conscious question: The Währinger has been allowed to remain in this condition in order to *remind* Vienna of something it needs to remember even if it also desperately wishes to forget. A person can only tell themselves a secret by telling someone else, says Phillips. In their seeming silence, are the stones of the Währinger actually breaking a confidence about an increasingly unbearable secret?

It may be true that, at some perhaps more conscious level of the Viennese psyche, the Währinger is indeed meant to be a reminder: that the persecutory impulse still exists and that fear should be taken seriously. After all, the graffiti on the cemetery's walls now is a "Get out" message addressed to all outsiders, as though to say, "We did this once; we can do it again." In fact, Professor O'Donogue suggests that one meaning of the Währinger's having been left in a state of public ruin was that it concretized "a fantasy of a posthumous Nazi victory." But there is a second unconscious possibility, which does not exclude the other. Might the Währinger also signify that the psyche or mind of Vienna is split in some way and in dire need of *re-minding*. I use that word in a double sense, to denote not only the work of remembering but also the work of psychic reintegration, of bringing together parts of the mind that have been split off and projected into others. Before this can happen, the Viennese psyche must hold its symptom, this disturbing Thing called Währinger, in some middle distance—not formed as memory but not really obliterated either.

Vienna's insistence on its post-war rehabilitation can sound defensive, very much in the direction of the *totalism* Erikson described (1959, p. 133). The Nazi bad is out there; the Austrian good is in here. But does that insistence mask despair about Erikson's *essential wholeness*, and is the Währinger the disguised, repudiated signifier of what Vienna, so far, has not been able to integrate within itself? Vamık Volkan (1981) might think of the Währinger as a *linking object*, something that links to the lost other while also arresting the mourning process—placing it in some frozen, dissociated, buried place—until the person is strong enough, or has the right human resources for, coming to grips with grief. Diane calls the Währinger a "phantasm," and it is. It's a ghost that haunts—and is allowed to haunt—Vienna. Efforts to destroy it can be seen as mad efforts to kill a ghost, to re-repress a repressed that always returns.

Broken glass

Glass shards and barbed wire on top of the walls surrounding the Währinger, in an effort to protect it from vandals, did not keep them out. Diane wonders, "What is kept in, and what kept out?" in this stark way. Or perhaps, what is kept separate by this wall? From one angle, the wall may well represent the split in the Vienna political psyche characteristic of what the psychoanalyst Melanie Klein calls the paranoid–schizoid position (1946). That is, in an effort to keep separate the good and the bad—played out by the Nazis as an ethnic distinction, but played out now in the city's fight with vandals—the Viennese psyche may be making what it feels to be an existentially necessary effort to keep separate the good and bad within itself.

One of the government's responses to early efforts by Professor O'Donoghue's group to restore the Währinger was that, because the cemetery was so badly in disrepair, it was actually dangerous for workers to enter it. Might we wonder if these stones were speaking to Vienna on a deeper level, a level at which entering the Währinger might truly be dangerous? A further clue in this direction also lies on the mantelpiece. The subtitle of Diane's presentation was "Desecration and Responsibility along Vienna's *Gurtel*." The first word was used several times throughout the paper, and the theme of desecration was prominent. The second word—responsibility—disappeared completely. What happened to the question of responsibility and does its disappearance speak to the core problem?

Indeed, might we imagine that, unconsciously, the purpose of desecration—the motive behind the cemetery's destruction and abandonment—was to make responsibility disappear? As though those who enacted the Viennese psyche were trying to de-sacralize the very martyrs their ancestors helped to create. Rather than "desecration and responsibility," perhaps it's "desecration *because* responsibility," because the guilt implicit in that responsibility would be unbearable. Might we think of the enactments around the Währinger as *repeating*, and also preserving in the service of *remembering*, history? If so, what would *working through*—the third term in Freud's trilogy (1914g)—look like?

All Saints' Day

At the moment she learned that she and the tour guide could form a descendants' advocacy organization for the Währinger, Professor O'Donoghue experienced a "seismic shift of identity." From what to what, I wondered? As I heard how this astonishing story played out, it seemed to me that the shift was from gifted, passionate, careful academician to *unwitting therapist*. How often have we therapists heard at the beginning of treatment the anxiety that some problem or story or relationship issue cannot be safely entered? But, in the face of Vienna's and their own anxiety, Diane and her colleague actively *decided* to enter. They finished the necessary paperwork, and, after considerable resistance, on New Year's Eve, 2009—the night of Vienna's world-renowned ball and the day before people make new resolutions—the government *decided* to approve their petition. It's worth remembering that the word *decide* has the same root as the word *homicide* or *suicide*; at some level, the alternative is over, and the parties to this decision are in a new, if also conflicted, place.

Further, because, even after the agreement, funding from the city was slow in coming, Diane's Viennese colleagues made the amazing decision to ask for help in cleaning the cemetery from the Viennese public. From the angle of psychotherapy, this is an intuitively brilliant decision because it invites the patient into treatment. It invites the Viennese public—carrying, among other things, an emotional legacy related to perpetration—to enter a process of both mourning and potential healing, a process of feeling and coming to terms with history, a movement from the paranoid–schizoid position to what Klein called the depressive position (1946).

What was the response to this powerful invitation? Professor O'Donoghue calls it "a gesture of breathtaking humanity." On All Saints' Day—a holiday in Austria and a holy day of remembrance—a stunningly large number of people showed up to clean and repair the cemetery, most of whom were not Jewish. A prominent but now terminally ill Nazi sympathizer, through the intercession of the next generation, owned his denied Jewish identity and recanted his past. A terrified Jewish family spoke the names of long-dead relatives for the first time in their son's memory, as he traced the largely effaced letters on the stone. The daughter of a Nazi grave destroyer said: "I *decided* the time had come ... Now the stones can be seen again." It was as though a psychological barrier had been dissolved; stones were *touched* repeatedly and, with that touch, feeling returned to those doing the touching. Contact with the dead brought life back to the living.

A child shall lead them

In the fall of 2012, the Erikson Institute, having devoted considerable study to the transmission of trauma from one generation of victims to the next, held a conference on generational trauma within the families of perpetrators. It was an extremely powerful event, as reported in Chapter 7. Among other things, it illustrated how very hard it is, even generations later, to break free from group dynamics in which old roles are mobilized again. It also made clear that the offspring of perpetrators are often completely devoted to—if not at times obsessed with—reparation. One complication of that drive is that their offspring—the third generation—often want to live their own lives, unburdened by the crimes of the first generation and the debts of the second. But, in Vienna, in the case of the Nazi sympathizer who owned his Jewish ancestry, it was the second generation who first came for a tour of the Währinger and the third generation—a fourteen-year-old schoolboy—who showed up, with his classmates and his family's blessing, to participate in the restoration.

There are at least two points to be made about this therapeutic process. First, as just noted, a child shall lead them. This kind of societal repair/reparation process is most likely to be led by the next and next next generations. A few years ago, a folksinger named Clare Burson released an album called *Silver and Ash* (2010), which told the story of her grandmother, who had escaped Leipzig in 1938, just before Kristallnacht, and who lost her parents in the Holocaust. Clare wanted to learn whatever she could about these terrible experiences, despite being warned by her mother that her grandmother had never been able to speak about them. Later, Clare said that her grandmother had spent "so much time trying not to remember that she successfully blocked the memories" (Jacobs, 2010).

During her college years, Clare decided to study in Germany. Her grandmother was shocked when she learned this: "Why in the world ...?" "She thought I was crazy," Clare said (Jacobs, 2010). They then had a "frank conversation," in which Clare, for the first time, used "incredibly charged words," like "Nazi" (Lunden, 2010). At the end of their talk, her grandmother asked Clare a stunning question: "And why haven't you invited me to go too?" Dumbfounded, Clare responded, "I never dreamed you would want to go." Her grandmother responded: "I will, for you." Clare writes: "The following spring, the memories began to flow ... We walked through the market square. She pointed out where her boyfriend Berny had a jewelry shop ... the building of her father's business ... the building she grew up in" (Jacobs, 2010). "It used to be so green," her grandmother said (Lunden, 2010). Clare Burson's *Silver and Ash* helped to heal a "rupture ... where there was no continuity between my past and my future ... It's our duty to hear the stories and incorporate them into our own lives ... I'm a grandchild of someone who fled Nazi Germany. I've lived my life feeling the effect of that. And I know I'm not alone" (Jacobs, 2010).

The psychoanalyst Dori Laub (2018), himself a Holocaust survivor, writes that the treatment of trauma, whether in the first or subsequent generations, involves the communication of "testimony" to a witness "[willing] to be totally present to the survivor, and [to] receive as well as experience what he/she wants to transmit" (p. 102). The transmission of trauma from one generation to the next can be seen as an ambivalent effort to give testimony and to find a witness. This is potentially dangerous for both parties but it is often so important to a person who has found herself in the role of unconscious witness to a parent's societal trauma. As Clare Burson so beautifully shows us, the task of the child-now-adult shifts from living out silent family suffering to bearing witness, so that the family's deeply personal story of tragedy is no longer dissociated from the human narrative. This can be a healing process not only for the younger generation, but also for the older ones who have suffered so profoundly.

A child shall lead them, via a process that involves *decision*—a conscious, courageous break with, even the risk of betrayal of, the older generation—in the service of healing. It's an effort toward the psychic wholeness of the family—and of a society—who desperately need, as the father of the fourteen-year-old schoolboy put it, "to figure things out." This kind of leadership risks the transmission of trauma upward, so to speak, from child to parent. This schoolboy, and all those who dared to enter the Währinger, re-minded the older generation of its traumatic past and traumatizing actions. They spoke to the split-off lost mind of that generation and brought the warded-off Bad into proximity with the defensively brittle Good. This kind of action potentially triggers genuine identity crisis, if not actual psychosis, but it also holds together the mix of good and bad elements necessary for depressive position maturation. From this angle, the Währinger's destruction could be seen as Vienna's transmission of trauma—trauma heaped upon its citizens and committed by its citizens—and its continued existence could be seen as its call for potentially healing testimony. Indeed, "I will, for you"—whether from a suffering relative, a group of volunteers or a government—is a profound statement of love.

The political psyche

Professor O'Donoghue and her colleague provided a *clinical* intervention into this transmission, and the public's response on All Saints' Day suggested a powerful *readiness* within the Viennese psyche to come to terms with their own traumatic past as perpetrators or descendants of perpetrators. They unwittingly stepped into and opened up a societal psychotherapy process, and took that society into psychotherapeutic care—for better or worse. In mobilizing a powerful reparative drive, they also opened up a process of great pain, which inevitably evokes resistances.

Among the most powerful of those resistances—woven into its postwar large-group identity—was the way that the effort to restore the Währinger triggered a sense of victimization. From one angle, we might conceptualize government as the conservative, if not defensive, center, the sometimes far too brittle ego, of a country's psyche. While the ego has the task of acknowledging reality—so that critical adaptations can be made—it may also be willing to sacrifice that task in the service of protecting collective self-esteem. One way some large groups do this is by developing a narrative of themselves as victims of another group's perpetration, and therefore as not responsible for the actions they too participated in. I mentioned earlier that the word *responsibility* disappeared from Diane's paper. Actually the word was used one more time, when city officials declared the restoration of the Währinger to be the responsibility of the Jewish community, not of the city. In fact, the Jewish community was a tiny, aging group whose small size was the direct result of German and Austrian actions, and who bore no responsibility whatsoever for the destruction visited upon the cemetery.

But, as Professor O'Donoghue noted, "cracks" in the defensive structure were developing. The examples she gave from that amazing All Saints' Day could "be seen as a subversion of the function this space (the Währinger cemetery) has been designated to play," the function of warning foreigners to get out. While this is true, the examples can also be seen as the *fulfillment* of another unconscious function it was designated to play: the function of reintegrating the Viennese psyche via the resumption of a warded-off mourning process.

This function of reintegration or *wholeness* is captured beautifully in a story Diane referred to, of a young girl (Wolf, 1980) who became *able to feel again*. She accomplishes this through the experience of sadness, for which she did not have a name. Having been trained to believe that some emotions are "improper," this little girl "had long ago begun to cheat herself out of her true feelings." As had the Vienna psyche cheated itself out of the true feelings of sadness, compassion, and a guilt so crushing it was felt—perhaps to some degree accurately—as unsurvivable: at least until a new generation—with the kind of help Diane and her colleagues provided—could risk "the beautiful, free correlation between emotions and events" (Wolf, 1980).

It is precisely this freedom—to feel whatever is to be felt in relation to human events—that mends the split psyche and restores wholeness to a society. In the years since that All Saints' Day, the cleaning of the cemetery has become an annual event with many more opportunities to assist in cleaning and take tours. Thousands of people have taken the tour and many have contributed to the cemetery's restoration. Members of the progressive party successfully petitioned the city to fund major repairs. Even further, in a gesture that declares "they are us," this political party led a movement to have the Währinger officially designated as a National Property, at a future time to be associated with the city's historical museum. Last year, with the help of Professor O'Donoghue, her colleagues and two forensic archaeologists, a rabbi led a service to re-bury the remains of Währinger's deceased. "Breathtaking humanity" indeed, and a profound moment in the long arc from historical trauma to cultural healing.

CHAPTER 13

Traveling through time: a group intervention in Northern Ireland

In 2013, several members of the International Dialogue Initiative were invited to design and facilitate a set of meetings to address an outbreak of violence in Belfast, the capital of Northern Ireland. Over the course of thirty years, sectarian violence between Protestants and Catholics—a period known as The Troubles—had led to more than 3,500 deaths. A lengthy, sometimes turbulent peace process culminated in the Good Friday Agreement of 1998, which, more or less, ended the fighting and established a power-sharing government. The agreement has held for two decades, though outbreaks of violence do occur periodically—this one over escalating tensions about the protocol for flying the Union flag. Given this terrible history, such a resurgence is always of great concern.

This particular Retreat brought together high level representatives from all five of Northern Ireland's major political parties as well as civic leaders from various segments of society (senior police officers, the Gaelic Athletic Association, clergy, a business executive, and leaders of NGOs, including a representative of a victims' organization). Organized by an ecumenical group, the meeting was held over two days at a remote

Retreat house on the north coast. Five formal one-and-a-half-hour sessions took place over this time; members of the Retreat, the ecumenical group, and the facilitating team shared meals and engaged informally outside the sessions.

There were twenty-one invited participants and a team of five IDI facilitators, of which I was one. The team was led by Dr. Vamık Volkan (2013, 2020), whose study of societal conflict, as reported in Chapter 11, was galvanized by two moments: the first when his medical school friend was killed in the civil war in Cyprus; the second when Anwar Sadat, the then president of Egypt, said that the trouble between Arabs and Israelis was "70% psychological." Dr. Volkan, while carrying on a psychoanalytic practice, immersed himself in projects related to the psychological understanding of societal conflict, working over long periods of time with Turks and Kurds, Israelis and Arabs, Estonians and Russians, among others. Later, as a Scholar at the Erikson Institute of Austen Riggs, he founded the International Dialogue Initiative. The IDI is now an independent network of professionals from various nations and various disciplines whose task is to develop psychological understanding and interventions to address large-group conflict.

At the Retreat, the agreed-upon task was to explore and diagnose underlying *psychological obstacles* to a more peaceful and stable Northern Ireland. The IDI team's aim was not to focus on individual dynamics, except to the degree that they might represent the larger group and societal dynamic. Participants in this kind of meeting—because they are embedded in the identity of their groups and because the immediate group dynamic pushes for it—inevitably function as informal spokespersons for the groups they represent. By listening to personal stories and observing interactions among the participants, the team tried to understand, name, and describe various processes that occur in and between large groups in Northern Ireland: Catholics and Protestants, Unionists and Nationalists, and various political and community organizations. Our effort was to help participants go beyond political statements and talk openly about emotional issues that might be very difficult to speak about. In this way, we hoped to explore what was going on in the communities in conflict and how the emotional legacy of The Troubles was manifesting itself currently.

Bullets through time

"Bullets don't just travel through skin and bone. They travel through time." As noted in the Introduction, this statement was tattooed onto the shoulder of a young woman whose father was shot during The Troubles. It captures the emotional legacy of trauma, the way that the next generation and even subsequent generations must deal with what happened to people they loved and are deeply connected to. Sometimes this transmission leads to further violence, sometimes to mourning and reparative efforts. One way or the other, it's on the skin, so to speak; it's an inescapable part of a person's emotional life.

In Northern Ireland, real resolution of emotional difficulties has been difficult to achieve. There is considerable suspicion and a resigned weariness about reconciliation efforts. Some participants in the Retreat wondered if this set of conversations would be genuinely useful or, as one participant put it on the first day of the gathering, "just going around in the cement mixer again." As we have seen throughout this volume, spontaneous metaphors are revealing. "Going around in the cement mixer" seems fruitless, but it also prevents a dangerous hardening. The metaphor raises a question about this sort of peace-making effort: Whether or not a given intervention proves valuable, is the continued work preventive in itself? Does it at least keep things in motion and some measure of hope alive?

The hand

The day before the Retreat began, my IDI colleague, Dr. Robi Friedman, arrived and brought a small gift to the member of our team who had initiated the project, Lord John Alderdice. A citizen of Northern Ireland himself, Lord Alderdice was deeply involved in the peace process for years (Alderdice, 2010) and, when the Good Friday Agreement was finally negotiated, he was elected the first Speaker of the Assembly. The gift was a porcelain hand making a sign of peace. That evening, Dr. Friedman and I encountered a different hand. As the sun was setting, we walked down the hill, along the coast, and into a small town, where we visited a pub. We sat at the bar, ordered our pints, and chatted about the upcoming meeting. The atmosphere was jovial on the surface but edgy underneath. A man seemed to be singing loudly into his friend's ear. The young woman behind the bar looked at her regulars with resigned exasperation.

Then a young man—perhaps in his thirties—sitting next to my colleague abruptly introduced himself, welcomed us to the pub, and asked where we were from. He seemed completely drunk, an impression confirmed by his garrulous speech and by his repeatedly thrusting his hand toward us for handshakes over the next half hour. We were taken aback, not just by his raucous intrusion but by the fact that all of the fingers on his right hand had been cut off at the knuckle. This man seemed to have been the victim of an industrial accident. He was both very friendly to us but also very angry, and he seemed to want us to see what, from a psychoanalytic angle, was his castrated hand. As we walked back to the Retreat house, my friend and I felt we had encountered something profoundly painful in Northern Ireland's current culture.

Leadership

In the formal meetings of the Retreat, four members of the IDI facilitating team sat in a large circle with enough chairs for the other twenty-one invited participants. A fifth IDI facilitator sat with the small ecumenical group outside the circle. They remained silent during the discussions, taking up an observer role, perhaps representing, psychologically speaking, the Northern Ireland public in general, on whose behalf the main group was working. After each session, the IDI facilitator met with them separately, collected their impressions about what they had observed, and helped them understand the interventions of the facilitating team. The IDI facilitators also met privately after the sessions, evaluating what they had observed and learned, listening to reports of the observers' views, and making decisions about how to proceed during the next session. At the end of the last session, a summary of the facilitators' findings and the observer's perceptions were shared with everyone in the room for general discussion.

As the first meeting was about to begin, we learned that one participant had had to drop out and another would be arriving late. Thus there were two empty chairs in the large circle, which happened to be the two chairs on either side of the lead facilitator, Dr. Volkan. This may seem like a strange coincidence, but, in my experience, when people enter a group—especially an emotionally charged group—they pay subtle attention to where they sit. What did it mean that no one sat next to the lead facilitator? One hypothesis would be that he represented authority, perhaps authority attributed to him as an accomplished person, but also the authority of someone who represented the risky task they were about to take up. Thus there may well have been some fear in the group's reactions to Dr. Volkan. Perhaps also, in such a bitterly contested larger environment, no one wanted to be seen as trying to curry favor with the person in authority by sitting next to him.

But this potential pairing dynamic—that is, the wish to gain advantage by forming a power couple with the person in authority—seemed present in an informal moment just before the session began. This moment too involved a hand. A young charismatic politician from one of the Nationalist parties—a party that wants Northern Ireland to unite with the larger Republic of Ireland—reached out to shake hands with Dr. Volkan, and said "Welcome to Ireland!" Not "Welcome to Northern Ireland." The struggle to have the person representing authority on one side and not the other seemed to have begun. In fact, the desperate search for a leader was the first major theme of the conversation. In various ways, people communicated an intense need for someone who had the power to contain and tame aggression, someone or something that could function as a stabilizing third structure. First, the police officers in the group were turned to. When the senior police representatives tried to explain *logically* how the Northern Ireland police institution worked—that it could not serve a partisan purpose or, in an effort to manage such widespread aggression, turn the society into a police state—disappointment ensued. The officers felt "caught in the middle" in this group as they also felt themselves to be in the society.

Then the participants searched for other symbolic "leaders," such as religious institutions and even business organizations. The clergy in the room at times attempted to fill this role, sometimes movingly, other times with frustration. One clergyman's story of how he called on his community to reclaim their church square from militants was a concrete and, it turned out, successful example of a citizen's effort to claim the societal space. Then a business leader pleaded that the economy and education were crucial bridging issues, if only groups could get past their rage. Finally, someone petitioned for a "bill of rights." The facilitators spoke to the participants' preoccupation with finding a stabilizing "leader," an institution, a focus (in psychoanalytic terms, a "shared superego") to help contain frightening, potentially destructive feelings. Since the overall population was fragmented, no one leader in Northern Ireland was currently able to do that. No one was able to help this traumatized large group restore its basic trust in each other and in a way of living together.

Dr. Volkan's leadership was exercised primarily in the management of the event. Sessions started and ended on time. Dr. Volkan set out the task at the beginning, invited people to speak openly and personally about their problematic experiences, and asked the group for a critical authorization. "I ask you, with all due respect, to allow me to say 'Shut up!' if I feel someone is giving a speech," he said. This elicited laughter and easy consent from the group, but it was extremely important to the group's confidence that, at least in the microcosm of the Retreat, someone would indeed manage aggression. And, managing it made it possible to talk about it specifically and directly. Another important intervention early on was Dr. Volkan's question to a man who reported having been in jail for a considerable period of time. "What were you in jail for?" Dr. Volkan asked. "Murder," the man said, in front of police officers, though he added that, from his point of view, he was a soldier who had killed in combat.

The group and the community

During the initial session, the women—none of whom were politicians—were completely silent. This eventually came to represent the silence of almost all of the non-political leadership, who seemed to be living out one person's idea that they were "spare parts." Again, an interesting metaphor; "spare parts" conveys a sense of being useless, but in fact, they are essential when something breaks down. On the other hand, the politician members of the group spoke easily, although in ways that sounded at first like party platforms. As a way of grounding themselves in their political identities and establishing security at the beginning of an anxiety-arousing discussion, this way of speaking made a certain kind of sense. But it was not a dialogue across representatives of different groups nor was it personal. The team noted that real dialogue across the political/non-political boundary was difficult, and so for a while the conversation was in a state, as one member put it, of "suspended animation," just as the politics of Northern Ireland were.

When this was noticed and understood, women among the participants were able to find their voices and to include the feelings they had kept silent about. One set of feelings erupted in response to a story one of the clergy told, a poignant story about having bought a new tie for a family celebration and then, to his shock, being greeted with a bitter question about whether he was ashamed to wear his collar. Initially, the group did not pick up on the obvious pain this man brought to the discussion. But when a facilitator noted the potential emotional obstacle of shame, another member burst into a rage: "How dare you speak about shame?" she said to the facilitator. "There is so much shame in all of us that, if we allowed ourselves to feel it, we would all kill ourselves."

This almost primal outburst highlighted two emotional obstacles to the group's and perhaps the community's moving forward. First, to speak the feelings made them real. It was as though the facilitator had not simply heard what the clergyman had just said about shame; he had made it real by speaking it. In this sense, he had inflicted it on the group. Second, having become real, the shame was now dangerous, dangerous to the very community essential to getting through these terrible feelings. "We would all kill ourselves" is a profound statement about the community-in-the-mind: that it simply would not survive the intense feelings of its members. These participants seemed to be saying that there was no holding environment for them, no collective capacity to contain together the shame of actions done to each other over so many years. Hence the longing for some Third outside the community to serve this function.

Betrayal

Other intolerable feelings eventually came into the conversation: guilt for abandoning past injustices, wishes for retribution intermixed with, and sometimes identified with, demands for justice, and existential fear of the other group. To some degree, the emotional engagement around shame seemed to free members, especially among the non-political subgroup, to join the discussion, while those in political leadership seemed more invested, and perhaps more stuck, in their positions. Was this the result of how powerfully they were carrying their constituencies' pain, grievances, and difficulty grieving? Ironically, the phrase "political class" was used a number of times, a phrase that could suggest being "above" the people. But did this distract all concerned from how embedded political leadership is in the most basic and stubborn feelings of the people? Is this one reason that it can be difficult to exercise real leadership in the face of constituents' resistance?

This brought up the nature of the loyalty to one's group. Actual feelings of loyalty to one's group intermixed with fear of being seen as disloyal, and seemed to bind members of the same group together, both in the meeting and probably in the society as well. As one member put it, "I'm part of a group that will be suspicious of you, so I'm morally bound to be suspicious." And, more frighteningly, should one be or appear to be disloyal, "… the danger is from our own group." The history of The Troubles is full of lethal punishment for real or suspected disloyalty. This question of loyalty presents an enormous problem for political leaders, who are elected by a part of the community but must lead the whole community. In the context of violent rivalries, there is a major risk—to electability and perhaps to safety—in being seen as betraying one's own group. But real leadership sometimes requires what a colleague calls "virtuous betrayal" (Krantz, 2006), that is, a leader's taking decisions that may betray a narrow, emotional, and even self-defeating interest of a constituency in favor of a greater, encompassing good. One politician described how his bipartisan work on the damage sectarian fighting had done to children's education was met with a grandmother's rage that he would dare talk with the people who had killed her grandson. "My dilemma," he said, is: "I betray the past or I betray the future."

Grievance and grief

This grandmother's pain captures the distinction between grievance and grief. The legacy of The Troubles is full of deep grievances that, at a psychological level, function as a powerful defense against grief. Grievance looks toward a future in which revenge of some sort or at least some compensatory righting of a grievous wrong will occur. Grief, on the other hand, is about a loss that is now in the past. Whatever has been lost, usually a person, is irrecoverable. In one sense, there is no future, certainly for the lost loved one, but also, as it is felt by those left behind, for the grief-struck as well. The only real way forward is through mourning, but the trauma of sudden loss makes opening up the mourning process very difficult, especially for those who have suffered so many losses over so long a time.

As the sessions proceeded, we began to hear more personal stories, which were very moving. Because the group had begun to work with each other and with us, and because time was short, Dr. Volkan made a critical intervention:

> I am sure that most you in this room and perhaps all of you have experienced losses during The Troubles. You lost family members, friends, things that you deeply value. Psychologically, it is obligatory that after important losses, people mourn. People die, things disappear, but their images, their "mental doubles" remain in our minds. We have an internal relationship with these mental doubles, which goes on until we say goodbye to them over time, until they become futureless, so to speak. If everything goes well such internal relationships slowly come to rest. But, in Northern Ireland such losses were linked to severe traumas and conflicts. So, my hunch is that such mental doubles are still very much around. What do they tell you?

Initially there was anger about this intervention because it invited the participants to open up very difficult emotions. At least two participants stated that they were not there "to be psychoanalyzed." They even suggested that the facilitator needed their permission before making this statement. Clearly, a frightening question had entered people's thoughts; if the community might kill itself because of shame, how could it survive the unbearable grief built up over so many years? Soon, however, the dynamics changed when one member dared to speak his own mind. "Are you kidding?" he said to the more resistant group members. "Ghosts are everywhere in Northern Ireland!"

Following this, participants began to talk about lost friends and relatives, and about what those "ghosts" were telling them, so to speak. They began to realize that, without going through and dealing with their complicated grief reactions, unspoken feelings remained alive in the mourner. At a group level, being stuck in a shared but warded-off mourning process forces traumatized communities to unconsciously hold on to other problematic emotions: survival guilt, wishes for revenge, shame for being friendly with the opposite side, guilt for abandoning past injustices, an unending list of grievances, and confusion about how to deal with victims. This discussion showed that even rational people must deal with "ghosts." Without the presence of a stabilizing "leader," this group (representing Northern Ireland's various communities) seemed to need outsiders (the facilitators) to help open and care for these "wounds." Now they were beginning to see how the intensity and pervasiveness of traumatic loss had become a profound emotional obstacle to peacemaking.

Another hand

One of the Nationalist leaders repeatedly stated how his party was extending its open hand to political opponents in order to "move forward," but that that gesture was always rejected. The facilitators noted that representatives of the Unionist parties—who want Northern Ireland to remain a part of the United Kingdom—were suspicious of these overtures. They felt that Nationalists had not really renounced what for the Unionists was an existentially threatening strategy, but had simply changed their tactics. Nationalists might give lip service to the reconciliation process but not really engage with it. The Nationalist side seemed unable to understand or alter this part of the dialogue. To them, the Unionists in the group seemed split among their various parties, unclear about their stance, silenced by their own colleagues, and not ready to meet the offer of an "open hand."

Did this stalemate represent what was happening with the majority of the silent electorate, who might themselves feel culturally and politically disempowered? Were Unionists worried about simply surviving (in contrast to the main Nationalist party's sense that it was thriving)? Were they worried about feeling abandoned by the British Government, or something else? We did not have time to fully understand all of these issues. Nationalists did not seem curious about their opponents' refusal to join them and did not present their own genuine arguments for societal change. Nor was empathy for the other's experiences a part of the culture of communication between these groups; it was as though empathy risked betrayal of one's own side and humiliation by the other. Meanwhile, "The Hand" once again emerged as a metaphor for working toward peace or refusing it.

In this context, Lord Alderdice found himself thinking about the mythic origins of Northern Ireland, and he brought to the facilitators' and the participants' attention the meaning of the Irish symbol, the Red Hand. According to mythology, the North had no rightful owner and was claimed by the two most powerful clans in the South. The clans' leaders agreed to a race between the fastest runner from each clan; whoever's hand first touched the land of the North would be its owner. As the two runners neared their goal, one saw that he was about to lose and so cut off his hand and threw it ahead onto the soil of the North. Thus, a claim was made and the battle started. The bloody "Red Hand of Ulster" is actually a ubiquitous symbol in Northern Ireland and emerged in the discussion as a powerful metaphor, capturing a deep, life-or-death sense of rivalry between two warring groups. The story—a story not only of rivalry but of bad faith agreements—and its being told in this moment, felt like a powerful intervention. An important historical and cultural context—a Genesis story really—had been discovered, one that cast grave doubts on what it meant to work together.

The myth of the Red Hand of Ulster brought to our attention another "hidden" emotional factor that most likely plays a role in preventing a settling of The Troubles in Northern Ireland: a stubbornly enduring, conscious and unconscious culture of rivalry, which stirs the adrenalin even if its actual goals are mythic and its means of achieving them unfair. After the Retreat, we learned more about how the symbol of the Red Hand is very much "alive" in Northern Ireland. It is part of the provincial and political flags of Northern Ireland. Its image is deployed frequently by the Ulster Volunteer Force and other loyalist paramilitaries (including the Red Hand Commandos). The Gaelic Athletic Association uses it for one of its county teams. A Red Hand marks burial plots maintained by the National Graves Association, adorns stained-glass windows in

Belfast's City Hall, and even advertises the services of Indian palmists. For decades, the Red Hand was the logo for the Northern Ireland Tourist Board, though it has since been replaced by a heart. As we saw in Chapter 6, people sometimes put right there on the mantelpiece a critical signifier of their trouble, which then becomes unconscious to them, the kind of secret, Adam Phillips (1996) says, that one can only tell oneself about by telling someone else.

Respect

In the final session, a young Unionist, who to that point had been the only silent member of the group, said to a Nationalist: "You extend your hand, and say you want us to join you but, when we don't, you interpret that as our problem, rather than asking us *why* we don't join you." He was pointing out how real curiosity was missing from the Nationalists' approach, in favor of presumptions and defensive certainty. It was as though Nationalists felt they already knew the answers, so didn't need to ask the questions. Indeed, it was generally true for the entire group that inquiry into why someone felt a certain way or hesitated about joining was largely missing, as though to genuinely explore issues across this highly charged political boundary was dangerous.

The Unionist then added, referring to a comment made earlier in that session: "And why do you want us to respect your dead? I respect my own dead; I don't need you to respect them." Then, one of the Nationalist members—to that point a jovial, collaborative sort of person—spoke with genuine feeling: "I'll tell you why. When I was growing up, people didn't acknowledge that my mother and father and grandmother even existed, and when they did, they treated them like dirt. So, if they weren't respected in life, I want them respected in death." An NGO leader, formerly a senior police officer, responded, in a way that joined with the facilitators: "That's what they mean by the *ghosts of the past*." Then he said to the Nationalist: "I won't remember much of the political talk here, but I will never forget what you just said."

Words that are unforgettable—unforgettable because so profoundly and personally true—are one of the most important outcomes of any intervention into trauma. In the relatively short time of the Retreat, we noted a number of hopeful progressions. Over the course of five sessions, there was increasing emotional engagement throughout the membership, an increasing capacity to tolerate the expression of feeling, and increasing strength in the voices of the civic leadership. Related to this, there was more person-to-person talk, including, very importantly, the political leaders' speaking personally. After phases of resistance, members joined the facilitating team's consultation and opened up personal experiences of trauma and loss. Finally, new leadership emerged, as did important bridging issues and a number of hypotheses that might shed further light on the emotional dynamics of this conflicted but very appealing community.

The IDI facilitating team left the Retreat feeling very grateful to the participants for the risks they had taken and for their growing trust in our capacity to contain and make sense of the strong feelings they expressed. For various reasons, this was a one-time intervention, the outcomes of which, whatever they were, were carried back by individual members into their political and societal roles. We learned that there were some behind-the-scenes communications between a few participants that seemed to move in a constructive direction. While it was probably being planned long before the Retreat, the Centre for Democracy and Peace-Building was founded in Belfast not long after the Retreat. Led by two of the Retreat's participants, the CDPB institutionalizes the larger task, of which the Retreat was a part. It tries to find "entry points" within Northern Ireland's political and social dynamics for *actions* that might diminish the power of the psychological obstacles that emerged in the Retreat. In doing so, it works to counter community fragmentation and despair. Traumatized societies are seriously at risk of collapsing back into traumatizing conflict. It is a testament to the Good Friday Agreement and to the perseverance of people, like those who organized and participated in the Retreat, that so far this battered, tenacious, and passionate country has managed to get on with the task of trying to live together.

AFTERWORD

When there are so many: two moments during the pandemic

During the spring of 2020, as the pandemic was reaching its first peak in the United States, the Erikson Institute hosted a series of online conversations, focused broadly on mental health challenges. Participants were invited to speak spontaneously about what they were hearing from their clients as well as what they themselves were struggling with. In providing this opportunity, the Erikson Institute (and I as the host of the event) hoped that "Talking it through"—the title of the series—would lead to deeper understanding and mutual support. We were surprised that so many people attended, but not by the urgency with which they participated.

Identity

"I'm a social person," a younger member of the group said, describing a challenge to her identity, in the Covid context, different from that for a person who might say "I'm a bit of a loner anyway." This was the first theme to emerge in these discussions. A performance artist spoke about not being able to be onstage. There was, he said, desperation—not simply economic—within this community, a feeling of "Please don't forget us," a kind of "out of sight, out of mind" anxiety. A therapist related this to her own "out of office, out of touch" anxiety. Psychotherapy relies on the therapist's getting in touch with a patient's emotional life, which registers in how they look, speak, and move. It seemed so difficult, or at least so much of a slowly developing skill, to do that work online.

These and other experiences required people to find ways to anchor themselves and their sense of identity in this new, strange, anxious context. In some organizations, meditation, mindfulness work, and clearly defining priorities, among other focused activities, were extremely useful in creating space for clear thinking and developing routines. But the Covid crisis also attacked the vulnerabilities—the "pre-existing conditions"—within organizations. For example, one person spoke of the guilt she felt and the resentment she felt from others because her job allowed for online work while theirs did not.

These tensions, which may have been there in some form all along, were heightened in the context of Covid fear. They became a challenge for leadership, whose difficult job required "holding" all these feelings and putting them in the perspective of how every role in its way is contributing to the accomplishment of a critical task. Team restoration became an essential activity, as did building intentionally the opportunities for connection that occurred informally when workers occupied the same space. In a context where anxiety, interpersonal tensions, and loss can tear at the organizational fabric, a sense of communal solidarity was seen as crucial to people's morale and even to their mental health.

Fragility

Organizational fragility during Covid mirrored fragility within the client systems: the fragility of families already suffering chronic stress, the fragility of marginal youth tenuously tethered to sources of help, and the fragility of children trying to hold on to hard-won developmental achievements. In many cases, this fragility too was already there but now more visible. This exposure of family problems, and of severely limited resources to deal with them, made some parents feel vulnerable to the judgment of others, adding to their frustration. Indeed, during the pandemic, parents felt even more charged to manage something they didn't have the power or understanding to manage. How that frustration might be enacted within the family was cause for great worry to those in the mental health community.

The various ways this group of professionals was trying to meet these challenges was impressive. In the face of so many needs and such limited resources, they described their efforts to build a vast safety net of therapist-initiated check-ins, parenting groups, warm lines, psychoeducational sessions, peer support meetings, and other outreach activities. This net couldn't hold everyone—and those building it felt that keenly—but it worked well for many, against the odds in some cases. The essential importance of holding the client in mind came through clearly, especially given the ways that a mind-set of social distancing and online work pull away from that holding. Though the number of volunteers stepping forward and the level of community contribution was very heartening, the stress on the helpers was real: "The work feeds our souls," one said, "and we also tear our hair out."

This stress included the strained boundaries between home life and work life, the difficulty of holding onto mission while feeling disconnected from work, and the different levels of risk staff might be facing with clients. Some mental health staff were "frontline" workers, while others were not, a difference which itself can lead to strain in the system. All of this calls for effective leadership. For some leaders, their view of their role seemed based on having the "answers" in the face of problems. But no one had the answers to Covid, and, for these leaders, their identities and their organizations were shaken. This included parents too, who, as CEOs in the family, struggled with not knowing what everyone, including them, wanted them to know. What emerged in the discussion was the importance of holding the mission as the guiding North Star, being transparent about what one knew and didn't know, and conveying the confidence that "We'll figure it out together."

Surprise

Sometimes this stance required, as another person put it, "Holding on to your hats!" In response to the pandemic, these mental health professionals had gone through a number of phases in rapid succession: initial panic and confusion, surprisingly quick adaptation, learning how to organize their work, a feeling of "Enough now," then anxious anticipation of how reopening might undo everything. There were so many unknowns on the horizon, in the spring of 2020, that people longed for certainty, even though nobody had that, and they dreaded the next hill on the "roller coaster."

A key to adapting seemed to be being open to surprise and learning from it. For example, a peer support group for troubled adolescents was continuing via Zoom, and the young people were showing up! The resources they were bringing to the work and their commitment to it were surprising to the therapist, something she didn't know she could count on. Similarly, clinicians were surprised that they and their child patients were finding ways to do play therapy online. Other things perhaps should not have been so surprising but were; for example, therapists knew that a student's going off to college was a developmental achievement but hadn't fully realized how much being sent home might undo it and invite regression. And college mental health professionals, for the first time, had to think about how to work with the families of their homebound students.

Embracing flexibility is difficult under any circumstances. It's even harder in the face of so many demands and stresses, and in the face of what needs to be given up, at least for a time. One person spoke of the grief she felt in moving from a known, comfortable way of working—one in which her clients had thrived and in which she knew who she was—to whatever new way was emerging. She and others spoke about how the experience of "being with" the client was changing, how it was moving from an easy, natural physical presence to a visual one, which demanded more cognitive focus and, at least until one got used to it, was exhausting. But people also spoke about the two-way visual window into the client's and the clinician's space, an interesting experience in itself leading to interesting questions, for example, about what the therapist's authority was in this new space. A pervasive theme was how important connection was for everyone in these trying times: on social media, through increased team meetings, through calls to clients, and so on. Everywhere, including in these discussion groups, people were "desperate to talk."

Disruption/rethinking

There were so many Covid-related disruptions, large and seemingly small, which required these professionals to rethink things they had "taken for granted." For example, a relief check, designed to help people through the economic consequences of the crisis, opened up for some a craving for substances, which had been tenuously held in check. Or a family used to spreading out during the work day was suddenly confined to a small space, leading to eruptions of frustration, even to domestic violence. Or a child normally at school was exposed to TV images of police brutality and was traumatized. Or a support group functioning well over a period of time was suddenly out of touch with each other because basic survival needs came first and because members had no access to computers or the internet. One first reaction to the latter was "Who knew!" and a second was "How did we not know?"

The pandemic had made visible, indeed had magnified, the disparities that have been there all along, and the vulnerabilities as well. The risk factors for suicide—isolation, unemployment, substance abuse, the presence of guns in a house, and so on—had all increased during Covid. Calls for help and general attention to mental health had as well, but there was great worry in the group about "deaths of despair." The protests that erupted following the killing of George Floyd, which occurred as these conversations were taking place, added to this feeling of disease. One participant said she saw a new "urgency to reckon with" things in her work, particularly where patient and therapist were of different races. She now found that she wanted to bring things into focus more and to have face-to-face conversations about differences, which both parties may have previously avoided in an effort to preserve the other's positive feelings. Though it might seem counterintuitive, risking conversation about negative but honest feelings, as we saw in the Prologue to this volume, leads to a sense of conviction that the relationship "can take it," a strengthening that is a sign of real progress. The loneliness and vulnerability the pandemic has brought are transcended in these encounters, and a trustworthy presence, willing to speak honestly about failures, both in the treatment relationship and in the larger system, is established.

The Covid-19 crisis has opened up various heretofore unseen or unappreciated gaps in society, including in its systems of care. For this group of mental health professionals, it also brought new urgency and creativity to working with those gaps, and gave them a precious opportunity to rethink the future intersection of the delivery of care and of justice. One moving result was the profound gratitude clients expressed when their treaters were willing to take this opportunity.

When there are so many we shall have to mourn

About eight months after these sessions, on February 22, 2021, the United States recorded its 500,000th death from the Covid-19 virus, this in just over one year. It's a staggering number—more than all U. S. casualties in WWI, WWII, and Vietnam combined, a 9/11 death toll every day for five and a half months. W. H. Auden's poem "In Memory of Sigmund Freud" (1940a), with which we began this volume, frames one aspect of the nation's challenge in that first line above. How does loss on such an immense and ongoing scale affect the task of mourning?

Mourning, as my colleague Vamık Volkan (see Chapter 13) often says, is an obligatory process. Human beings do not have a choice about whether the mourning process occurs, only a degree of choice about how it is taken up. Though it has its biological and social dimensions, mourning is, first of all, a psychological process, a process of allowing images and memories of the lost loved one to come to mind, with feeling, in order to integrate them into the internal relationship with that person and to say goodbye to the external relationship. It is a conscious and unconscious process that has its own trajectory, its own pain, and, to be sure, its own complications. For example, unfinished emotional business with the lost other, especially to the degree that it involves negative feelings, may well lead to depression—or, as Freud put it, melancholia (1917e)—rather than mourning. But mourning is made bearable through the help of others and the "holding" sociocultural rituals of bereavement.

The Covid context has profoundly affected this process. It has heightened two kinds of anxiety referred to throughout this volume: a paranoid–schizoid anxiety associated with harm coming from the other person and a depressive anxiety associated with harm I myself might do. To the degree that these forms of harm are linked to less conscious feelings and fantasies about oneself and others, anxiety is amplified. Moreover, the social distancing, necessary to protect oneself and others, affects the mourning process in at least two ways. Certainly, it has interfered with the social and religious rituals of mourning. Wesley Carr, former dean of Westminster and a leader within the field of group relations, designed and conducted the funeral of Princess Diana in 1997. He described in an earlier work (and elaborated later) how the flow of a funeral liturgy is meant to carry mourners into, hold them through, and bring them out of a regressive emotional experience, a collective relaxing of defenses in the service of healing (Carr, 1985; Shapiro, 2019). In the context of Covid, when people cannot gather in this way, how does this happen? Have mourners adapted and found creative ways of doing this? What happens if they haven't?

The second way social distancing has affected mourning occurs in the dying process itself: Loved ones and the person they are losing cannot physically be with one another. In many cases, they can't see and certainly can't touch each other. To the trauma of loss and of helplessness is added the trauma of aloneness for both parties. As we have seen throughout this volume (see Chapter 9), exposure to trauma is mitigated by the emotional presence of others, and intensified by their absence. We might describe dying during the pandemic in the language of Winnicott (1974) from Chapter 1: Covid has introduced a profound emptiness into the dying process, a traumatic moment of "nothing happening" when something extremely important needed to happen.

We have all learned to live with social distancing and to do without the ordinary physicality of human relationships. Largely, people have adapted, from elbow bumps to kisses blown through a mask to closing emails with "Hugs." But for mourners-to-be and for the loved ones they are losing, these adaptations don't work. Even if loved ones view each other through a windowpane or a small screen, it is still "through a glass darkly," and often an excruciating experience of being so near but prevented from the longed-for touch that nearness yearns for. At this point in the Covid trajectory, we don't know what the effects of this emptiness will be on mourners, how they will recognize it within themselves, and how they may find meaningful ways of filling it.

The frailty of our conscience

The next few lines of Auden's poem frame another aspect of mourning in the aftermath of Covid, at least in the context of the United States:

> *When grief has been made so public, and exposed*
> *To the critique of a whole epoch*
> *The frailty of our conscience and anguish;*

As we saw in Chapter 10, rituals of bereavement are affected not only by protective restrictions, like social distancing, but also by society's attitude toward its institutions. For example, in post-WWI Britain (Newcombe & Lerner, 1982), immense loss did not lead to increased churchgoing, as one might expect; in fact, just the opposite. Why? One answer has to do with that society's profound change in attitude toward authority: the governmental authority that had, seemingly so blithely, sent young men to their deaths and the clerical authority that supported it. In their anger and grief, people left divine authority alone on Sunday. Within the field of group psychology, authority became a new area of study.

Trauma—whether traumatizing horror or acute loss—occurs in a context, even if awareness of that context is obliterated in the traumatic moment. Part of healing is the restoration of context, both as a holding environment but also for the task of understanding its contribution to the traumatic experience. We have seen in Chapters 2 and 10 how moral injury—sometimes in the form of traumatic disillusionment—is a major factor in trauma; indeed, in some instances, it *is* the trauma. Is moral injury—witnessing or participating in actions that violate, at the deepest level, a person's sense of what's right—part of the trauma of Covid?

During the first surge of the virus, a mask-less partier on spring break in Tennessee proclaimed "Nashville is undefeated!" In his outburst of protest against Covid restrictions, this young man was representative of a set of attitudes—lived out in super-spreader events—that undoubtedly have contributed to the number of Covid casualties. The politicization of science, of governmental authority, and of what it means to be strong or weak, among other things, reshaped a medical crisis into a social and moral one. In Auden's words, it has exposed "the frailty of our conscience," such that people have acted recklessly, indifferently and cruelly toward others, and thereby brought a new level and kind of "anguish" into American life.

How do members of a society mourn when a significant part of that society is implicated in the loss? How do we deal with the "frailty of conscience" that has brought this about? How is a mourner's grief affected by a powerful grievance against one's community, sometimes one's own family? There may well be, for many mourners, a feeling of moral injury for continuing to participate in such a system. In their anguish and anger, mourners may feel that the community they have been a part of did not deserve their lost loved one, nor do they as mourners want to return to it.

Anguish

There are many other layers of pandemic-related anguish in addition to the anguish of personal loss—the anguish of unemployment, of feeling left behind and discriminated against, perhaps even of Lost Cause humiliation in that rambunctious assertion that "Nashville is undefeated." But Covid anguish also includes a sense of betrayal by both leadership and fellow citizens, a failure of its and our responsibility to protect each other. Largely, this is carried by mourners and health care workers. Indeed, the latter have been one of the groups most traumatized by the pandemic. Of the many powerful accounts of their experiences, a very moving one, by Rana Awdish, is called "The Shape of the Shore" (2020). Awdish describes the chronic gut-level fear frontline health staff feel, fear that they will die of Covid—and they had seen what that was like—or harm those at home. She describes their maddening sense of helplessness, as they face wave after wave of illness and death. She describes the nausea, exhaustion, and desperation to flee. And she describes the cumulative, eventually overwhelming sense of grief, expressed in tears that couldn't be wiped away for fear of touching one's face.

Awdish tells us too how the effort to treat so many Covid patients assaults the health care worker's basic sense of identity. People whose purpose in life is to heal feel like abject failures when they lose so many patients, "the passive drape of their arms off the sides of the gurney …

still silently begging us to save them." One staff member said: "I don't recognize myself anymore, I don't know who I am here. I kept a mother from her own baby. I had to treat her as if she was a threat to her own child." Capturing the guilt and self-loathing, another said: "What kind of a person is so afraid of her own patient that they don't immediately run in to help them? I watched my patient suffocate through a window." Another tried to shock an already dead patient back to life: "It felt like torture … I felt inhuman."

The traumatic feelings of health care workers mirror on a collective scale the deeply personal feelings of the families of the dying, and they share the pain of those last moments. "We used to leave the room when the families would say their goodbyes. It felt sacred, and private. Now I stand there stupidly … I don't want to be the only human contact they have at the end of their life." A dying man's daughter "couldn't bring herself to come in alone, so she asked me to take a picture of her dad's body for her. I didn't know if it was OK … I said a prayer and I took it. I'd never done that before." The task of a doctor resigns itself to the task of a minister.

Like the traumatized veterans of Chapter 10, frontline health staff experience a crazy-making disconnect between their home and work lives. A sense of "absurdity" crept into ordinary tasks, including helping kids with their homework: "No one seemed to understand how little remained of us." And despite the public shows of support—the 8pm candles or grateful noise-making—cynicism also crept in: "The news and our neighbors had labeled it a war. We read it as an attempt to keep us cordoned in the infected city while they remained sheltered in their suburban nests … They hung white ribbons on our own trees and doors, as if we had already gone missing." Psychologists brought in to help fell victim to this cynicism, and some of their interventions seemed to deepen it. Indeed, as we also saw in Chapter 10, well-intentioned help can sometimes minimize the depth of health workers' suffering, such that their accepting it would feel like a denial, even a betrayal, of their actual experience: a moral injury in itself.

Of whom shall we speak

On February 22, 2021—the day the United States reached the "grim heartbreaking milestone" of 500,000 Covid deaths—President Biden addressed the nation's loss and the way that trauma-related defenses work against acknowledging it. With 500 candles in the background, he said that "We have to resist becoming numb to the sorrow. We have to resist viewing each life as a statistic … We must do so to honor the dead. But, equally important, to care for the living." The process of mourning means that those left behind *need* to feel this sorrow, in order to go on as whole persons, and they need to feel it in the company of people who can feel it with them. The black bunting, lowered flags, and moment of silence that followed were meant to lead this process on a collective level. In large and small, traditional and innovative ways, others across the U. S. are doing that too.

Recovery from Covid-related trauma requires this kind of leadership into collective mourning. Beyond acknowledging, remembering, and feeling personal loss at an individual level, something more encompassing is needed by the nation. And, to the degree that the U.S. as a society has not been "in it together," to that degree the healing process requires a larger set of rituals or acts of communal remembering that can be joined over time, even by those who failed to appreciate the level of suffering when it was happening. Memorial moments—and perhaps eventually anniversary ceremonies and monuments—established by national and local leadership assert that those lives mattered. In providing places and times to remember and to honor, to empathize and even forgive, leadership helps people recognize that, in the act of speaking about those we have lost, their lives will speak back to us, and that that process will be healing.

The path forward after the pandemic should include a recognition that what Dr. Awdish and her colleagues—and so many others—experienced "was not a diagnosis but a tragedy" (2020). Traumatic experience is certainly debilitating and can become a diagnosis, especially if there are pre-existing emotional conditions within a person's and a family's life. But healing from traumatic experience, as we have seen throughout this volume, needs a kind of witnessing, a truthfulness, and a being with, at the family, community, and societal levels. Witnessing recognizes the shared nature of the tragedy and resists the drift toward denial, the latter being a primary condition for what makes trauma traumatic. While another "Roaring Twenties" might well be on the horizon, relief and euphoria do not have to become denial, despite pre-existing conditions within American society that might push in that direction. Anniversary rituals, memorial ceremonies, monuments, personal testimonies, and similar forms of honoring, to use a term from Chapter 10, "inscribe" the tragedy, and allow for a healthy "forgetting" because they make space for shared remembering.

EPILOGUE

Anna Freud's drapes

In the early 2000s, quite out of the blue, a woman whom I didn't know called me. Her name was Joan Corell, and she had spent her career teaching psychology at a college about an hour's drive from the Austen Riggs Center, where I was then the director of the Erikson Institute. She said that she was closing her college office and paring down her many possessions. Among those were Anna Freud's drapes, which she felt she could no longer keep. She asked if I wanted them. I said, "Yes, indeed!" and thanked her for thinking of us.

Soon thereafter, a box addressed to me arrived in the Riggs mailroom. It contained two quite large plastic bags of material. Not yet having a plan for them, I put the bags in my office closet, where—given a busy schedule of patients and Erikson Institute activities—I forgot about them, except for the occasional twinge of "Oh yes! What are we going to do with them?" To my shock and embarrassment, considerable time went by, until I came to my own closing up tasks as I prepared to retire from Riggs. At that point, I began to rummage through the closet: its file cabinet, pictures, mugs, and, of course, plastic bags.

When I opened the bags, there, in my hands, were Anna Freud's drapes: long swaths of thickly woven, soft but heavy silk, which felt like chenille; each had thin vertical stripes in creams and golds on a deep brown background, with the occasional wider horizontal band in those lighter colors. They conveyed an aura of warmth, luxuriance, privacy, and old-world formality. Their pattern and texture were close to fabric produced in Vienna by the eminent designer, Josef Hoffman, in the early years of the twentieth century, suggesting that they had perhaps traveled with the Freuds as they escaped Austria in the late 1930s.

In one of the plastic bags, there was a note from Professor Corell, with the following story:

> In 1975, I had a sabbatical leave from my position in the Psychology Department of Westfield State College and went to study for a while at the Tavistock Institute in Hampstead, London. I soon learned that the neighborhood housed the Institute that Anna Freud ran (now called the Anna Freud Centre) and I would go there for public lectures. I was able to have a few conversations with Anna Freud which meant a great deal to me. In 1982, Anna Freud died. It must have been in 1983 when I was visiting in Hampstead and decided to drop in at Anna's Institute. The Freud house was only down the street at 20 Maresfield Gardens. When I went by, I could see and hear activity going on at the house. It was obviously being renovated (in preparation for its becoming a museum). Just as I passed, a man came out carrying a load of brown and gold drapes and threw them in the rubbish tip. "Can I have those?" I asked. "Carry them off," he said. There were four very large panels of heavy woven material. The weight almost knocked me over and their dust was soon all over me. But somehow I managed to haul them through the underground, up and down steep escalators with people staring in disbelief. When I got them to the postage-stamp size hotel room, there wasn't really any place to put them since three of us were staying in the room that was already full of our belongings and us. My friends were not happy troupers. I jammed them under the beds for the night and in the morning, found a cleaners and had them cleaned and boxed … [and] sent home … They reminded me of my experiences in Hampstead and were a pleasure to have. When I retired, they retired to plastic bags in the bottom of a closet. Now is the

> time for a more appropriate life for them. I am very pleased that Austen Riggs will accept them for their archive.

When Professor Corell called me, Riggs didn't really have an archive. It had a basement, in which the occasional, and completely accidental, discovery would be made: for example, the sketched time line Erik Erikson had drawn as he was writing *Gandhi's Truth*, along with an early draft of that manuscript. These items found their way to the Center's excellent library, but Otto Will's handwritten seminars remain in the basement to this day. What else from Riggs' long psychoanalytic history might be found there has now been entrusted to its new librarian, who, thankfully, is an archivist as well.

But back then, Professor Corell's verbal offer made no mention of an archive and included no stipulation about what was to happen to the drapes. Despite my occasional efforts to remind Riggs of this inheritance, the Center never found a way to use this nearly century-old furnishing, nor could it figure out a way to build on its historical significance. So it fell to me to decide what to do. The reference in Professor Corell's note to an archive we did not yet have made me feel that they should somehow become part of Riggs' legacy. Not infrequently, when faced with questions like this, I turned to my wife, to whom this book is dedicated, and who, to my great good fortune, is both a librarian and a decorator. She had a wonderful idea: turn the drapes into pillows and offer them to close colleagues, especially those who would be taking up leadership roles that I and other Riggs staff were leaving. And so Anna Freud's drapes found their way to a local friend who was also a talented seamstress and craftsperson. Loving the back story, she energetically dove into the project and, in a week or so, produced *seventeen* beautiful pillows! Plus, from one of the remnants, a small, elegant shoulder purse for my wife.

In the early 1920s, a struggling young artist, suffering what he had not yet come to call an "identity crisis," wandered into a job at a nursery school in Vienna. It turned out to be the school for the children of the adults who had come to Vienna for analysis with Sigmund Freud. Anna Freud was one of its directors. Erik Erikson, the struggling artist-turned-teacher, became her protegé in the newly developing field of child psychoanalysis. In the early 1950s, now famous for his conceptualization of the identity crisis, Erik Erikson joined the staff of Riggs, and his artist wife, Joan, began a program of creative activities there. Among those activities—amazingly enough—was a nursery school where patients could apprentice themselves to a Montessori-trained teacher and learn what Erikson had learned long before. At the heart of the activities program was what patients lovingly referred to as "The Shop," where they could study and work with any number of artists and craftspersons, including one who wove beautiful fabric.

In 1956, Riggs held the first (and only) Stockbridge Congress on Child Psychoanalysis. It was a large, international gathering, honored to have, among its attendees, Ms. Anna Freud. A wonderful photo of her leaving the front door of The Shop hangs in the Riggs library to this day. And one of her drapes-turned-pillows now rests on the couch of its reading room. The others I gave to various staff members and friends, some of whom, as I was, were present at the end of the Erikson era and some of whom were taking up new leadership roles, sustaining and developing the tradition of clinical and theoretical work we all had inherited. Dreams may be told by people resting their heads on some of those pillows, but most, I would guess, will provide comfort and support—maybe backbone—to people working through personal suffering.

When I presented the pillows—wrapped in soft paper with ribbon around them and accompanied by framed copies of Professor Corell's letter—to these new leaders, they were, to a person, excited, moved, and grateful. They understood that this was more than a gift; it was a *transmission*, a performative moment of one generation's authorizing the next to carry on a precious mission: an "I dub thee" or "I now pronounce thee" moment, not having to do with anything royal or priestly, but rather with the full circle aspect of Erikson's life cycle: the way that at the end there is something given "in trust" so to speak, which establishes anew the essential basic trust—the foundational "Yes"—at the heart of a successful beginning, whether to a life or to a task.

Someone once commented that any photograph of William Shakespeare, no matter how dark or blurry or tattered, would be worth more than the most precisely rendered portrait. Why? Because a photograph captures the light that really touched someone. In that sense, it's more than a representation; it's a relic. And so it is with those pillows. I hope that both Anna Freud and Joan Corell would be thrilled with how the pillows turned out, with how those drapes have traveled through time and with where they currently live.

The poet William Stafford (1998) wrote that "The authentic is a line from one thing along to the next … It holds together something more than the world, this line." As we have seen, trauma too threads its way through the history of families, organizations, and societies, but the playing out of trauma too often forces upon people the inauthenticity of suppressed speech and "cut-out" stories. For the Freuds, who narrowly missed the horrors of Nazi Vienna in 1938, the arc of their work was from trauma to speech. To a small but, I hope, meaningful degree, Anna Freud's drapes bequeath that task to Riggs' staff, just as she and her father bequeath it to however psychoanalysis can find its voice in today's trauma-filled world. Here is the ending line of Stafford's poem: "Are you coming? Good. Now it is time."

References

Alderdice, J. (2010). Off the couch and round the conference table. In: A. Lemma & M. Patrick (Eds.), *Off the Couch: Contemporary Psychoanalytic Applications* (pp. 1–15). London: Routledge.

Alderdice, J. (2012). Speech to the United Nations General Assembly, New York, September 13.

Auden, W. H. (1940a). In memory of Sigmund Freud. In: *Another Time*. New York: Random House.

Auden, W. H. (1940b). Musee des Beaux Arts. In: *Another Time*. New York: Random House.

Awdish, R. (2020). The shape of the shore. *Intima: A Journal of Narrative Medicine*, ISSN 2766-628X.

Barthes, R. (1981). *Camera Lucida*. New York: Hill & Wang.

Beradt, C. (1968). *The Third Reich of Dreams*. Chicago, IL: Quadrangle.

Bion, W. R. (1961). *Experiences in Groups*. New York: Basic Books.

Bion, W. R. (1967). Notes on memory and desire. In E. B. Spillius (Ed.), *Melanie Klein Today, Vol. 2: Mainly Practice* (pp. 17–21). London: Routledge, 1988.

Bion, W. R. (1997). *War Memoirs, 1917–19*. F. Bion (Ed.). London: Karnac.

Bloland, S. E. (2005). *In the Shadow of Fame*. New York: Viking.

Bollas, C. (1987). The unthought known: Early considerations. In: *The Shadow of the Object* (pp. 277–283). London: Free Association.

Bollas, C. (1989). The trauma of incest. In: *Forces of Destiny: Psychoanalysis and Human Idiom* (pp. 171–180). London: Free Association.

Bollas, C. (2002). *Free Association*. Cambridge: Icon.

Braceland, F. (1946). Psychiatric lessons from World War II. *American Journal of Psychiatry, 103*: 587–593.

Bragin, M. (2002). The destruction of metaphor: Examining structure and meaning among responses to extreme violence. Presented at the "September 11: Psychoanalytic Reflections in the 2nd Year" Conference, New York.

Brenner, I. (2001). *Dissociation of Trauma: Theory, Phenomenology, and Technique*. Madison, CT: International Universities Press.

Brown, C. (1993, February 8). I now walk into the wild. *The New Yorker*, pp. 36–47.

Burka, J., Sowa, A., Baer, B., Brandes, C., Gallop, J., Karp-Lewis, S., Leavitt, J., & Rosbrow, P. (2019). From the talking cure to the disease of silence: Effects of ethical violations in a psychoanalytic institute. *International Journal of Psychoanalysis, 100*(2): 247–271. DOI: 10.1080/00207578.2019.1570218.

Burson, C. (2010). *Silver and Ash*. Nashville, TN: Rounder Records.

Carney, M. J. (2007). *The End of the Neubacher Project*. Documentary film written and directed by Marcus J. Carney.

Carr, W. (1985). *The Priestlike Task*. London: SPCK.

Caruth, C. (Ed.) (2014). *Listening to Trauma: Conversations with Leaders in the Theory and Treatment of Catastrophic Experience*. Baltimore, MD: Johns Hopkins University Press.

Christie, G. (1964). Therapeutic community and psychotherapy: The Austen Riggs Center. *Medical Journal of Australia, 1*: 457–460.

Coates, S., Rosenthal, J., & Schecter, D. (Eds.) (2003). *September 11: Trauma and Human Bonds*. Hillsdale, NJ: Analytic Press.

Covington, C. (2016). *Everyday Evils*. London: Routledge.

Covington, C. (2020). *For Goodness Sake: Bravery, Patriotism and Identity*. Bicester, UK: Phoenix.

Davoine, F., & Gaudilliere, J.-M. (2004). *History Beyond Trauma*. New York: Other Press.

Doerries, B. (2016). *The Theater of War*. New York: Vintage.

Duhigg, C. (2016, February 25). What Google learned from its quest to build the perfect team. *The New York Times Magazine*.

Eliot, T. S. (1920). Gerontion. In: *The Collected Poems and Plays, 1909–1950*. New York: Harcourt, Brace & World, 1952.

Erikson, E. H. (1950). *Childhood and Society*. New York: W. W. Norton.

Erikson, E. H. (1954). The dream specimen of psychoanalysis. In: R. P. Knight & C. R. Friedman (Eds.), *Psychoanalytic Psychiatry and Psychology: Austen Riggs Center, Vol. 1* (pp. 131–170). New York: International Universities Press.

Erikson, E. H. (1958). *Young Man Luther*. New York: W. W. Norton.

Erikson, E. H. (1959). *Identity and the Life Cycle*. In: G. S. Klein (Ed.), *Psychological Issues* (pp. 1–171). New York: International Universities Press.

Erikson, E. H. (1961). The roots of virtue. In: J. Huxley (Ed.), *The Humanist Frame* (pp. 145–165). New York: Harper.

Erikson, E. H. (1969). *Gandhi's Truth*. New York: W. W. Norton.

Erikson, E. H. (1970). Autobiographic notes on the identity crisis. *Daedalus, 99*: 730–759.

Erikson, E. H. (1977). *Toys and Reasons*. New York: W. W. Norton.

Fonagy, P., Gergely, G., Jurist, E., & Target, M. (2002). *Affect Regulation, Mentalization and the Development of the Self*. New York: Other Press.

Fraiberg, S., Adelson, E., & Shapiro, V. (1975). Ghosts in the nursery. *Journal of the American Academy of Child Psychiatry, 14*: 387–421.

Freud, A., & Burlingham, D. (1943). *Children in War*. New York: Medical War Books.

Freud, S., & Breuer, J. (1895d). *Studies on Hysteria. S. E., 2*. London: Hogarth, 1958.

Freud, S. (1900a). *The Interpretation of Dreams. S. E., 4–5*. London: Hogarth, 1958.

Freud, S. (1913i). The disposition to obsessional neurosis. *S. E., 12*: 311–326. London: Hogarth, 1958.

Freud, S. (1914g). Remembering, repeating and working-through. *S. E., 12*: 145–156. London: Hogarth, 1958.

Freud, S. (1915a). Observations on transference-love. *S. E., 12*: 157–171. London: Hogarth, 1958.

Freud, S. (1917e). Mourning and melancholia. *S. E., 14*: 237–258. London: Hogarth, 1958.

Freud, S. (1920g). *Beyond the Pleasure Principle. S. E., 18*: 1–64. London: Hogarth, 1958.

Freud, S. (1923b). *The Ego and the Id. S. E., 19*: 1–66. London: Hogarth, 1958.

Freud, S. (1926e). *The Question of Lay Analysis. S. E., 20*: 177–258. London: Hogarth, 1958.

Freud, S. (1933a). *New Introductory Lectures on Psycho-Analysis. S. E., 22.* London: Hogarth, 1958.

Freud, S. (1939a). *Moses and Monotheism. S. E., 23*: 1–137. London: Hogarth, 1958.

Frie, R. (2018). *History Flows through Us.* London: Routledge.

Friedman, L. (1999). *Identity's Architect.* Cambridge, MA: Harvard University Press.

Friedman, R. (2019a). *Dreamtelling, Relations and Large Groups.* London: Routledge.

Friedman, R. (2019b). *Beyond the Soldier's Matrix.* London: Routledge.

Friend, T. (2003, October 6). Jumpers. *The New Yorker.*

Fromm, M. G. (1989). Winnicott's work in relation to classical psychoanalysis and ego psychology. In: M. G. Fromm & B. L. Smith (Eds.), *The Facilitating Environment: Clinical Applications of Winnicott's Theory* (pp. 3–26). Madison, CT: International Universities Press.

Fromm, M. G. (2000). The other in dreams. *Journal of Applied Psychoanalytic Studies, 2*: 287–298.

Fromm, M. G. (2007). The escalating use of medications by college students: What are they telling us, what are we telling them? *Journal of College Student Psychotherapy, 21*(3/4): 27–44.

Fromm, M. G. (Ed.) (2012a). *Lost in Transmission: Studies of Trauma across Generations.* London: Karnac.

Fromm, M. G. (2012a1). Treatment resistance and the transmission of trauma. In: M. G. Fromm (Ed.), *Lost in Transmission: Studies of Trauma across Generations* (pp. 99–114). London: Karnac.

Fromm, M. G. (2012a2). Afterword: Lost and found. In: M. G. Fromm (Ed.), *Lost in Transmission: Studies of Trauma across Generations* (pp. 215–220). London: Karnac.

Fromm, M. G. (2012b1). Impasse and transitional relatedness. In: *Taking the Transference, Reaching toward Dreams: Clinical Studies in the Intermediate Area* (pp. 1–19). London: Karnac.

Fromm, M. G. (2012b2). The therapeutic community as a holding environment. In: *Taking the Transference, Reaching toward Dreams: Clinical Studies in the Intermediate Area* (pp. 187–204). London: Karnac.

Fromm, M. G. (2012b3). What does “borderline” mean? In: *Taking the Transference, Reaching toward Dreams: Clinical Studies in the Intermediate Area* (pp. 20–33). London: Karnac.

Fromm, M. G. (2013). What are we treating? Festschrift for Vamık Volkan. *Clio's Psyche, 20*(2). ISSN 1080-2622.

Fromm, M. G. (2014a). Dimmesdale's ailment, Hawthorne's insight. In: M. G. Fromm (Ed.), *A Spirit that Impels: Play, Creativity and Psychoanalysis* (pp. 35–48). London: Karnac.

Fromm, M. G. (2014b). Interview with Frank Ochberg, M.D. *Psychoanalytic Psychology, 31*(2): 206–216.

Gaudilliere, J.-M. (2020). *The Birth of the Political Self.* F. Davoine (Trans.). London: Routledge.

Gould, L. (2002). Managing depressive anxieties: Consulting to the United States Holocaust Memorial Museum. Presentation given at the Austen Riggs Center, January 11.

Green, A. (1999). *The Work of the Negative.* London: Free Association.

Guntrip, H. (1968). *Schizoid Phenomena, Object Relations and the Self.* New York: International Universities Press, 1969.

Halbfinger, D., & Rasgon, A. (2020, May 18). Israeli settler found guilty of murdering Palestinian family in 2015 arson attack. *The New York Times.*

Hamburger, A., Hancheva, C., & Volkan, V. D. (2020). *Social Trauma—An Interdisciplinary Textbook.* Cham, Switzerland: Springer.

Hawthorne, N. (1850). *The Scarlet Letter.* Oxford: Oxford University Press, 1990.

Herman, J. (1992). *Trauma and Recovery: The Aftermath of Violence—From Domestic Abuse to Political Terror.* New York: Basic Books.

Jacobs, J. (2010, September 19). Silver and ash. Interview with Clare Burson. *Pittsburgh Jewish Chronicle.*

Jaques, E. (1955). Social systems as a defense against persecutory and depressive anxiety. In: M. Klein, P. Heimann, & R. Money-Kyrle (Eds.), *New Directions in Psychoanalysis* (pp. 478–498). London: Tavistock.

Kennard, D. (1998). *An Introduction to Therapeutic Communities.* London: Jessica Kingsley.

Khan, M. M. R. (1983). Secret as potential space. In: *Hidden Selves* (pp. 97–107). New York: International Universities Press.

Klein, M. (1940). Mourning and its relation to manic-depressive states. *International Journal of Psycho-Analysis, 21*: 125–153.

Klein, M. (1946). Notes on some schizoid mechanisms. *International Journal of Psycho-Analysis, 27*: 99–110.

Kogan, I. (1995). *The Cry of Mute Children: A Psychoanalytic Perspective of the Second Generation of the Holocaust*. London: Free Association.

Kohut, H. (1969–70). On leadership. In: P. Ornstein (Ed.), *The Search for the Self: Selected Writings of Heinz Kohut, Vol. 3* (pp. 103–128). New York: International Universities Press, 1991.

Kohut, H. (1971). *The Analysis of the Self*. New York: International Universities Press.

Kohut, T. (2012). *A German Generation*. New Haven, CT: Yale University Press.

Krakauer, J. (1996). *Into the Wild*. New York: Villard.

Krantz, J. (2006). Leadership, betrayal and adaptation. *Human Relations, 59*(2): 221–240.

Krystal, H. (Ed.) (1968). *Massive Psychic Trauma*. New York: International Universities Press.

Lacan, J. (1962–63). *Book X: L'angoisse*. Paris: Seuil, 2004.

Lacan, J. (1977). *Écrits*. New York: W. W. Norton.

Laub, D. (2018). Testimony as part of the therapeutic process in psychoanalysis. In: E. J. Schreiber (Ed.), *Healing Trauma: The Power of Listening* (pp. 97–108). New York: International Psychoanalytic Books.

Lawrence, W. G. (1991). Won from the void and formless infinite: Experiences of social dreaming. *Free Associations, 2*: 259–294.

Leduff, C. (2001, December 5). A bleaker Santa's-eye view: Bell-ringer sees more anxiety and less giving. *The New York Times*.

Litz, B. (2014). Clinical heuristics and strategies for service members and veterans with war-related PTSD. *Psychoanalytic Psychology, 31*(2): 192–205.

Loewenberg, P. (1995). *Fantasy and Reality in History*. London: Oxford University Press.

Lunden, J. (2010, October 15). *Clare Burson: Songs of a Haunted Past*. National Public Radio interview with Clare Burson.

Margulies, A. (2013). Presentation at the Harvard Medical School Conference on "Therapeutic Action: Concepts of Cure," Boston.

Mellow, J. R. (1980). *Nathaniel Hawthorne in His Times*. Baltimore, MD: Johns Hopkins University Press.

Miller, A., & Ochberg, F. (2012). *Instructor's Manual for Psychotherapy for Chronic PTSD*. Psychotherapy.net.

Miller, Z. (2021, February 22). Biden mourns 500,000 dead from COVID-19 in White House ceremony. *PBS News Hour.*

Milner, M. (1937). *An Experiment in Leisure.* London: Routledge, 2011. (First published under the pen name, Joanna Field; re-published in 1957 with the title *On Not Being Able to Paint.*)

Muller, J. (1996). *Beyond the Psychoanalytic Dyad.* New York: Routledge.

Muller, J., & Richardson, W. (Eds.) (1988). *The Purloined Poe.* Baltimore, MD: Johns Hopkins University Press.

Newcombe, N., & Lerner, J. (1982). Britain between the wars: The historical context of Bowlby's theory of attachment. *Psychiatry, 45*: 1–12.

Niebuhr, R. (1952). *The Irony of American History.* Chicago, IL: University of Chicago Press.

Niederland, W. G. (1968). Clinical observations on the "survivor syndrome." *International Journal of Psychoanalysis, 49*: 313–315.

Obama, B. (2016, May 28). Excerpts from "The memory of the morning of August 6, 1945, must never fade." *The New York Times.*

Ochberg, F. (1996). The counting method for ameliorating traumatic memories. *Journal of Traumatic Stress, 9*(4): 873–880.

Ochberg, F. (2013). An injury, not a disorder. *Military Review,* March–April: 96–99.

O'Connor, S. (1990). *I Do Not Want What I Haven't Got* [CD]. New York: Ensign Records.

O'Donoghue, D. (2014). A cemetery's lament: Desecration and responsibility along Vienna's Gürtel. Paper presented at an Erikson Institute Forum, April 5.

Parsons, M. (1990). Marion Milner's "answering activity" and the question of psychoanalytic creativity. *International Review of Psycho-Analysis, 17*(4): 413–424.

Phillips, A. (1996). *Terrors and Experts.* Cambridge, MA: Harvard University Press.

Phillipps, D. (2015, September 19). In unit stalked by suicide, veterans try to save one another. *The New York Times.*

Pritchett, V. S. (1964). *The Offensive Traveler.* New York: Alfred A. Knopf.

Rapaport, D. (1959). A historical survey of psychoanalytic ego psychology. In: G. S. Klein (Ed.), *Psychological Issues* (pp. 5–17). New York: International Universities Press.

Rifkind, G. (2019). Preparing the psychological space for peacemaking. *New England Journal of Public Policy, 31*(1): Article 7.

Rycroft, C. (1979). *The Innocence of Dreams*. London: Hogarth.

Sands, P. (2016). *East West Street: On the Origins of "Genocide" and "Crimes against Humanity."* New York: Alfred A. Knopf.

Scholz, R. (2020). The German "Welcoming Culture"—Some thoughts about its psychodynamics. In: A. Zajenkowska & U. Levin (Eds.), *A Psychoanalytic and Socio-Cultural Exploration of a Continent: Europe on the Couch* (pp. 85–98). London: Routledge.

Schulz, K. (2015, July 13). The really big one. *The New Yorker*.

Senfft, A. (2007). *Silence Hurts: A German Family Story*. Winner of Deutscher Biographiepreis, 2008. Berlin: Ullstein.

Shaffer, P. (1973). *Equus*. London: Penguin.

Shapiro, E. (2019). Wesley Carr, religious institutions, and institutional integrity. *Organisational and Social Dynamics, 19*(1): 103–111.

Shapiro, E. (2020). *Finding a Place to Stand: Developing Self-Reflective Institutions, Leaders and Citizens*. Bicester, UK: Phoenix.

Shapiro, E., & Carr, A. W. (1991). *Lost in Familiar Places: Creating New Connections between the Individual and Society*. New Haven, CT: Yale University Press.

Shay, J. (1995). *Achilles in Vietnam: Combat Trauma and the Undoing of Character*. New York: Touchstone.

Shay, J. (2002). *Odysseus in America: Combat Trauma and the Trials of Homecoming*. New York: Charles Scribner's Sons.

Shay, J. (2014). Moral injury. *Psychoanalytic Psychology, 31*(2): 182–191.

Sherman, N. (2010). *The Untold War: Inside the Minds, Hearts and Souls of our Soldiers*. New York: Oxford University Press.

Sherman, N. (2014). Recovering lost goodness: Shame, guilt and self-empathy. *Psychoanalytic Psychology, 31*(2): 217–235.

Silverman, L., & Hirky, E. (2002). Thematic and countertransferential shifts in working with the survivors of both the 1998 African Embassy bombings and the 2001 New York terror attacks. Presented at the "September 11: Psychoanalytic Reflections in the 2nd Year" Conference, New York.

Soble, J. (2016, May 28). An embrace for a survivor who studied the bombing. *The New York Times*.

Sontag, D. (2002, April 28). Who was responsible for Elizabeth Shin? *The New York Times Magazine*.

Souter, K. (2009). The *War Memoirs:* Some origins of the thought of W. R. Bion. *International Journal of Psychoanalysis, 90*: 795–808.

Springsteen, B. (2002). *The Rising* [CD]. New York: Columbia Records. (Songs referenced include "Nothing Man," "The Rising," "Empty Sky," "You're Missing," "My City in Ruins," and "Paradise.")

Stafford, W. (1998). An introduction to some poems. *The Way It Is: New and Selected Poems*. St. Paul, MN: Graywolf.

Stern, J. (2003). *Terror in the Name of God*. New York: Harper Collins.

Stern, J. (2010). *Denial: A Memoir of Terror*. New York: Harper Collins.

Stern, J. (2014). A case study of a Swedish Neo-Nazi and his reintegration into Swedish society. *Behavioral Sciences and the Law*. wileyonlinelibrary.com. DOI: 10.1002/bsl.2119.

Sullivan, H. S. (1940). *Conceptions of Modern Psychiatry*. New York: Basic Books.

Tillman, J. (2006). When a patient commits suicide: An empirical study of psychoanalytic clinicians. *International Journal of Psychoanalysis*, *87*: 159–177.

Tronick, E. (2007). *The Neurobehavioral and Social-Emotional Development of Infants and Children*. New York: W. W .Norton.

Van der Kolk, B., McFarlane, A., & Weisaeth, L. (1996). *Traumatic Stress: The Effects of Overwhelming Experience on Mind, Body and Society*. New York: Guilford.

Volkan, V. D. (1981). *Linking Objects and Linking Phenomena*. New York: International Universities Press.

Volkan, V. D. (1997). *Bloodlines: From Ethnic Pride to Ethnic Terrorism*. New York: Farrar, Straus and Giroux.

Volkan, V. D. (2004a). Actualized unconscious fantasies and "therapeutic play" in adults' analyses: Further study of these concepts. In: A. Lane (Ed.), *Power of Understanding: Essays in Honor of Veikko Tahka* (pp. 119–141). London: Karnac.

Volkan, V. D. (2004b). *Blind Trust: Large Groups and Their Leaders in Times of Crisis and Terror*. Charlottesville, VA: Pitchstone.

Volkan, V. D. (2013). *Enemies on the Couch: A Psychopolitical Journey through War and Peace*. Durham, NC: Pitchstone.

Volkan, V. D. (2015). *A Nazi Legacy*. London: Karnac.

Volkan, V. D. (2019). *Ghosts in the Human Psyche*. Bicester, UK: Phoenix.

Volkan, V. D. (2020). *Large-Group Psychology: Racism, Societal Division, Narcissistic Leaders and Who We Are Now*. Bicester, UK: Phoenix.

Volkan, V. D., Ast, G., & Greer, W. (2002). *The Third Reich in the Unconscious: Transgenerational Transmission and Its Consequences*. New York: Brunner-Routledge.

Voss, T. (2019a). *Where War Ends: A Combat Veteran's 2,700 Mile Journey to Heal*. Novato, CA: New World Library.

Voss, T. (2019b, November 11). Veterans and moral injury. [Letter to the Editor.] *The New York Times*.

Waslekar, S. (2012). Report of the 9th Meeting of the International Dialogue Initiative, London. www.internationaldialogueinitiative.com.

Wilke, G. (2012). Brochure for the Erikson Institute Conference on "The Legacy of Perpetrator Trauma," Austen Riggs Center, September 2012.

Wilke, G., Binney, G., & Williams, C. (2005). *Living Leadership*. Harlow, UK: Pearson Education.

Wilson, L. (2017). Report of the 15th Meeting of the International Dialogue Initiative, Vienna. www.internationaldialogueinitiative.com.

Winnicott, C. (1980). Fear of breakdown: A clinical example. *International Journal of Psychoaanalysis*, *61*: 351–356.

Winnicott, D. W. (1941). The observation of infants in a set situation. In: *Through Paediatrics to Psycho-Analysis* (pp. 52–69). New York: Basic Books, 1958.

Winnicott, D. W. (1951). Transitional objects and transitional phenomena. In: *Through Paediatrics to Psycho-Analysis* (pp. 229–242). New York: Basic Books, 1958.

Winnicott, D. W. (1954). Metapsychological and clinical aspects of regression within the psycho-analytical set-up. In: *Through Paediatrics to Psycho-Analysis* (pp. 278–294). New York: Basic Books, 1958.

Winnicott, D. W. (1960a). The theory of the parent–infant relationship. In: *The Maturational Processes and the Facilitating Environment* (pp. 37–55). New York: International Universities Press, 1965.

Winnicott, D. W. (1960b). Ego distortion in terms of true and false self. In: *The Maturational Processes and the Facilitating Environment* (pp. 140–152). New York: International Universities Press, 1965.

Winnicott, D. W. (1963a). Hospital care supplementing intensive psychotherapy in adolescence. In: *The Maturational Processes and the Facilitating Environment* (pp. 242–248). New York: International Universities Press, 1965.

Winnicott, D. W. (1963b). Communicating and not communicating leading to a study of certain opposites. In: *The Maturational Processes and the Facilitating Environment* (pp. 179–192). New York: International Universities Press, 1965.

Winnicott, D. W. (1969). The use of an object. *International Journal of Psycho-analysis, 50*: 711–716.

Winnicott, D. W. (1971a). Playing: A theoretical statement. In: *Playing and Reality* (pp. 38–52). New York: Basic Books.

Winnicott, D. W. (1971b). Playing: Creative activity and the search for the self. In: *Playing and Reality* (pp. 53–64). New York: Basic Books.

Winnicott, D. W. (1974). Fear of breakdown. *International Review of Psycho-Analysis, 1*: 103–107.

Wolf, C. (1980). *A Model Childhood.* New York: Farrar, Straus and Giroux.

Wolf, E. (1995). Psychic trauma: A view from Self Psychology. *Canadian Journal of Psychoanalysis, 3*(*2*), 203–222.

Index

'*Traveling through Time* is a vivid, nuanced, integrated portrayal of trauma as it exists across time and across social groups. Based on his deep professional engagement with familial, organizational, and societal trauma, Fromm brings to life the experience of the individual in each of those contexts. His psychoanalytic approach emphasizes the dignity of the individual and demonstrates the value of curiosity to understanding such important matters as moral injury and the fear of repetition of trauma, whether conscious or unconscious. He shows us that mourning is required to move beyond grievance to grief, to join past to present, and to create space for an adaptive future. This is a sophisticated book written in accessible language. It is a must read for anyone living or working with trauma.'

Harriet Wolfe, M.D., President, International Psychoanalytical Association

'What happens to us in the face of unbearable pain? How do our efforts to manage traumatic experience shape our family life, our children's capacities, our institutions, our society's development? In this moving book, Dr. Fromm, a master clinician, takes us through these questions with powerfully evocative stories from his long career. He brings our psychological theories to life, illuminating for the general and professional reader aspects of human development that echo across the generations. A stunning collection.'

Edward R. Shapiro, M.D., Former Medical Director/CEO, Austen Riggs Center; Clinical Professor of Psychiatry, Yale Child Study Center; author, *Finding a Place to Stand: Developing Self-Reflective Institutions, Leaders, and Citizens*

'This eloquent book examines trauma as it moves through time and takes shape in an "unconscious task deposited into the future," an unacknowledged history or untold story passed on and enacted in families, in organizations, and in society. Fromm compellingly recounts the stories of children delegated to bring their parents' unspoken pasts into the present, of organizations whose fragmentation unconsciously communicates a censored history, and of societal structures bound up with what the social or the political realm has not yet assimilated. At the center of this remarkable book is Fromm's own delicate, subtle act of listening, grounded in his clinical experience and turned not only toward the patients and institutions he encounters but also toward the great psychoanalytic theoreticians, whose work, as he reveals, emerges as a unique task of personal witness. In its movement between individuals and institutions, this book is consistently surprising. And it reminds us, importantly, that the reenactment of trauma demands "the dignity of our listening," and that the contact with the dead, as Fromm so beautifully shows us, brings life back to the living.'

Cathy Caruth, Class of 1916 Professor of English, Cornell University; author, *Unclaimed Experience: Trauma, Narrative and History* and *Listening to Trauma: Conversations with Leaders in the Theory and Treatment of Catastrophic Experience*

'The true-life stories brought together in this volume really open up the experience of working with traumatized people and communities. But that does not begin to describe its value. This is a book you will come back to again and again. Every few pages you will find a valuable insight or memorable remark. The personal stories of psychoanalytic greats such as Erikson, Bion, and Kohut are fascinating. They shed a new light on the characters and inspired me to return to reading them again. The way the pathology of individuals, families, and communities is woven together is also of great interest. I found myself inspired by the work of Fromm and his colleagues at the Austen Riggs Center's Erikson Institute. You will be too.'

John, Lord Alderdice FRCPsych, Senior Research Fellow, Harris Manchester College, University of Oxford